Social Service Politics in the United States and Britain

Social Service Politics in the United States and Britain

Willard C. Richan

Temple University Press/Philadelphia

Library of Congress Cataloging In Publication Data

Richan, Willard C
  Social service politics in the United States and
Britain.

  Bibliography: p.
  Includes index.
  1. Social service—United States—Case studies.
2. Social service—Great Britain—Case studies.
3. United States—Social policy.   4. Great Britain—
Social policy.   I. Title.
HV95.R52   361.6'1'0941   80-27534
ISBN 0-87722-216-9

Temple University Press, Philadelphia 19122
© 1981 by Temple University. All rights reserved
Published 1981
Printed in the United States of America

Contents

Part Three
Analysis

Acknowledgments

NO STUDY OF THIS KIND IS A ONE-PERSON EFFORT. SPECIAL THANKS
for their advice and encouragement go to Dr. Robert Morris,
Brandeis University; Dr. Neil Fraser, University of Edinburgh;
Dr. Alfred J. Kahn, Columbia University; and Dr. Edward
Newman, Temple University. Many thanks are also due to
David Jones, director of the National Institute for Social Work,
and Professor F. M. Martin, University of Glasgow, for aiding
with field study contacts and arrangements in Britain. For their
comments and suggestions on portions of the manuscript, I
would like to thank Myles Johnson and Bernard Plawsky of the
National Association of Social Workers; Baroness Serota and
Robin Huws Jones, formerly of the Seebohm Committee;
Phoebe Hall, Department of Health and Social Security; Nancy
Drucker, University of Edinburgh, and Michael Ames, Temple
University Press. Needless to say, the many persons who
agreed to be interviewed for the study provided an essential
ingredient in the final product; their generosity and patience is
deeply appreciated. Finally, a special word of thanks to the au-
thor's wife, Anne Richan, for her careful reading of successive

drafts of the manuscript, and her helpful suggestions, support, and encouragement.

Field research for this study was made possible by a grant from the English-Speaking Union.

Social Service Politics
in the United States and Britain

Introduction

THE PREPARATION OF THIS BOOK TOOK PLACE AT A MAJOR TURNING point in British and American social service policy. The author carried out field work in Britain at the height of the 1979 election campaign that swept into power the Conservative government of Margaret Thatcher. Unlike earlier Tory prime ministers, Thatcher interpreted the election as a mandate to dismantle many basic social welfare programs, thus bringing to an abrupt end the virtually uninterrupted growth of the welfare state. The completion of the manuscript coincided with the American presidential campaign of 1980, which saw a similar turn to the right. Goaded by public disenchantment with social programs and a challenger with a reputation for extreme conservatism, President Jimmy Carter began to sound more like a Republican than a Democrat. It was clear that, whatever the outcome of the election, the erosion of welfare programs will be accelerated in the coming years.

These events were watched with no small amount of distress by American and British social workers, as they saw the gains of recent decades slipping away. Few social workers have experienced such a profound sense of defeat. Even in the 1950s, when social work "turned inward" and political conservatism prevailed, social services continued to grow. In Britain, the basic trend was one of general expansion of social programs dating from the postwar advent of "socialism." Moreover, there is every indication that the rightward turns in the two countries are not transitory phenomena, but rather the outward signs of a basic reorientation to social services. The arithmetic of age distribution will force on both societies an increase in certain kinds of basic provisions in the coming decades, but the spirit of enlightenment and emancipation of those in want, which has characterized the model of modern social services, if not always the reality, appears likely to suffer.

In times such as these, it is tempting for social workers to give in to a sense of futility, and withdraw from the arenas where decisions about social services are made. It is of the nature of social workers, however, to be perpetual (and sometimes insufferable) optimists. Just as they believe that somehow their special magic will set things aright in even the most depressing case situations, they never quite give up on the hopes of progress in the societal arena.

This spirit of hope is captured in the story of three friends on a small island in the path of an immense tidal wave that was due to sweep over it in a few days' time. One was a soldier of fortune, the second was a divine, and the third was a social worker. "I am going on one last, gigantic binge," said the soldier of fortune, eyeing his whiskey supply nearby. "I shall pray to Almighty God to deliver my soul to heaven," said the divine, who immediately fell to his knees in an attitude of supplication. The two then turned to the social worker and asked what he would do while awaiting his fate. "Practice swimming," was the reply. American and British social workers will be swimming upstream in the coming years. This book is intended to help them improve their aquatic skills.

The November 1972, issue of *Social Work,* the journal of the National Association of Social Workers, carried a commentary that closed with the words,

I do not question the judicious use of political action as an appropriate social work tool, but I do question its *extensive* use. The assumptions that are presumed to support such use are open to question, and there has not been a thorough consideration of possible harmful side effects. The question social workers must answer for themselves is whether the gains made by increased political activity will outweigh the resistance it creates. (Orten 1972, p. 106).

The letter expressed sentiments that were widely felt among American social workers as the activism of the 1960s created its own backlash of doubts and hesitancy. In the same month in which the above letter was published, the National Association of Social Workers had refused to take a position in the election campaign which led to the re-election of Richard M. Nixon. American social workers were indeed ambivalent about their proper role in the political arena. Yet, within a few months, new developments in Washington would resolve the question, as the social services came under increasingly sharp attack. In response, social workers and allied groups united to fend off the threat.

There was a basic difference between the activism of the 1960s and that which occurred in the early 1970s. Underlying much of the former there was a kind of altruistic heroism, in which the social services themselves were frequently the target of protest. The social workers certainly benefited from the out-pouring of federal funds during the crisis of the sixties, but the chief protesters were frequently not the chief beneficiaries. The political activity of the early 1970s was much more clearly a merging of the concern for the consumers of services with the workers' concern for their own career interests.

A word should be said at this point about the meaning of "social services" as used in this book. The social services referred to here are what are called *personal* social services. They are helping activities, under governmental or nonprofit auspices, that involve the direct intervention of an agency in the consumer's life. They do not include financial assistance, non-psychiatric medical care, housing or education, although they may be employed to facilitate a person's use of these resources. They may involve the provision of concrete services (for example, transportation) or counseling and other forms of "soft" services.

"Social workers," as discussed in this study, are persons employed in the provision of social services. They are not necessarily professional in the sense of having specific educational credentials, but they are viewed as social service specialists; and they are often closely identified with professional or quasi-professional associations.

The present study is based on an analysis of several case histories concerning the development of social service policies in two countries, and other issues involving social workers themselves as political constituencies. The cases are drawn from the United States and Great Britain. Both were at the center of the flowering of political and economic liberalism in the nineteenth century; and both have, over the years, experienced dilemmas regarding philanthropy, especially that mediated through government. The United States has modeled many of its social welfare institutions on British forerunners, even to adopting the same names.

Yet, the development of social welfare policy in the two countries has differed significantly. The United States has been far more uneasy with the notion of a welfare state and with governmental intervention than has Britain. Conversely, the class-consciousness of the British, especially as this has found political expression, has created a receptive climate for welfare activity not found in the United States. Moreover, the diffusion of governmental responsibility in this country has retarded policy innovation, as compared with the more centralized system in Great Britain.

At the same time, both countries, as capitalistic democracies, have provided environments which tended to foster the development of social services at a more advanced level (though not necessarily on a more generous scale) than is true elsewhere. Such societies tend both to acknowledge the existence of social problems and interpret them as being amenable to social service intervention. The fact that Britain and the United States have approached this task in very different ways means we may be able to identify characteristics that are shared by different kinds of capitalistic democracies. That is, if social service professionals have reacted to political challenges and opportunities in similar ways in these two countries, then one can expect to find a similar response in other nations with a comparable political-economic structure.

The analysis in this inquiry was directed to two basic questions: Are social workers able to influence policy decisions in areas of greatest concern to them? And what factors are associated with the ability to influence? In addressing the first question, the author selected policy issues concerning the personal social services and the social service work force itself. It is these areas that have the most direct impact on the career concerns of social workers, as well as on their clients.

Among the factors in political influence, *money* is the most versatile, since it can be converted into other resources. *Votes,* either in general elections or within a deliberative body, are most directly translated into influence over decisions in a formal sense. And *formal authority* is the legitimized power to make decisions. These are potent assets in the policy-making process, but they are also assets in singularly short supply among social workers. Thus, if our inquiry were restricted to these three factors, it would be a brief inquiry indeed. Such a limited perspective, however, ignores several other important elements.

One such element is *information*. This term is used in two senses here: (1) *strategic intelligence,* knowledge of the decision-making process, key actors, and patterns of influence; and (2) *evidence,* or backing for arguments with which to persuade audiences. While access to information is not entirely within social workers' control, they can increase it by diligent effort. Similarly, *personal relationships* with strategic individuals are determined in part by outside circumstances, but can be cultivated by social workers. *Time* is an exceedingly precious commodity in the policy-making arena. There are externally imposed limits on the availability of time; yet, they can be stretched, and priorities in the use of time can be changed.

The factor that is fully within the control of social workers is their own *investment* in an issue; that is, their readiness to commit resources to it. While it would be naive to suggest that investment alone is sufficient to assure that one will prevail in the policy-making process, it is the author's belief that it can offset differences in more tangible assets.

The chapters that follow are organized into three parts. Part I deals with the two national contexts, their policy-making structures, political patterns, and respective approaches to social service policy. Part II presents the six case studies. While these descriptions include interpretive and analytical material, the main analysis is found in Part III.

The case studies, which constitute Part II, are presented in chronological order. They fall naturally into several groupings. The first two involve laws enacted in the British Parliament for the reorganization of personal social services in the local authorities. The similarities and differences between the acts covering Scotland, on the one hand, and England and Wales, on the other, help to illuminate key factors in the political process. Two cases concern policy initiatives by the Nixon administration as it sought to bring personal social service management and funding under greater control. Finally, we examine two episodes directly concerning the vital interests of social workers themselves: in Britain, a series of strikes in local social service departments; and in the United States, a campaign for the enactment of state licensing laws for social workers. The fact that all of these incidents occurred within a fifteen-year period increases their comparability.

The *Social Work (Scotland) Act of 1968* was the basis for reorganizing the personal social services in Scotland. It was followed by a major expansion and upgrading of services, all the more dramatic because of the low level of service development which preceded it. Aside from a few limited references in the professional literature (see Weber 1974), the act has been virtually ignored by American social workers. The events surrounding its development and enactment have had very little exposure to British social workers as well (see Carmichael 1969). Yet social workers played an important role, first in redirecting the thrust of the evolving policy, then getting it acted on in Parliament.

The *Local Authority Social Services Act of 1970* and the Seebohm Committee Report on which it was based are familiar to many American, as well as British, social workers. Now, thanks to an excellent study by Phoebe Hall (1976), the account of this act's evolution into law has been widely circulated in Britain, although less so in the United States. Here again, social workers had a major hand in the development of policy that drastically changed the delivery of public personal social services.

The *Allied Services Act* had the full prestige of the Secretary of Health, Education, and Welfare behind it, with the blessings of the Nixon administration, yet it failed to get beyond the stage of committee deliberations in the House of Representatives, in three attempts to have it enacted. The bill was not particularly controversial: its support came from both parties, and it did not involve the outlay of significant amounts of money. Nevertheless, it was effectively killed by a combination of opposition from certain social service professionals and a general lack of enthusiasm for its passage, either in Congress or among social workers.

The fourth episode concerns attempts by the Nixon administration and congressional conservatives to restrict federal spending for personal social services. Two pieces of legislation are involved: an amendment to the *Revenue Sharing Act of 1972,* which placed a 2.5-billion-dollar ceiling on federal social service funds that had previously been "open-ended," that is, available to states to the extent that they came up with matching money; and the *Social Services Amendments of 1974* (Title XX of the Social Security Act). This case was not a total victory for either the administration forces or the social workers and their allies. The Title XX episode is useful for looking at the place of coalition politics in social policy development.

The final two cases are of a different order from the others, since they deal directly with social service work force issues and not social service policy, per se. A series of bitter strikes in social service departments in Britain in 1978 and 1979 had major ramifications both for the internal relations of the social work community and the profession's external image. It is the disruptive impact on the professional community itself that is the major focus of this case history. The struggle over licensure of American social workers is an episode that continues as of this writing, although in more subdued fashion than was true in the mid-1970s.

The record of British and American social workers in the political arena is mixed, but the pluses should be encouraging news for those social workers who find it hard to believe that their professional community is ever listened to. An examination of the factors that maximize or detract from the professionals' effectiveness in influencing policy should also be of service to the social work community. The last section of the book is devoted to such an analysis.

The research evolved out of the author's long-standing interest in the organization and delivery of personal social services, and in the political role of social workers. It was his involvement in the evaluation of a large-scale project in social services integration that led him to recognize the crucial importance of national policies in determining the nature and success of such efforts at the local level. To what extent can social workers affect these policies? As against a prevailing skepticism about their political potential, there are specific instances when social workers have, in fact, altered the direction of policy. Rather than simply accept the conventional wisdom that social workers "lack political clout," the author decided to make a more systematic study of the social work role in influencing policy.

Considering the importance of the question, there is surprisingly little in the way of empirical evidence on the politics of personal social services at the national level in either the United States or Britain. One reason for this may be the aforementioned newness of such services as a subject of national policy. This is especially evident in the United States, where the federal government did not even try to enunciate a national policy on the personal social services until the 1960s.

Handler's (1973) analysis of social services in public welfare and Mott's (1976) study of the social and political history of Title XX of the Social Security Act still stand apart as major American political studies of this kind. In Britain, Hall's (1976) history of the Seebohm Committee and the Local Authority

Social Services Act, and some of the case studies presented by Hall, Land, Parker, and Webb (1975) represent a kind of analysis of which there are too few examples (see also Lees 1972).

The author read extensively in the available literature on social service policy, the social service work force, and the political contexts in the United States and Britain. He also had access to fugitive documents, including minutes, memoranda, and correspondence. Nearly forty experts and participants in the episodes, in this country, England, and Scotland, were interviewed in connection with the study. The author devoted special attention to the cases which had received least coverage in the professional literature. Thus, the author interviewed those involved in the Social Work (Scotland) Act and the Allied Services Act most heavily.

In the interviews, the nature of the case, information gaps and areas of confusion, and the special knowledge and perspective of the informant determined the questions to be asked. Each respondent was encouraged to expand on his or her areas of interest. In several instances, informants differed in their recollections and interpretations of events; in each case, the apparent discrepancies were pursued, in an effort to gain an accurate picture. The same approach was used when an informant's account was at variance with documentary information or previous studies.

It is the author's hope that this book will contribute to knowledge about the politics of social services, particularly as it relates to the ability of social workers to wield influence. It is intended as a beginning probe into an important and, as yet, little explored subject.

Part One
The Political Context

1

The Contrasting Political
Environments of the
United States and Britain

"CENTRALIZATION" IS PROBABLY THE KEY TERM FOR AN UNDER-
standing of the differences between the British and American
political systems. The history of the American system has been
one of attempts to bring cohesion among quasi-independent
elements, while in Britain there has been a struggle to constrain
the power of central authority. In neither case, of course, have
the efforts been consistent or unanimous. In fact, the best way
of describing the American response to the centralization/decen-
tralization issue is to say it consists of a series of zigzag movements, always with great ambivalence, in the overall direction
of greater centralization. Since World War II, the forces for
centralization in Britain have been much stronger than those for
decentralization.

THE LEGISLATIVE FUNCTION
Although superficially similar in structure and function, the
American Congress and the British Parliament are vastly differ-

ent bodies. Because of much greater party discipline in Britain, the government in power can usually count on legislative support of a kind that is virtually unknown to American presidents except on rare occasions of national emergency. The individual member of Parliament is told that he or she represents the nation, not a local constituency; this is underscored by the fact that it is not even necessary to reside in the "home" district (Beer and Ulam 1962, p. 77; Crossman 1972, p. 90). The notion that members of the national legislature should give in to pressure from the constituents who elected them—considered an integral part of "grass-roots democracy" in the United States—is frowned upon in Britain (Pym 1974, pp. 105–109).

The late Richard Crossman described the deflating experience of campaigning for a "safe" Labour seat in Commons as a young man; of standing out on the street speaking earnestly through a loudspeaker, but getting no response, Crossman says:

> There was nobody else on that empty street except a very old man who was mowing his grass in his front garden, and he looked up at me and said, "I wonder, boy, why you waste your time talking like that. You do realize, I suppose, that Coventry East would vote for the back end of a jackass if it was labeled Labour" (1972, p. 91).

From then on Crossman knew that staunch Labour party supporters cared only about the party platform and had little interest in the personality or views of the backbencher they sent to vote for it.

Americans accustomed to frequent revolts and other forms of maverick behavior in Congress may find rather surprising the degree of party solidarity expected within Parliament, especially on the Labour side. On one occasion Crossman, as whip in the House of Commons, was criticized by Prime Minister Harold Wilson for allowing a sizeable though not crucial defection from Labour's ranks over defense policy. Wilson later wrote,

> In my short speech to the (Party) meeting I said simply that we could not go on in this manner. The last thing I wanted to do was to move back to any tightening of discipline. But many of those who embarrassed the

Government did so in the safe knowledge that their revolt was sufficiently limited in numbers to avoid a crisis which might force the Government to resign or go to the country. . . . This led me . . . to say that every dog is allowed one bite, but if biting becomes too much of a habit its owner tends to have doubts about renewing the license when it comes up (1971, pp. 377–78).

The strong national control of the parties in Britain is exercised in a most tangible way: an individual must have the national party's approval in order to bear the official party label. Thus a frown from the head of the party is taken very seriously.

It appears, however, that here, as in other matters, the only truly safe generalization is that there are no truly safe generalizations. Recent studies have indicated that the reputed party solidarity in Parliament has been weakening over the years (Schwartz 1980). Yet, in comparison with members of the American Congress, backbenchers in Parliament are still a relatively obedient lot.

The contrast between the two legislative systems is particularly sharp in relation to fiscal matters. Money measures not only originate in the Cabinet (Beer and Ulam 1962, p. 102), but Parliament is not permitted to change the Budget Resolution once it is presented by the government (Crossman 1972, p. 39). Thus, it is left only with the opportunity to criticize the budget after the fact. Not only has Congress traditionally had a central role in working over and significantly changing the president's budget before passage, but in recent years its fiscal control has been increased with the establishment of the Congressional Budget Office (Reiselbach 1977, p. 53). Government departments are the predominant source of new policies in Britain. The limited time available for "private members' bills" (that is, those coming from individual members of Parliament) assures a near-monopoly of government-inspired measures (Pym 1974, p. 100). Add to this the fact that the member so presumptuous as to initiate a proposal must in effect become his or her own "whip" to muster votes in its behalf (p. 82). Occasionally there is enough strong momentum in the country behind a policy to get it through this formidable gantlet. This happened, for instance, in the liberalization of anti-abortion laws in the late 1960s (p. 80). Such instances are exceedingly rare.

It is true that most major United States legislation also emanates from the administration. Yet, in contrast with British practice, such measures often end up in virtually unrecognizable form after they have been through the congressional mill. Moreover, congressional committees frequently produce their own bills.

The functions of the national legislatures are also different: in the United States, the function is to deliberate upon and enact legislation, with a major sharing of responsibility with the executive; in Britain, the role is more accurately depicted as one of advising and, to a lesser extent, watchdogging policy (Beer and Ulam 1962, p. 133). This does not mean that Parliament has no influence on policy. Ironically, however, the government worries far more about its own partisans in Parliament than about the opposition. The members of the latter are assumed to follow their own leadership's commands; their major function is to try to embarrass the government with sharp questioning (Crossman 1972, pp. 47ff). The real concern of the government is to hold its own party in line. For the reasons stated above, the prime minister and the members of his cabinet have at their disposal many kinds of weapons for enforcing their will with backbenchers.

The committee system—that bane of all American presidents down through the years—is also present in the British legislature, but it is a pale imitation of the powerful baronies of Congress. The expanded system of parliamentary committees to oversee government policies was launched with much fanfare in the mid-sixties by Richard Crossman. A decade later Miller (1977) observed, "rather than a watershed, the Crossman reforms appear as a mere bubble on a placid lake" (p. 125). Crossman himself described them only half jokingly as a way to "provide occupation to our frustrated backbenchers" (1972, p. 102).

Reforms with an opposite intent—to weaken the great power of committee chairpersons in Congress, and thereby democratize that institution—were undertaken in both the House and Senate between 1971 and 1975. While the iron law of seniority was broken, thus ending a few longstanding fiefdoms, most of the powerful figures either held onto their control or passed from the scene for reasons unrelated to the reforms (Reiselbach 1977, pp. 41–67).

One reason why the power of committee chairpersons has survived such reform efforts is the fact that their power is less structural than personal. Key chairpersons have moved up through the ranks by continuing to be re-elected over long periods of time, becoming virtuosi in the ways of the congressional labyrinth, using their power to give and withhold rewards among their colleagues, and—a point often ignored—coming to know more about the substance of policies under their domain than presidents and cabinet officials, whose tenure is normally much shorter than theirs (Polsby 1971, p. 73).

Given the central role of Congress in policy making, strong committees are a necessity for effective functioning. Many observers have noted the difference in style between the Senate and the House of Representatives. Although almost four and one-half times larger, the House operates more efficiently. This is because its procedures are more streamlined, it caters less to the whims of its members, and principal committee chairpersons are able to wield more power than is true in the other chamber. Senators are more likely to be national figures and thus demand more individual autonomy; they need to be generalists because there are fewer to go around in filling committee posts; and they maintain a generally more informal atmosphere than the House. All these things exact a price in legislative inefficiency (Polsby 1971; Galloway 1955, pp. 34, 59).

Of the two houses of Parliament, the more crucial is Commons. The House of Lords, once a major power in British government, can do little more than delay policies approved by the other chamber (Galloway 1955, Beer and Ulam 1962, pp. 123–57). The sitting government can easily vitiate any threat of revolt in Lords by the use of its unlimited power to add more peers to that body (ibid.). Thus the rebels can easily be outnumbered by fiat.

A central item in the conventional wisdom of American government has been that the power of the presidency has grown enormously vis-à-vis that of the Congress (see, for example, Williams 1963, p. 232; also Beloff 1975, p. 11). That the executive does indeed have great leverage in relation to legislative branch, some of it deriving from factors outside of the formal division of powers, is unquestionable. With the apparatus of government at their disposal (with a research capacity unmatched by anything available to Congress), the ability to command the attention of the country through the mass media, and powers of appointment and frequent opportunities to bestow special projects on favored geographical areas, American presidents have tremendous influence in the political arena. Privy to secret information regarding tension spots around the globe, they can—and do—manipulate international crises to their political advantage.

Yet, despite this awesome power, virtually every president in modern history has had an uphill battle to get his legislative program enacted; the "victories" involve bills that come out of Congress bearing only a slight resemblance to the form in which they were introduced. The exceptions to this general rule involve measures passed in times of national crisis, such as wartime, the Great Depression of the 1930s, and the perilous period following the assassination of President John F. Kennedy. A major reason for Congress's ability to frustrate the executive will is the complex system of deliberation geared to diverse sectional and special interests. The advantage is with those who wish not to act. When individuals in Congress seek to promote their own pet policies, they run into exactly the same kind of resistance.

THE EXECUTIVE FUNCTION

The American president is obviously the most powerful single official in the country. Elected in a quadrenniel national plebiscite, he fulfills the functions of prime minister and king, since he is the symbolic, as well as the governmental, head of the nation. Commander-in-chief of the armed forces and the one who determines foreign policy, insofar as any single individual does, the president more than anyone else is responsible for protecting American interests in the world. But just as Congress and the Supreme Court are significant counter-influences in national policy, the executive branch of government is only partly under the president's control. This is particularly true of domestic policies, because of the influence of vested interest groups, which bring pressure to bear at strategic points.

In contrast, the British prime minister has virtually total control over the top echelon of government officials. Not only does he or she have a free hand in selecting or dismissing cabinet ministers, but the make-up and size of the cabinet is decided by the prime minister. Contrary to the case in the United States, department heads do not automatically sit on the cabinet (Beer and Ulam 1962, pp. 102–122). Cabinet minutes are a sanitized version of the prime minister's summary of the deliberations rather than a verbatim record; and substantial secrecy surrounds cabinet meetings (ibid.; Crossman 1972, pp. 35–36).

There is great pressure on the individual cabinet member to support the results of deliberations, however much these are pushed in a particular direction by the prime minister, lest the government be endangered. This extends even to decisions that were arrived at in the cabinet minister's absence (Crossman 1972, p. 55).

Next to the prime minister, the most powerful government official is the chancellor of the exchequer. Together they determine the budget, which is made known to the rest of the cabinet the day before it is presented to Parliament, effectively precluding any voice of the cabinet in the final product. Unlike the backbenchers in Commons, cabinet members are not even free to criticize or question what is offered (pp. 39, 56). Are cabinet ministers without significant leverage on policy? The most drastic means of influence of course is resignation from the cabinet—it has the same shock value as suicide, which is what it amounts to, politically speaking. There are less dramatic and risky ways of making an impact on the prime minister's decisions. One is the cabinet committee, through which several ministers may act in concert. Unfortunately, the prime minister does the selecting of committee members, and may preside at committee meetings if he so chooses, sharply limiting their influence on him (p. 43).

The more significant means of influence available to cabinet ministers is through informal contacts with the prime minister. There have been many instances in the past when decisions have been affected in this way, although all concerned are aware that, in the end, it is the prime minister who must decide (Crossman 1977, p. 375). Then, of course, having been given a rather free hand in running their respective departments, the ministers are able to affect policy in operation. However, here they run into the permanent civil service and its not inconsiderable power over government activities. (The role of the civil servants in Britain and the United States is discussed below.)

Although American presidents also choose their cabinet members, they have much less control over this than do their British counterparts. Not only are the positions that go to make up the cabinet clearly established, but such appointments need confirmation by the Senate. While senators are hesitant to challenge seriously any such appointments, especially of a new president, there is always that possibility. At the very least, a cabinet designee who is the least bit controversial can expect to go through a stiff questioning period by one or more Senate committees. Such confirmation hearings are open to the public, and, depending on their news value, may be televised. The opportunity these forums provide for making political capital and possibly embarrassing a president of the opposite party is not lost on senators.

Unlike its British counterpart, the United States cabinet is not a deliberative body, and presidents sometimes neglect even to convene them for months at a time. Also, it is not unusual for both major parties to be represented in the same cabinet. In recent decades, the importance of the cabinet has been further eroded by the expanding role of the Office of the President and particularly the White House staff. Increasingly, an amorphous group of individuals, whose shape and size changes with each successive administration, surrounds the president, providing much the same consultative function as that available to the British prime minister (Nicholas 1975). The American chief executive is probably even more free than his British counterpart to ignore advice from either set of counselors, who are under less pressure to maintain the image of solidarity. It is said of President Abraham Lincoln, for instance, that once when he found his cabinet solidly opposed to a proposed course of action, he announced the following tally: "one aye, seven nays—the ayes have it."

The president is also free to dismiss a cabinet member at will, and though he must be concerned about the political impact of such an act, the appearance of a breach of solidarity in the ranks is less serious than it is for the prime minister. However, presidents have other significant constraints on their action regarding high administration officials: the close ties that may develop between cabinet secretaries and powerful congressional committee chairpersons (Nicholas 1975, pp. 21–25; Vale 1975, p. 38). All members of the United States cabinet are department heads, with the exception of the chief delegate to the United Nations. Since they preside, at times, over thousands of civil servants, and provide services to important interest groups, cabinet members are usually well protected against presidential discipline; and it is only when they become particularly embarrassing that they are likely to be fired.

The degree of autonomy with which department heads may administer their programs varies greatly in both countries. In Britain, much responsibility is delegated to the individual minister, but there is always the concern that he not embarrass the government or weaken the party's standing in the public eye. In the United States, partly because of the vastness of the undertaking and partly because there is less need for an image of solidarity, secretaries have a great deal of autonomy. President Richard Nixon, in inaugurating his first term, hoped to concentrate his attention on foreign policy. He told one interviewer, prior to his election, "I've always thought this country could run itself domestically without a President. . . . All you need is a competent Cabinet to run the country at home" (Evans and Novak 1971, p. 11). However, in time he found that he could not ignore the operation of the domestic machinery. His solution was to shift more power for domestic affairs to the White

House staff, despite his earlier announcement that the cabinet should have increased power and the White House staff be cut (pp. 12, 51).

The options open to the respective heads of government in the two countries and the constraints upon their power also differ in significant ways. The American president comes into office with an uncertain mandate from a fickle electorate, and may be an outsider to the mainstream of his party. This was truest for Dwight D. Eisenhower, who was believed likely to be nominated by either party in 1952, before he aligned himself with the Republicans. Aside from this tenuous hold on party leadership, the president faces the aforementioned independence of Congress and the Supreme Court.

The British prime minister has much more control over the affairs of state. The power is derived from three main sources: the position as head of the ruling party; authority over an obedient cabinet, with its base in a supportive parliamentary majority; and control over patronage (Crossman 1972). At the same time, the prime minister must stand ready to defend the party's program before the withering challenge of the Opposition. This is a kind of pressure that American chief executives are not exposed to; even the right to call cabinet members before their committees has been denied the congressional leadership on grounds of executive immunity from control by the legislative branch. Overhanging the prime ministership at all times is the fact that lack of support in Parliament may force the ruling party to "go to the country" for a renewed mandate. No American president has ever been removed from office in midterm except by death, although Nixon averted such a step only by resigning.

THE BUREAUCRACY

The American and British political systems are most similar in their civil service apparati (Presthus 1974, p. 327). In each case, politically appointed department heads preside over bureaucracies, many of which are massive and unwieldy. The civil servants stay on while their masters come and go—giving the subordinates much influence over policy (Mosher 1968, chaps. 3 and 4; Crossman 1972, pp. 58–59, 65–66).

The storied impartiality of the British civil servant is perhaps best illustrated by the major leap which took place following World War II. Despite their upper-class background and "public" school preparation, the functionaries of the Whitehall bureaucracy turned to the business of carrying out the Labour party's drastic reforms without dissent (Beer and Ulam 1962, pp. 158–63). An apolitical image among civil servants is assiduously cultivated. For example, when a cabinet officer is to address a political meeting, his press department melts into the woodwork and turns the task of coverage over to the party organization (Crossman 1972, pp. 62–63). This is not to say that civil service administrators are purely technicians carrying out mandates from above with total impartiality. Through shadings in language, selective communication, and timing they do, in fact, seek to influence policy. The process, however, is circumspect and goes on within carefully defined limits.

In contrast, incoming American cabinet members assume that holdovers from the previous administration are likely to sabotage many of their attempted reforms. For the civil servants ranged below, ties with counterparts on congressional staffs are frequently the most salient (Nicholas 1975, p. 22; Vale 1975, p. 50). The alliance of Congress and the bureaucracy against the top echelon of the administration is most graphically demonstrated in the recurrent efforts of recent American presidents to rationalize and simplify the federal machinery (Vale 1975, p. 50; *National Journal* 1973).

The differences between the American and British bureaucracies should not be exaggerated. While the United States civil servant may be more freewheeling and avowedly political in his or her orientation than the British counterpart, the latter is far from neutral, as has been suggested. In the British bureaucracy, there is apt to be significant hostility to the influence of "outsiders," even cabinet ministers. There is pressure on the minister from below to become an advocate for his or her department's interests. Nor can the minister ignore this sort of concern, for, in the words of the late Richard Crossman, "If Whitehall gangs up on you it is very difficult to get your policies through, or even to get a fair hearing for a new idea. . . . Departments know that they last and you don't" (1972, pp. 65–66).

While theoretically a new minister could bring in trusted supporters to aid him or her—for instance in the strategically important position of permanent secretary (second in command in the department)—the civil servants below would be able to neutralize such an individual very quickly. In this sense, the British bureaucracy seems more resistant to change than the American. One factor contributing to this is the tendency for the civil service to be a long-term career in Britain. Several of the Britons interviewed for this study confirmed this pattern, based on their personal observations and experience. Once in government, a person seldom leaves it for a career outside.

There is a special problem for intellectuals who move into the British civil service: they are often perceived as having capitulated to the system and, thus, as having poorer credentials for serious scholarship. One young woman who has a growing reputation in policy research experienced this kind of reaction when she became a researcher in the Department of Health. She is convinced that unless she moves out of government within a relatively short time she will have very little choice but to stay.

In the United States, it is fairly common practice for scholars to move into government positions for a period of time, then return to the campus or go into some other endeavor, such as private consulting (Sharpe 1975). This movement in and out of government gives the federal bureaucracy a degree of openness not to be found in its British counterpart. In the latter instance, the experts are more likely to remain outside, perhaps serving as volunteers on committees of inquiry (p. 12). This probably protects the integrity and independence of the experts better, but it may also make the bureaucracy more ingrown.

A distinctive pattern in the British civil service, not found in the American federal bureaucracy, is the clear line of demarcation between administrators and professional advisers. The administrators—"proper" civil servants—are the disinterested bureaucratic virtuosi who are trained to be administrators but are complete generalists. Their skill lies in their ability to grasp the nub of a situation quickly and ask relevant questions, regardless of the subject matter (Crossman, 1972, p. 56; Sharpe, 1977, p. 69). Within the bureaucracy they hold the balance of power; but the professional advisers consider them "colleagues," and are not in a direct line below them.

The professionals have ordinarily spent a period of time in a career outside of the central administration before entering it. Unlike the administrators, they are subject specialists. The relations between these two kinds of civil servant are complex. Professionals coming into government must learn intricate rules for transmitting information and ideas; the rules are both formal and informal.

Given structural relationships, it is not surprising that there is tension between the two groups of civil servants. Some professional advisers who were interviewed complained that administrators were "hard to pin down on anything," and expressed a degree of mistrust. One professional who had served many years in government felt that colleagues needed to learn that administrators "don't wear horns." This individual welcomed the fact that the administrators are challenging and force one to be very clear about what one is putting forth.

There is general agreement that civil service administrators do fulfill their image of impartiality and integrity. When an administrator defects from this standard, he is roundly condemned. One man who helped to write policy regarding personal social service administration, then became a candidate for a lucrative post he had helped to create, was strongly criticized.

In the United States, there is not the same line of demarcation between administrators and professionals. Instead, there is a mixture of careerists who stay in government and others who float in and out; all are likely to develop careers within a subject area. In neither case are there the tight strictures against becoming "political" that exist in the British bureaucracy. Communication channels are also much looser. As a result, the neophyte in the federal service must rely on informal relations to understand the complexities of the system.

Given a legislative body that plays a secondary role, a government constantly concerned about being ejected, a compliant cabinet, and what has been described as a bureaucracy lacking in creativity (Crossman 1972, pp. 74–75), one may wonder how Britain has managed to generate bold and creative social policies over the years, often seeming to be light years ahead of the United States. In terms of political structure, an overriding factor has been the role of the parties in Britain.

POLITICAL PARTIES

"The battering ram of change" is how Crossman has referred to political parties in Britain (1972, p. 82). Quite clearly his reference was to the Labour party. It was with the advent of Labour as a major force in British affairs that the concept of a mass party, with grass-roots participation in policy deliberations, emerged. Prior to that, says Rose (1971, pp. 209–10), policy was determined by small coteries of party leaders in Parliament. But whether with wide or narrow bases of participation, British parties have been organized in such a way that they could be the major source of policy initiatives. They are national organizations, with strong control at the top. They are thus able to speak with a unified voice on policy issues (D. J. Wilson, 1975). The drafting of the party platform is, accordingly, a serious business, and elections are interpreted as national mandates (Beer and Ulam 1962, p. 78). Candidates for national office are pledged to uphold the platform, and the pledge is something they are held to.

The central organization of the parties can be seen very clearly in their relations with their local counterparts. Both the Labour and Conservative parties have regional offices to coordinate the work of the local parties. These are basically administrative arms of the national party organizations, helping to facilitate their work. Local parties have complained long and hard about the onerous burden of sending regular reports to the regions, but with little success (D. J. Wilson 1975, p. 48). The locals send recommendations to the national party conferences, where they are considered, and, in return, are expected to support the decisions that come out (Rose 1971, pp. 297–302).

With so little dispersion of authority in such large and far-flung organizations, it stands to reason that actual control of party affairs is entrusted to a relatively few hands. In the Labour party—which was in power during the period dealt with in the case studies—the two major policy-making bodies are the National Executive Committee (NEC) and the Parliamentary Labour Party (PLP). The NEC, which is elected by the mass party, has wide-ranging powers concerning party administration and organization, endorsement of candidates and substantive policy positions (Crossman 1972, pp. 89–92). The PLP, made up of the party members in Parliament, is formally independent of the NEC. It cannot alter the party mandate, arrived at in annual conference, but it can delay acting upon it. But the PLP's most important function is to name the prime minister when there is a change of leadership. There is much overlapping in membership between the NEC and the PLP, although a person may serve on one and not the other. Sitting astride the two, and thus dominating party affairs, is the party chairperson. When his or her party is out of power, this person leads the Opposition forces in Parliament. And when the party achieves an electoral majority it is to this same individual that the Queen turns to to form a new government.

From what has been said about the structure of decision making in the British system, it is easy to see that the majority party has the potential for fashioning and enacting major policy initiatives. Yet it would be wrong to see parties as monoliths in firm control of British public life. The Labour party, in particular, has often faced serious factional disputes; it tends to be more vulnerable than other parties because of the strong emphasis on ideology. Local Labour affiliates have sometimes been accused of causing dissension and pressing the party toward extremism, but Rose's research (1971) challenged this assumption. Kavanagh suggests that the trend toward centralization will have the effect of creating more tension, both between local and national government and between local and central party organizations (1977, p. 195).

Some of the threats to major party hegemony are coming from without. The rising challenge from the Liberals and other minority parties in recent years has made it more difficult to talk in terms of *the* Government and *the* Opposition. From 1970 to 1974, the combined vote of the two major parties declined from 89.3 percent to 75.1 percent. In October 1974, only half of the registered electorate voted for either Labour or Conservative candidates. The defections are particularly noteworthy outside of England, where nationalist movements have been growing (Kavanagh 1977, pp. 200–201). Considering the seesawing between the two largest parties and their slim margins, the slackening support among the voters has been of major concern to party leadership. But one must view such threats in perspective. British political parties are still the major source of policy initiatives.

Such is clearly not the case in the United States. An American president is never referred to simply as the head of his party but always as "titular" head of the party. The modifier may give some indication of the limited significance of party affiliation in the governing of the country. More important to the internal affairs of the party organization is the party chairman, who is virtually unknown to the general public. His ultimate function—in fact, the function of the entire party apparatus—is to win elections, nothing more. Party platforms, rather than a mandate for action, are designed to include "something for everybody" and nothing too offensive to anybody. On rare occasions, platform committees have departed from that rule—as, for instance, in 1964, when Goldwater conservatives dominated the Republican platform committee; and again in 1972, when George McGovern's liberal supporters controlled the drafting of the Democratic platform. In both instances, the results were disastrous for the respective parties' fortunes in the elections that followed. Not that the platforms per se were of much importance to the electorate, but they reflected the sharp ideological images of the respective candidates: it is clearly the center that dominates American presidential elections (Dye and Zeigler 1975, pp. 237–38).

Notwithstanding Lord Bryce's observation that, "in America the great moving forces are the parties" (1915, vol. 2, p. 5), they actually bear little resemblance to the national organizations familiar to Europeans. In fact, it is questionable whether they can be referred to as "organizations" at all, in the sense of ongoing bodies with a formal membership committed to shared aspirations. Instead, they are skeletal structures, "unusually fluid and evanescent," run by relatively small cadres of activists who seek to mobilize the energies of the members periodically for the purpose of electing candidates (Sorauf 1968, pp. 79–80; Dye and Zeigler 1975, pp. 235–36; Crossman 1972, p. 74).

Insofar as the major parties are organized entities, they are highly decentralized. The election system, which emphasizes states and local congressional districts, contributes to the weakening of the national party structures. The closest thing to a powerful party system, in the British style, is actually found at the local level, in the political machines in large cities. Even here, the power has often been attached to a single personality rather than a durable party structure. Personal followings also tend to be the pattern in the process of nominating candidates for national office, in Congress as well as the White House (Bibby and Davidson 1967, p. 19).

The increase in the use of mass media in campaigning has been a major contributing factor to the decline in the importance of party organization. A series of election reforms over the years—such as open primaries and crossfiling—has also weakened party influence. A pattern of convergence of the major parties, noted in relation to Britain, has been far more long-standing and pervasive in the United States. There is much more ideological diversity within than between the major parties. Yet there are recognizable differences between the party postures, particularly in domestic policy. Mainstream Republicans are more conservative fiscally, more strongly opposed to government activity—especially in the social welfare area, and more pro-business and anti-labor than mainstream Democrats. Not surprisingly, the general composition of the two party memberships is also different, with Democrats being younger, more urban, and more likely to belong to ethnic and racial minorities (Dye and Zeigler 1975, pp. 229–30). A major component of Democratic party membership, that in the Deep South, departs from this pattern. The fact that the Democrats are a clear majority of the voters is offset to an extent by the factionalism within the party. The Republicans historically have been more homogeneous.

Party affiliation is of greater consequence within Congress than in the nation as a whole. The majority party organizes the Congress, determining the leadership in each house and on the all-important committees. While there is not the party discipline found in the British Parliament, nonetheless party membership does influence voting patterns. Dissident members can be punished by the party leadership when it comes time to make committee assignments. Furthermore, there are many perquisites and favors that party leaders can give or withhold. This kind of influence is most potent in the House of Representatives, especially with freshman members. But there are exceptions here, too—as when a coalition of reform-oriented newcomers pushed through changes in the rules in the post-Watergate period.

As is the case in Britain, there has been a decline in support of the two major parties in recent years. Between 1964 and 1972, for example, the percentage of eligible voters identifying themselves as Independents rose from twenty-three to thirty-four (Epstein 1980; Dye and Zeigler 1975, p. 249); and the number so labeled has remained around a third since then. Unlike the case in Britain, however, this disaffection has not crystallized in the form of sustained third-party support. By and large, Independents have a low rate of involvement in the political process.

Given the lack of ideological identity of the respective major parties, the meaninglessness of party platforms, and the lack of strong national organization, American political parties have little impact on the substance of policy. Thus policy initiatives must come from other sources. One is the group of professional and academic figures who move in and out of government. These have certainly been a major source of ideas. In addition, a wide range of special interest groups seek to influence policy. This latter influence is predominantly negative, however, in the sense of resisting rather than promoting new intiatives; this stems from the fact that they are generally preoccupied with averting changes that might affect their interests adversely.

SPECIAL COMMISSIONS AND COMMITTEES

The commission or committee specially appointed to deliberate on a problem and offer recommendations is a feature of both British and American systems, but their functions are different. The commission or committee of prominent citizens and experts that is established by the British government is expected to make substantive policy recommendations that are to be the basis for official policy positions. In other words, its recommendations are treated with the greatest seriousness. In one of the cases described in this text, such a committee, the Seebohm Committee, in effect fashioned the Local Authority Social Services Act (see Chapter 5).

Presidential commissions and committees in the United States are established primarily to gather information, provide political support for a position the administration wants to take, provide a forum for an exchange of views on a controversial question, or simply buy time until the issue becomes less heated or the pressure for action dissipates. Presidents have been known to establish such committees, then later quietly shelve their reports without comment. It is noteworthy that one committee that did have a major role in fashioning legislation—the Committee on Economic Security, which formulated the principles on which the Social Security Act of 1935 was based—was composed of cabinet members (Schlesinger 1959, p. 304).

A British institution which has no exact American counterpart is the *white paper,* a document justifying the Government's position on some matter. It is circulated to members of Parliament, regardless of party, and put on sale to the public. A white paper serves the function of assuring that the party in power cannot simply push through its policies with its compliant parliamentary majority, in the absence of a full airing and public debate. Thus, it serves as a protection to the democratic process in a political structure which provides a built-in advantage to the ruling regime (Muir 1930).

THE FEDERAL SYSTEM

The most obvious—and historically the most important—difference between the British and American political environments is the system of state governments in the United States. While on the surface the design of the United States Constitution settled the question of whether there was to be a single nation or a loose confederation of states, the issue has never been fully resolved. Rather, it has repeatedly intruded itself on the political scene, often at critical times in the nation's development.

The Civil War put an end to the one serious attempt by states to withdraw from the Union altogether. In the 1930s, a major barrier to nationalization was breached when the government moved boldly into the social welfare arena. The Supreme Court decisions of 1937, which affirmed the right of the federal government to collect taxes in order to provide income protection to its citizens, laid that issue to rest (Schlesinger 1951, p. 369).

States continue to be a major political institution. With some significant exceptions, the majority of social programs developed and enacted at the national level have, in reality, been state programs, in which the states agree to meet certain standards in return for federal financial support. One result of this federal system has been great disparity among states in the scope and quality of programs. For instance, in 1978, monthly welfare grants under the federal Aid to Families with Dependent Children (AFDC) program could be anywhere from twelve dollars per person to one hundred twenty-eight dollars per person, depending on the state in which the family resided (*Social Security Bulletin* 1979, p. 72).

The ongoing tension between state and federal governments has usually been cast in a liberal-conservative framework, with the federal end tending to be on the liberal side, that is, in favor of the expansion of programs for protection of the weak and equalization of opportunity. The most tortured history revolved around the questions of slavery and, later, the rights of racial minorities. "States' rights" was for years the rallying cry with which congressional representatives of the South fought civil rights legislation. Less publicized but significant battles have also been fought around the implementation of legislation already enacted. Federal agencies charged with enforcing standards have often been hesitant to press the issue with the states (see, for example, Bell 1965).

Although the role of states has diminished noticeably over the years, they are likely to continue to be a major force in governmental policy in the foreseeable future. One factor in this is the aforementioned political structure, in which candidates for national office are dependent on state-based election machinery. Even more significant is the fact that three-fourths of the state legislatures would have to ratify any changes in the constitutionally defined role of states. Not that major changes could not come about (they have from time to time in the past), but there is presumed to be a point beyond which state governments would not be willing to allow their power to be eroded.

In Britain, the relations between the central government and local authorities follow the same pattern as is exhibited in other political structures: a high degree of central control. Under the principle of *ultra vires,* local authorities have only those powers explicitly conferred on them by Parliament (Benjamin 1977, p. 152; Benemy 1965, p. 174). While local governments chafe under specific prohibitions and burdens imposed by Westminster and Whitehall, the basic system of control from above is understood and accepted (Scarrow 1971, p. 27).

Following World War II, there was a major erosion in the functions of local authorities. Since 1945, responsibility for electric and gas services, most income maintenance functions, agricultural services, tax assessment, certain aspects of road transportation, and hospitals and other health services have been removed from local jurisdiction. Thus, the smaller authorities have been left with few functions of major significance to the citizenry (Young 1977, pp. 214–15). Little wonder, then, that there is a lack of interest in local government (Scarrow 1971, p. 18)

Not only does the central government have basic control over the local authorities, but it has built in further constraints on their autonomy, vis-à-vis their constituents. For example, the Local Government Act of 1933 ruled that, in most urban areas, after the local council has voted for a bill, it is required to hold a public meeting at which the voters can reject the total bill or any of its clauses; it takes only one hundred voters to force a referendum on a clause (Scarrow 1971, pp. 4–5).

An argument for the increasing centralization of responsibility has been that all but the largest local authorities lacked the technical capacity to carry on most functions of modern government. But there also have been complaints that the local authorities were basically pressure groups needing restraint and possibly more interested in representing themselves than their constituents (Scarrow 1971, p. 22; compare Benjamin 1977 with Wiseman 1966, p. 213.)

Despite these trends, central government is sensitive to the reactions of the local authorities, which do, after all, have the most intimate contact with the electorate. Nor is this concern limited only to London and the other metropolitan centers, although understandably they are particularly influential. As the locals have banded together in the Association of Municipal Corporations and the County Councils Associations, they have been able to have a significant impact on national policy (Scarrow 1971, p. 15; Crossman 1977, pp. 633, 690; Hall 1976, pp. 54–55).

GENERAL POLITICAL PHILOSOPHY

There are, finally, pervasive assumptions about the proper role of government that guide and shape the British and American political experience. They are both cause and effect in relation to the systems described in the foregoing discussion. One must begin by acknowledging that the two systems have underlying values that are similar in many respects. Both spring from a common heritage that places a paramount value on the freedom of the individual. Its roots run back to the *udal* principle in Norse law, under which a man and his progeny held absolute title to his land without intervention of any secular power (Fergusson 1884, pp. 141–42).

The American colonies were founded at a time of intense consciousness about royal absolutism, by those who were most suspicious of higher authority. The hostility to central control—by both government and church—has been a continuing obsession in the American mind ever since. It is no accident that the philosophy of Herbert Spencer, Social Darwinism, which preached untrammeled right of exploitation of the weak by the strong, found more fertile soil in the American intellectual community than in its author's homeland, England (Hofstadter 1944). Whereas the British have interpreted individual rights in part as claims on the state for a share in its beneficence, Americans have seen rights more as a negative concept: the right to be left alone by government (Rimlinger 1971).

The two systems thus present contrasting environments for the process of developing social policy, despite their common heritage and adherence to a democratic form of government. Aside from the greater readiness of the British to use government as an instrument for social welfare, there are structural characteristics which have made it easier to bring about policy reform in that country: a far greater degree of centralization, both in relation to levels of government and as between the executive and legislative branches; and national parties whose formally adopted platform serve a policy-making function, not just as a means of garnering a few more votes at election time. These differences are reflected in the nature and boldness of the social service reforms that were undertaken in the respective settings in the late 1960s and early 1970s, their success or failure, and the role of social workers in relation to these efforts.

2
Interest Group Politics

"WITHIN A SOCIETY," WRITES FORMER PRESIDENTIAL ADVISER Richard Goodwin, "there is no 'public' interest; only individuals with common private interests" (1974, p. 312). Whether one views that comment as cynical or merely realistic, it is a view that is expressed with increasing frequency. A rapid proliferation of special interest groups and the dismal careers of countless reform efforts in recent years have led some government analysts to ask whether the United States is capable of being governed any more (see, for example, Herbers 1978). Indeed, lobbying by private interests has increased dramatically in the past five years: nearly double the number of paid lobbyists in Washington between 1973 and 1978, and two billion dollars spent annually on influencing national policy (*Time* 1978, p. 15).

But some of the reaction to "government by special interests" appears to have been triggered by a combination of diverse factors: a president lacking previous experience in the ways of Washington, a departure from a consistent pattern for virtually all of the presidents in this century; a Congress whose truculence is bolstered by new means of budgetary control; and the emergence of an array of single-issue groups in no mood to compromise. In reality, extra-governmental interest groups have been deeply involved in all aspects of the governing process in both the United States and Britain for generations. Far from spelling the demise of democratic political institutions, interest groups are seen by those most involved in government to be an essential element in its operation. In other words, if they did not exist they would have to be invented.

This last point should be clearly understood. It does not mean that interest group influence on public policy is "good," in the sense of enhancing the interests of the total society, nor that all interests are equally represented. Dye and Zeigler (1975) make a good case for the fact that interest group influence is basically unequal and that, on balance, it protects the status quo. Rather, the point is that the formal machinery of government is dependent on outside groups for its operation. It is not unusual, for instance, to find officials fostering the development of outside interest groups in order to drum up support for their policies (Presthus 1974, p. 281). The primary dependence on interest groups, however, is for information. A sample of members of Congress ranked such groups first among sources of information, followed by the party and newspapers (p. 280). If interest group politics is unfair it is because it is part of an unfair social-political system. The intent here is not to place a value on it but to understand it.

Given what has been said thus far about the political environments in the United States and Britain, we can anticipate that interest groups outside of government will adapt their approaches to these environments. For example, the legislative branch will be a much more important target of lobbying efforts in this country. Presthus's study of the United States and Canada is useful in this regard, because Canada has a parliamentary structure like that in the United Kingdom but with strong provincial governments that are analogous to the states in the United States. He found that the cabinet was a major focus of lobbying efforts in Canada, but that targets were more diffuse in this country, with Congress ranking first among all targets (p. 147).

THE AMERICAN SCENE

The Legislative Arena.   The U.S. Congress has been the butt of endless jokes over the years. Its work has sometimes been looked upon as more symbol than substance (Edelman 1964), but in recent years Congress has demanded new respect. The House and Senate budget committees play an increasingly important, if negative, role. Indeed, there were many points in the past when its actions were pivotal. The Social Security Act of 1935 and several amending acts since then, the many pieces of tax legislation enacted over the years and urban renewal measures, to name only a few, have had major implications for the distribution of real resources. On a less tangible but still vital level, the Voting Rights Act of 1965 laid the basis for significant shifts in political power in the South.

The complexity of congressional politics requires that those who would influence legislative decisions be highly sophisticated about its operation. Particularly strategic are chairpersons of certain committees, but much of the day-to-day contact is with committee staff. Here, as elsewhere, a principal resource for the interest group representative is information. The strategic importance of this resource depends on how knowledgeable the committee people are regarding the policy at issue. The image of the heavy-handed lobbyist who threatens reprisal at the polls is not realistic. Sophisticated interest group representatives may imply such threats, but to make them directly is to invite defiance on the part of the lawmaker and a challenge to back up the threat at the next election (Dye and Zeigler 1975, p. 267).

Ordinarily, a wide range of tactics is employed. Direct contact with public officeholders and their staffs, including giving testimony at hearings, ranks highest, with enlistment of one's constituency—for instance, for letter-writing campaigns—a close second. Coalition politics—that is, collaboration with other interest groups—is also a popular approach in the United States. Of lesser importance generally are publicity campaigns, although welfare interest groups make substantial use of this approach (Presthus 1974, p. 154).

Senior Administrative Officials. Cabinet members are a principal target of very few groups in the United States, in contrast with Canada, where they are a major focus of interest groups' attention (p. 147). One explanation for this may be that cabinent members in this country do not constitute a policy-making body. They are generalists who often enter office with little understanding of their specific sphere of responsibility, and who move on and off the scene with regularity. By the time he leaves office, it is not unusual for a president (most of whom do not get to serve out two full terms) to have a basically different cabinet from the one with which he started. One knowledgeable Washington observer has suggested that most persons who have filled the position of secretary of HEW have tended to cut themselves off from the program people who handle the nuts and bolts of policy within the department.

Civil Servants. In contrast to their limited contact with senior officials, interest groups are frequently involved with the bureaucracy. The interpenetration of professional interest groups and the civil service since World War II has had a major impact on policy (Mosher 1968, pp. 105–110). Among American interest groups in the social welfare field surveyed by Presthus, more than one-fourth listed civil servants as a primary target group; this was equal to the number citing Congress as a prime target (p. 147).

Particularly with respect to the civil servants, personal contact and personal relationships are important means of interest group influence. Administrative agencies, in contrast to the halls of Congress, lend themselves to direct negotiations with small, highly focused and highly informed interest groups (Dye and Zeigler 1975, p. 276). The low visibility of such agencies increases this tendency. This fact, and the crucial importance of information and personal trust in such relationships, helps to explain why there is only a limited relationship between a group's reputed political "muscle" and its success in influencing policy.

Effectiveness of Interest Groups. "Political influence," says Presthus, "is not, as common sense might lead one to assume, entirely a function of group affluence and large membership, nor is it confined to the great 'economic' associations of business, industry, labor, and the professions" (1974, p. 123). That assertion appears to be something of an understatement, judging from Presthus's own data. He found, for example, that organized labor was rated highest in effectiveness by both American legislators and government bureaucrats, yet in actual cases its success rate was rather modest. Conversely, welfare groups, which had a low reputation for effectiveness, had a very high success rating (pp. 206–207). Needless to say, one must avoid generalizing too widely from such findings. It may be that welfare groups are more likely than labor to pick issues on which they have a good chance of winning.

An apparent factor in labor's relatively poor showing, according to Presthus, is the low priority it gives to influencing public policy in the United States. But an additional element appears to be the tendency of many unions to put major reliance on elective sanctions and less on expert testimony and other means of providing information to officials (pp. 206–207). The information giving is part of a wider pattern of providing services:

> [It is] clear that politically effective directors spend their time somewhat differently than those who are less effective. They are more likely to emphasize highly-valued services such as providing information to legislators, compared to other directors who attempt to inform them about constituent opinion, an area where most legislators feel they have little to learn (p. 209).

Contrary to the conventional view of "pressure" group relations with government officials, in which the former browbeat the latter, the reality for the more successful groups is "a symbiotic, exchange relationship" with officials (Presthus 1974, p. 167). This appraisal is consistent with a view that interest group representatives, congressional staff, and civil servants are highly functional to one another. The pervasive anti-government attitude in the United States places a special burden on interest group spokespersons, who must at the same time cultivate close working relationships with officials, yet demonstrate that they are vigorous in promoting the interests of their rank and file.

One way in which such tension may be mitigated is through differential rates of participation in the political process by different segments of interest groups. Dye and Zeigler's notion of elites seems useful here. They identify three such subgroups: leaders, active followers, and passive followers.

> [L]eaders accomodate only those factions represented by active members, whose values are not necessarily reflective of the values of most members. Since in most cases the followers are not especially interested in political activities, lack of accurate representation is not crucial to their continued membership. Only when the leaders go beyond the limits of acceptable behavior, and thus become highly visible, will they encounter much opposition (1975, p. 266).

Actually, Dye and Zeigler might have added a fourth subgroup—the paid representatives of groups in the political arena. The fact that interest group representatives may have different views from those of their constituencies is illustrated by one member of a coalition of social service professionals which worked on the development of the Social Service Amendments (Title XX) to the Social Security Act. This person was asked to rate his own satisfaction and that of his organization with the initial version of the bill and a later version. His ratings for himself changed from "very low satisfaction" to "very high satisfaction." His ratings for the organization by which he was employed were exactly the opposite.

"The Iron Triangle." In recent years, a new term has entered the lexicon of the political analyst: the iron triangle. In the words of a panelist in a 1978 conference: "You have the executive branch and you have special committees in Congress and you have a few powerful special interest groups. Those three together, if they get together, can do whatever they want, regardless of what anyone else thinks." If one accepts both a simple three-way relationship among parties in the political process and rigidity in their approach to issues, then the iron triangle is an apt metaphor to describe what goes on; but the reality is that there are rarely only three parties involved. More typically a number of interest groups vie for ascendency or coexist in uneasy and shifting alliances. Veterans' groups identified with different wars find themselves working at cross-purposes (Greve 1979). Officials of general government and professional groups are often on opposite sides of a particular issue, as happened in the case of the Allied Services Act. Then too, federal agencies and congressional committees get involved in jurisdictional fights with one another. Rather than rigidity, the more typical pattern is one of mutual bending, of trading off secondary interests for primary ones. As a rhetorical device, "the resilient polygon" has less punch than the iron triangle, but it more accurately describes what goes on.

THE BRITISH SCENE

The myth that there was no lobbying in Britain died hard. Despite treatises on the subject as early as 1908, and well after Beer's study of the phenomenon (1956), there were still those who tended to deny it (McKenzie 1974, p. 277; Crossman 1972, p. 38). As might be anticipated, interest groups in Britain have adapted their targets and strategies to the existing political milieu. The lobbying since World War II has been different from what went before, for the advent of the welfare state since the war has altered the political environment considerably (Beer 1956, p. 233).

The major, though not exclusive, foci of interest group attention are the parties, the Cabinet ministers, and the civil servants. In the case of civil servants, however, the principle of impartiality makes such activity rather delicate. It is perhaps because of this and the tendency to deny the existence of lobbying altogether that Beer and Ulam found interest groups to be rather inconspicuous in their modes of operation (1962, p. 170).

Types of Interest Groups.   McKenzie (1974) makes a useful distinction between *sectional* (special interest) and *promotional* (cause-oriented) groups (p. 281). The latter tend to be outsiders to the policy-making arena and "lack political and economic sanctions" (Pym 1974, p. 14). The government can engage in various delaying tactics to wear such groups down. If the pressure is too widespread, there may be resort to a study commission or committee of inquiry (p. 52).

The Child Poverty Action Group (CPAG) is one of the more significant cause-oriented groups to be active in recent decades (Seyd 1976). From a small core of academic sociologists and social welfare workers in 1966, it grew in ten years to a membership of twenty-five hundred, with a paid staff of eleven full-time workers and an annual budget of sixty thousand pounds. Typical of outsider groups, it has focused almost exclusively on raising public awareness of poverty issues by relying on rational argument rather than emotional appeal. Its quarterly journal and frequent pamphlets carry well-researched articles designed to appeal to a select audience. It has also fed information to friendly members of Parliament for use in questioning the government.

One striking omission from its tactical arsenal, according to Seyd, has been direct contact with the civil servants in the Department of Health and Social Security, a major source of policy on poverty issues (pp. 198–99). The Labour government of Harold Wilson saw CPAG as an external critic, never satisfied with the government's efforts to improve the lot of the poor. Former Secretary of Social Services Richard Crossman saw some relief measures as having "spiked the guns of the C.P.A.G." (1977, p. 888), but the prime minister was worried about the organization's political impact (p. 809).

But while promotional groups get the headlines, it is the sectional interests which have the greater impact on policy. Their own members' self-interest is of paramount importance, although they sometimes take on characteristics of promotional groups. The classic case is the labor movement. This not only has been avowedly political, but unlike its American counterpart, has always had a strong ideological bent. Highly class-conscious, it has focused on public policies to improve general conditions (Fraser 1979).

Interest Groups and Political Parties. Given the important role of parties in shaping British policy, it is not surprising that they are a major target of interest groups. Concern has been expressed in some quarters that as pressure groups become more powerful, parties may degenerate into little more than brokers for competing interests (McKenzie 1974, p. 283; Stewart 1974, p. 291). Stewart believes that a major factor in maintaining party authority (that is, the ability to resist group pressures) is that the party, rather than merely seeking power as an end in itself, does so for a purpose: "The virtue of a party decision as opposed to a group decision is that the party . . . can be assumed to have considered more factors than the group" (Stewart 1974, p. 291).

A number of writers have noted the gradual convergence of the major parties' positions over the years, a fact which makes them especially vulnerable to interest group pressure (Beer 1956, pp. 3–4; McKenzie 1974, p. 285). As parties compete more and more for the same votes, especially with very narrow majorities, interest groups can play a very strong role by holding out the promise of pockets of votes.

It was mainly through involvement in the Labour party that certain intellectuals identified with social welfare developed close relationships with key officials in the Labour government of Harold Wilson. For example, Richard Titmuss and Brian Abel-Smith became close friends of Secretary of State for Social Services Richard Crossman, who frequently turned to them for advice (see Crossman 1977). They were instrumental in helping bring to fruition the efforts of the Seebohm Committee through their work with Crossman (Hall 1976). Titmuss and his associates are credited with having had a major influence on social insurance legislation (Klein 1976, p. 474).

Interest Groups and Government Officials. It is with cabinet ministers and civil servants that the sectional interest groups have the greatest involvement, reflecting the manner in which much policy gets formulated in Britain. The frequent consultations between government officials and interest group representatives is viewed as highly legitimate and is not thought of as lobbying, although in reality that is often what it is (Beer 1956, pp. 5–7). McKenzie asks rhetorically,

> Are there not a few great interest groups . . . whose leaders form a kind of inner circle of 'oligarchs' which deals frequently and intimately with senior ministers? And is it not the case that this handful of people decide the fate of the whole community, which is, for the most part, unaware even of the issues they are deciding? (1974, p. 285).

He also points out that the influence runs in two directions, and the minister (for his or her part) may ask the interest group representatives to support a certain policy. Stewart notes that "the machinery of consultation is particularly well developed. . . . The place of most groups is recognized. Their representatives sit upon government" (1974, p. 292). But there is the danger that,

> Civil servants and politicians whose daily routine involves contact with the groups, hearing their viewpoints and their problems, obtaining information from them and co-operating with them on committees, may come to accept the standards of the groups as their own. There is danger that departments may become mere pressure groups within the government (p. 293).

Concern has been expressed about a tendency of government to turn over to commissions dominated by private interests the task of developing policies that were previously the responsibility of governmental departments and ministers. For example, Grant (1977) cites the case of the Manpower Services Commission—representing the Confederation of British Industry, the Trade Union Congress, and government—which was given responsibility for developing health and safety policies (p. 174).

It appears that one can lose the "war," in terms of major legislation, and more than offset this disadvantage by winning the series of "battles" in ongoing negotiations with the bureaucracy. At least this is Eckstein's (1960) interpretation of the experience of the British Medical Association (BMA). He attributes much of the BMA's success to its style of negotiating with government officials, an interpretation which is contested by Marmor and Thomas (1972). But whether it is style or the power to pose credible threats that is responsible for BMA's effectiveness, the continuing—and, in Presthus's (1974) term, "symbiotic"—relationship with government has served BMA's constituency well.

The emerging public medical care system helped to convert the BMA from a scientific society into what was, in effect, a trade union. Its constituency consists of the general practitioners, who give the basic care under the National Health Service. In contrast with the monolithic American Medical Association, the medical specialists in Britain are organized in a series of Royal Colleges, which are separate from the BMA. At points, the government has been able to exploit these divisions by splitting one group off from another in regard to a specific policy (Eckstein 1960, p. 66; see also Pym 1974, pp. 75–76).

The main involvement, however, concerns the BMA. On its side, the government needs information and a means of getting individual physicians to support and carry out government policies. In return, it is able to offer concessions to the medical community. The BMA also provides a channel for grievances against official edicts. In order for it to serve the government's purposes, it must maintain sufficient credibility among its members. It can only do that as it is able to go to bat for its aggrieved members and obtain concessions for them (Eckstein 1960, p. 112). Klein (1974) suggests that the exchange is aided by the fact of a single organization dealing with the authorities (p. 473).

BMA leaders are also frequently placed on government committees and commissions. In Klein's words,

> Typically, policy has been made by setting up expert committees—usually dominated by medical membership—to report on specific policy problems. Thus, the emphasis has been not so much on policy analysis as on achieving a political consensus among those representing the very professions that would have to implement any decisions made (pp. 466–67).

By and large, BMA plays a low-keyed role in the political arena. For example, it shuns the heavy use of public propaganda for which the AMA is famous. However, it does not restrict its activity to the bureaucracy, and it has on occasion sought the support of friendly members of parliament through direct lobbying.

The Use of Overt Campaigning.   Although quiet politicking with cabinet ministers and civil servants is the favorite tool of established, "sectional" interest groups, most do have recourse to other tactics at times. Often this is a fall-back approach for occasions when private negotiations with officials do not seem to be working (Beer 1956, p. 9). Officials have no problem with this idea. To quote Stewart (1974), "There are further safeguards should the groups be treated unfairly. The government accepts the appeal to Parliament or to public opinion in that a decision may be modified in the light of the group's impact there" (p. 292). Understandably, the government prefers to handle things more discretely, thus avoiding an image of not being in control. This may lead to extended delays in submitting certain policies to Parliament for action, as happened for example in the case of the Local Authority Social Services Act (Hall 1976; Crossman 1977).

GENERAL OBSERVATIONS

Interest group activity is, then, part and parcel of the policy-making process in both Britain and the United States. Despite the major differences in the way in which decisions are made, the strategies used are strikingly similar. Much of the most successful activity appears to be the quiet consultation and negotiation with key policy makers, and particularly with their underlings who have so vital a role in shaping specific measures and interpretations. This process tends to exclude certain groups that either are viewed as too strident or lack the resources to employ full-time representatives who can become expert regarding certain policy areas. Direct threats of political retaliation are generally not effective, although more subtle indications of constituent strength can have impact. The greatest asset of the lobbyist is information. The less access the policy makers have to it, the greater the advantage for the interest group representative. Because of the importance of seemingly minor details in policy, the extreme complexity of the governmental process, the huge volume of information to be absorbed, and the need to be seen as a source that can be trusted, work in behalf of an interest group is time consuming. Organizations with meager resources must thus concentrate their attention on rather limited objectives if they hope to have a significant impact.

Aside from the obvious differences in the role of parties and of the legislative arm of government, there are other ways in which the American and British political arenas diverge. One is the career patterns of people in and around government. The British civil service is a career system; once in, a person generally remains there. But there may be substantial mobility among different areas of specialization. There is not the American penchant for glorifying the subject specialist. One offshoot of this may be less readiness to welcome outside experts than is true in the American federal bureaucracy. In the latter case, mobility is more likely to be within the same subject specialty but with fairly frequent shifting in and out of government, or between the federal department and the congressional staff. Related to all this is the pattern of drawing academicians directly into government in the American case, whereas they are more likely to remain external in Britain. This probably enhances their independence as critics, although it may lessen their actual impact on decisions made.

3
The Emergence of
the Welfare State

SOCIAL SERVICE POLITICS IS A CREATURE OF THE WELFARE STATE, "a state in which," according to Webster's dictionary, "the welfare of its citizens, with regard to employment, medical care, social security, etc., is considered to be the responsibility of the government." This is because it is only as the state allocates a large share of its wealth to social welfare that social services assume major importance in the political arena. In addressing the subject of social service politics, we are thus talking about a relatively young phenomenon.

While the United States and Britain share a common poor law heritage, in which government social service activity tended to be viewed negatively, there have been marked differences in their approaches to such activity, especially in recent decades. A major factor in the greater readiness of British governments to provide services for the citizenry, according to Fraser (1979), has been the more avowedly political role of the British labor movement. Its American counterpart was historically more oriented to collective bargaining than political action and for many years opposed progressive social legislation.

British class consciousness and relative lack of social and economic mobility were conducive to the development of a strong sense of labor solidarity, one, moreover, that found ready expression in political channels. Government was characteristically viewed as an instrument to redress grievances, as well as a potential source of repression that had to be guarded against. Contrary to the case of "individual rights" in the United States, where they are associated with minimal governmental interference in private affairs, rights for the Briton are more commonly viewed in terms of claims one makes upon the powers that be (Rimlinger 1971).

THE EVOLUTION OF THE BRITISH WELFARE STATE

Collectivism in Britain—in the sense of collective responsibility for the welfare of the individual—was already apparent in the nineteenth century. By the 1880s, the Marxist-oriented Social Democratic Federation and the more moderate Fabians were on the scene, and these movements led to the founding of the Independent Labour party in the 1890s (Larson 1924, pp. 743–44).

Two periods of intensive activity in social policy were the years between 1906 and 1911, and those from 1920 to 1925. With the Labour party posing a significant challenge for the first time, the government enacted the Workingmen's Compensation Act and the Provision of Meals Act (school lunches for hungry children) in 1906. These were followed in 1908 by the Old Age Pension Law and legislation to protect children and young persons (Larson 1924, pp. 755–56). In 1909 came minimum wage and housing reform laws, and in 1911, the National Insurance Act, which protected workingmen in three industries against the risk of unemployment. By 1913, social welfare represented 29 percent of all governmental expenditures (p. 497).

In the early 1920s, Britain was thrown into a depression, after a brief postwar boom, and, with Labour providing an added spur to action, the government enacted more social measures. In 1919 came housing legislation, and in 1920, the Unemployment Insurance Act, which extended protection to industrial workers generally (Mowat 1955, pp. 43–46). The Widows',

Orphans', and Old Age Contributory Pensions Act and National Health Insurance (covering wage earners) followed in 1925. It is worth noting that the moderate wing of the Conservative party, led by Neville Chamberlain and Winston Churchill, was a major force behind these measures. Their intent was at least in part to blunt the appeal of Labour, which was posing an increasing political threat (pp. 338–43).

The Beveridge Reforms. By the time of Britain's entry into World War II, the country had a wide-ranging set of social welfare provisions, but they were piecemeal and scattered, and many persons fell through the cracks. In 1941, a committee chaired by Sir William Beveridge began to put together a comprehensive plan for basic protection against economic want and related problems. Its report, issued the following year, charted a new course for British social welfare. In the midst of the agony of war, which affected the civilian population as directly as the military, all factions supported the reforms. Thus, although the welfare measures after World War II are associated with the Labour government, which came into power at that time, the basic reforms would have been enacted in some form regardless of which party assumed control (Handler 1973; Kavanagh and Rose 1977; Rimlinger 1971; Titmuss 1950).

The Family Allowance Act of 1945, the first of the measures to be enacted, provided benefits without a means test or provision for contributions from the beneficiaries, based simply on the number of children in the family; as is typical of social security schemes in Britain, the conception was bold but the actual benefits were pegged at a low level (Handler 1973; Rimlinger 1971).

The National Insurance Act, which went into effect in 1948, was a far cry from the 1911 act of that name. In keeping with the strictly universalistic philosophy underpinning the total Beveridge plan (that is, benefits not based on level of need but available to all equally), a flat rate of contributions and a flat pension were devised. This principle required that benefits be set at a low level, which, with the rising cost of living, forced extensive use of means-tested assistance in subsequent years, thus undercutting the principle of universalism (Handler 1973, pp. 23–24; Hoshino 1969).

A pillar of the Beveridge scheme was the National Health Service, begun in 1948. Like other elements in the system, it was a major expansion of programs that already existed. Instead of being a limited program for wage earners, as was the 1925 act, the new program provided a comprehensive, cost-free health care system for all persons (Handler 1973, pp. 23–24).

Personal Social Services.   The postwar period in Britain witnessed a similar expansion in the personal social services, nonfinancial welfare provisions. The Education Act of 1944 expanded the programs for physically and mentally handicapped children. The Public Health Act of 1946 gave local authorities responsibility for providing domestic help to sick and infirm people and to families in which the mother was absent from the home. The National Assistance Act of 1948 established the system of accommodation and other services to the elderly, the physically handicapped, and the homeless, to be provided by local authority welfare departments. The Children Act of 1948 created local children's departments, with wide-ranging responsibilities. And the National Health Service Act, which went into effect the same year, called for maternal and child welfare services, for the mentally ill and subnormal, home nursing, health visiting, and home helps (homemakers). Meanwhile, housing authorities were coming to see their role as including concern for social conditions and family well-being in the housing estates (Handler 1973, pp. 32–39; Seebohm Report 1968, pp. 24–25; Hall 1976, pp. 3–9).

The cumulative impact of these legislative initiatives can be seen in the growth in social welfare expenditures in subsequent years. Between 1952 and 1968, public spending for local welfare services rose 234 percent (adjusted to allow for inflation); for child care 127 percent; for education 189 percent; and for health, 95 percent. These all outpaced both the 74 percent rise in overall public expenditures during these years and the 58 percent rise in the gross national product. The most dramatic rises in social service outlays occurred in the early part of this period, the late 1950s and early 1960s (Hall 1976, pp. 8–9).

There appear to have been three major factors involved in these increases in Britain: the need to speed the nation's recovery from the effects of the war; the influence of the Labour party on national policy; and growing concern about child protection, youth behavior, and general family disorganization (Handler 1973, pp. 42–60).

SOCIAL WELFARE IN THE UNITED STATES

The task of tracing the evolution of the "welfare state" in this country is complicated by the historic division of responsibility between the federal government and the states. In the same general era in which social legislation was being adopted for all of Great Britain, some states in this country were enacting similar policies. However, not only were the progressive measures limited to certain portions of the country, leaving the rest untouched, but the coverage of state laws was extremely uneven.

The first Workingmen's Compensation Law was passed in Maryland in 1902; by 1917, all but ten states had enacted such legislation (Schlesinger 1951, p. 204). A major movement for mothers' pension laws (by which widows and orphans could be maintained in their own homes) began with the enactment of the Funds for Parents Act in Illinois in 1911; two years later nineteen other states had such laws (Axinn and Levin 1975, pp. 133–34). By the time of the Great Depression, seventeen states had some form of old age pension program (Schlesinger 1951, p. 330). These laws tended to be minimal in provision and punitive in their application, consistent with the American aversion to giving "something for nothing."

It was not until the Depression that anything approaching a comprehensive social insurance and assistance scheme for the country as a whole was enacted. Health insurance was many years down the road. The first unemployment insurance program was a state program—enacted in Wisconsin in 1932, as the economic collapse created strong political pressure for protection of workers (Schlesinger 1959, pp. 301–302).

The Social Security Act. The federal government had always been directly involved in welfare programs for special groups of Americans—war veterans, Indians, and newly-freed slaves. But great care had been taken to avoid committing the national government to responsibility for the welfare of its general citizenry. In a historic veto of a bill to provide federal funds for the erection of state mental hospitals, President Franklin Pierce declared in 1854, "It can not be questioned that if Congress has power to make provision for the indigent insane . . . it has power to provide for the indigent who are not insane, and thus to transfer to the Federal Government the charge of all the poor in all the States" (Axinn and Levin 1975, p. 71).

After the passage of the Social Security Act in 1935, which set up a comprehensive system of social insurance and assistance programs, the constitutionality of the federal role was in doubt until a series of decisions by the Supreme Court in 1937 (Schlesinger 1951, p. 369). Even today the issue of state versus federal prerogatives in welfare matters is far from dead. The Social Security Act laid out the basic framework for public welfare that continues today: a set of insurances to protect people against major economic hazards, and means-tested assistance programs for the destitute.

Over the years the insurance provisions have been broadened and strengthened, the most significant expansion being health insurance for the elderly, adopted in 1965; a companion provision provided medical assistance for the poor. The last significant challenge to the principle of a universalistic, contributory insurance system occurred in the early 1950s. Republicans sought to turn the retirement program into a pension financed from general revenues, thus subject to congressional control. The threat was beaten off by the moderate Republican administration of Dwight D. Eisenhower.

Changes in the public assistance provisions of the Social Security Act have been piecemeal, leaving intact the system of state-based programs, with the federal government contributing to the cost and setting standards. The result has been great inconsistency from state to state. A general catchall category—general assistance—has no federal subsidy and no federal standards.

In the past decade, two American presidents, representing both major parties, have sought to make major reforms in public assistance, but without success. Some progressive provisions in the original act—such as cash as opposed to in-kind assistance, confidentiality of information, and elimination of work as a condition of receiving assistance—have been eroded over the years. On the other hand, the courts have knocked down a few of the more restrictive conditions that states attached to the receipt of assistance.

Governmental Support for the Personal Social Services. The resistance to federal intrusion on states' prerogatives has been even stronger in the personal social services than in relation to income maintenance. The private, nonprofit sector of social services has fought against governmental encroachment at any level. The potential of such services for socialization and social control, especially of the young, appears to be a major factor in this. As a result, over the years, it was only in times of great crisis that government, especially federal government, became very active in this field. Federal programs for youth, enacted during the Depression, were phased out when the crisis ended. It was a similar story with wartime emergency programs, although social services for veterans became a permanent fixture (Axinn and Levin 1975, pp. 230–33).

Over against the resistance to governmental intervention by the voluntary sector, was the growing recognition that private philanthropic dollars were steadily shrinking, and that states were becoming less and less able to support services. In the years after World War II, the federal government became increasingly involved in subsidizing personal social services, with the states acting largely as a conduit to locally based public and voluntary agencies. The first major step in this direction was the National Mental Health Act of 1946 (actually not funded until 1948), through which community mental health services were supported (Axinn and Levin, p. 230).

The greatest impetus for an expanded federal role came in 1962, when the Social Security Act was amended to provide funds for personal social services to recipients or potential recipients of public assistance. The program was based on the belief that personal inadequacies of the recipient were a major factor in his or her poverty; proponents held out the hope that through personal social services the growing welfare rolls could be reduced. Meanwhile, an array of federal subsidy programs to deal with school adjustment, child care, juvenile delinquency, physical disabilities, and problems of aging appeared on the scene.

The scope of the growing federal involvement was staggering. In 1960, there were fewer than two hundred categorical grant-in-aid* programs under the aegis of HEW. By the early 1970s, the number had grown to more than one thousand (Iglehart, Lilley, and Clark 1973, p. 1). Federal grants to the states for social services, under the 1962 Amendments to the Social Security Act, amounted to less than two hundred million dollars in Fiscal Year 1963, 522 million dollars in 1970, and 1.6 billion dollars in 1972 (Mott 1976, p. 9).

Just as the Depression had been the occasion for a forward leap in financial welfare, another national crisis fostered the rapid growth in federal funding of the personal social services in the 1960s, reawakening for some the hopes, for others the fears, of fundamental social change. In this instance, as in the Depression, what resulted was more on the order of moderate social reform, clearly within the existing framework. Whether one accepts the analysis of Piven and Cloward (1971), who saw the growth in social welfare as an attempt to lessen the impact of the political unrest, or of Galper (1975), who views the "welfare state" generally as a means of propping up the capitalist system, it is clear that the reforms were time limited, leaving only a residual system of welfare programs that did not disturb the basic economic and political relationships in the country. The present study is less concerned with the underlying reasons for the growth than with its consequences.

THE CREATION OF A MAJOR INDUSTRY

Social welfare is now a major element in the national lives of the United States and Britain. In 1976 more than one-seventh of the

*Formula grants to the states for carrying out programs meeting federally established guidelines and regulations.

gross domestic product in the United States was accounted for by federal government expenditures for health, education, welfare, and related activities. In Britain, the figure was one-fourth, almost equalling the volume of industrial activity for that year (United Nations 1978, pp. 729, 809, and 862). Strict comparisons between expenditures by the respective central governments in the two countries are somewhat misleading because of the decentralized pattern in the United States. Nonetheless, national public social policies clearly loom large in both countries, and central government social policy decisions have a major impact on the total economy.

In both countries, the growth in social welfare was accompanied by a major expansion in the social service work force. Between 1940 and 1960, social welfare employment in the United States rose gradually from seventy thousand to ninety-five thousand, then shot up to two hundred sixteen thousand by 1970 (Siegel 1975, p. 5). While some of this increase was for the administration of cash income programs, the most dramatic rises were in personal social services. For example, social work personnel in health settings went from nine thousand eight hundred in 1960, to more than twenty-four thousand in 1970. In public education settings, the rise was from six thousand three hundred to over sixteen thousand (p. 6). In public child welfare, there were fewer than seven thousand six hundred full-time workers in 1960, and twelve thousand five hundred in 1969 (Richan 1978, p. 248).

Nor should these increases be at all surprising. A distinctive characteristic of the human services is the extent to which they involve personal contact, the direct laying on of hands. An expansion of such programs means an expansion in personnel. Thus, during both the postwar era in Britain and the 1960s in the United States, armies of paid helpers were created. But unlike military forces, these armies could not just be brought in for a transitory crisis and then disbanded. In short, the expanded cadre of helpers had a vested interest in careers within the social service field.

Of particular importance was the expansion of an organized and articulate cadre of social work professionals. In the

United States, the number of people with some graduate study in social work rose from 38,604 in 1950, to 66,886 in 1970, according to government estimates. During the same period, the number of persons with a Master of Social Work degree went from 11,136 to an estimated fifty-nine thousand (Siegel 1975, pp. 10–11). In 1955, several social work professional associations came together in the National Association of Social Workers (NASW). A similar process led to the formation of the British Association of Social Workers in 1970.

A concomitant trend has been the unionization of social service personnel, mainly in the governmental sector. The largest public employees' union in the United States is the American Federation of State, County, and Municipal Employees (AFSCME), many of whose members are in the human services. Thus, unionization has been an added spur to the development of a constituency that has a major stake in the expansion and continuation of the social services and is increasingly politically sophisticated.

Another characteristic of the personal social services is the imprecise nature of the demand for service. Unlike income assistance, the need for which tends to follow economic and demographic trends, personal services are responses to vaguely defined "needs." This problem has plagued every task force that has sought to make projections of personnel shortages and requirements. For example, a working party that studied social work staffing in Scottish local authorities in the late 1950s found difficulty in estimating the numbers of persons in current caseloads needing different levels of service:

> No information exists on which such estimates could be based, but they are essential to sound decisions about appropriate staffing and deployment of staff. We recommend a variety of studies to determine types of need and appropriate ways of meeting them. We ourselves would expect the proportion requiring skilled casework to be substantially higher among persons discharged from mental hospitals and their families, than, for example, amongst the elderly (Great Britain 1959, par. 563).

The Seebohm Committee, whose report was the basis for the Local Authority Social Services Act of 1970, found the same problem in assessing the insufficiency of services (Great Britain 1968a, pars. 74, 75). A major criticism of its work was the reliance on general statements of opinion without empirical data. (See Hall 1976, p. 82; Smith 1971; Townsend 1970.)

In the United States in 1965, a task force at HEW forecast astronomical shortages of trained social work personnel for public programs, based on the numbers of positions that would become available in existing programs (Departmental Task Force 1965). This, in fact, is one of the characteristic ways in which estimates of personnel needs are made: the number of positions funded or expected to be funded. The other is to make simple forecasts of population growth. Both bases have major limitations.

In reality, "need" for personal social services is an amorphous and elastic concept. For example, a Declaration of Rights of the Child, adopted by the United Nations General Assembly in 1959, asserts that the child shall, wherever possible, "grow up in the care and under the responsibility of his parents, and in any case in an atmosphere of affection and of moral and material security" (United Nations, General Assembly 1960, p. 19).

The 1962 amendments to the Social Security Act, while more modest in their aims, had among their purposes,

- To prevent and solve problems that result in the neglect, abuse and delinquency of children.
- To protect and care for homeless, dependent, and neglected children.
- To promote the welfare of the children of working mothers.
- To strengthen the home and to provide adequate care for children away from their homes (Coughlin 1973, p. 16).

If carried out literally, such a mandate would easily require many times the number of persons available for child welfare work. Obviously, the intent is a much more limited conception of service. Just as obviously, there are no clear boundaries to the amount of service or service personnel required to meet "the needs of children." Far more crucial than any external and objective measures of need, in determining the numbers of children for whom service is provided, is the availability of funding. The level of funding, in turn, is based on a series of political decisions.

The upshot of these developments is the emergence in recent years of a major enterprise or "industry" in the United States and Britain, one in which decisions involving large sums of money lack precision and empirical validation, and in which large organized constituencies have a vital stake. Under these circumstances, one can anticipate that the policy-making process will be highly politicized.

Yet, it is a political process attended by ambiguities not found in other sectors. The rhetoric of human service professionals is dominated by the image of selfless servants of the public good. Social workers have been described by Lubove (1965) as "professional altruists." Unlike industrial union members, those in the human services are constrained to justify their bread-and-butter demands in terms of the public interest and quality of service to consumers (Deaton 1972). As a result, political activity by social service workers in their own behalf cannot be overtly self-oriented. Nor is this necessarily a calculated attempt to befuddle the public. In a real sense, social workers themselves need to be convinced of the moral rightness of their political activity.

The Political Context

Part Two
The Case Studies

4
Social Service Reform in Scotland

IN THE AFTERMATH OF WORLD WAR II, GREAT BRITAIN WAS FORCED to come to terms with a set of circumstances drastically different from those it had experienced before. Abroad, its empire was crumbling; at home, the economy was reeling from the devastation wreaked by the war. Old assumptions regarding class and custom had been shaken to their roots. In response, the country turned to the left politically, some industries were nationalized, and the welfare state came into being. These changes in themselves added to the trauma for many Britons, even while reducing the hazards of life for the population.

A second response was to focus on social problems with a more familiar ring—family breakdown, child neglect, and juvenile delinquency. Reports of the effects on children of being uprooted during the war, a rising youth crime rate, and scandals involving maltreatment of children under local authority jurisdiction created a sense of national crisis. The problems were defined in terms that seemed to lend themselves to treatment by professional intervention. With basic protections built in under the welfare state and a rising sense of optimism, it was natural to view human difficulties as a matter of individual and family malfunctioning.

Beginning in the late 1940s, a series of prestigious committees and legislative enactments helped give form to this outlook in what Handler (1973) has called a "unified theory of deviance." The emphasis was on preventive intervention, with poorly functioning families the main target. Quite naturally, a major focus of attention was the organization and staffing of the personal social services.

The distinctive character of social service reform efforts in Scotland relates in part to the fact that social services there were in a much less developed state than in England. Carmichael (1969) attributes the primitive level of services to the historic absence of involvement of the Scottish middle class in charitable activities, reinforced by a religious outlook which held that the thrifty could survive. On the other end, radical Labour politicians saw social work and social welfare benefits as capitalism's means to avert social change. Another reason for the distinctive social service development in Scotland was that nation's legal structure.

The legal tradition in Scotland is that of the Roman law, "in which main positions are arrived at by argument from first principles," in contrast to the English Common Law, built up from a large number of case decisions (Carmichael 1969, p. 36). Scotland has its own criminal justice system, based on three kinds of courts: the High Court of the Justiciary, which deals with the most serious crimes; the sheriff's courts, which hear criminal cases of a less serious nature; and district courts, which handle minor offenses. It is the sheriff's courts which traditionally dealt with juvenile offenses (Great Britain Central Office of Information 1978, p. 25).

THE KILBRANDON AND McBOYLE COMMITTEES

In 1956, the Ingleby Committee was established to study the problems of juvenile delinquency and child neglect, as they pertained to England and Wales. In Scotland, the responsibility was split between two different bodies: the Kilbrandon Committee (delinquency) and the McBoyle Committee (child neglect). The rationale for the division of responsibility between Kilbrandon and McBoyle was that child protection would be easier to incorporate in legislation for the total United Kingdom than would anti-delinquency measures, which more directly involved the legal system. As it turned out, the McBoyle Report (Great Britain 1963b) was rushed to completion just in time for its recommendations to be included in the Children and Young Persons Act of 1963.

The McBoyle Report was much bolder than the Ingleby Report in examining the underlying causes of neglect, citing as one such cause financial adversity of the family (par. 20). It recommended that local authorities have the duty to provide comprehensive services—including provision of cash or in-kind aid—for families in order to prevent child neglect. And, like the Ingleby Report, the McBoyle Report called for better coordination among public and voluntary agencies. Section 1 of the Children and Young Persons Act of 1963 drew upon McBoyle in requiring local authorities to make advice, guidance, and assistance available to families (Campbell 1978, p. 28).

Social work professionals had objected to splitting the responsibility between the McBoyle and Kilbrandon Committees, arguing the essential indivisibility of children's problems, and feeling that the issue of child neglect would get too little attention as a result (Professional Caseworkers' Working Party 1962). To be sure, the McBoyle Committee was overshadowed by the more prestigious Kilbrandon Committee, yet its ideas continued to influence policy development years after its work was finished.

The Kilbrandon Committee had been formed in 1961 by the Secretary of State for Scotland. Its assignment was to consider the provisions of the law of Scotland relating to the treatment of juvenile delinquents and juveniles in need of care or protection or beyond parental control and, in particular, the constitution, powers, and procedure of the courts dealing with such juveniles . . . (Kilbrandon Report 1964).

Lord Kilbrandon's eminent standing and the high caliber of the other committee members assured from the beginning that its ideas and recommendations would carry considerable weight. The membership was predominantly from the justice system; there were no social workers included. While evidence was invited from social workers and other professionals, they felt they got a much better reception from the McBoyle Committee. One informant noted that when the Professional Caseworkers' Working Party (PCWP) met with the Kilbrandon Committee, it was a rather informal session, and the chairman was absent. In all, the committee heard from thirty-seven organizations, a few of them representing social work, and fifteen individuals.

One finding by the committee was that the rate of juvenile offenses, while rising, had not assumed anything like the epidemic proportions that the escalating public concern had seemed to suggest. Between 1950 and 1962, male delinquency had risen from 44.9 per thousand to 52.3 per thousand, while for females the figures were 2.4 and 4.2 (app. A).

The Kilbrandon Report called for a major overhaul in both the juvenile justice system and in services in the field. One explanation for its more radical departure from the status quo than was true, for instance, of the Ingleby Report, is the aforementioned difference in legal traditions in England and Scotland. The Kilbrandon Committee broke new ground while the Ingleby Committee drew on present practices and attempted no fundamental analysis of root problems; their respective approaches are consistent with, on the one hand, the Scottish legal system of argument from first principles and, on the other, the English common law tradition (Carmichael 1969, p. 36).

Of at least equal importance was the existing state of services in Scotland. Separate juvenile courts existed in only four jurisdictions; and social work services were at a very primitive state of development throughout the country. Thus, politically, proposals for major changes would meet less formidable opposition from vested professional interests than would be true in England.

The primary focus of the Kilbrandon Report was the justice system itself, particularly the operation of the courts. This is not surprising, perhaps, in view of the heavy representation of jurists on the committee. A major strength of the document was its emphasis throughout on a humane and enlightened approach to juvenile offenders, an important contribution in the light of the strongly moral and even punitive tone that pervaded a major part of juvenile justice system. The most innovative proposal was the replacement of the existing adjudication machinery for juveniles with a system of citizen panels, consisting of three persons who either by knowledge or experience were considered to be specially qualified to consider children's problems. The citizen panels would be essentially lay bodies: while in practice their numbers might well include members of the legal profession, doctors, teachers, and local authority members, none would be appointed by reason of any existing official position or specialist qualification, but simply on the basis of personal qualities (par. 94).

In practice, the scope of responsibility of panel members would be somewhat limited. Questions of fact in contested cases would remain under the jurisdiction of the courts, although this involved fewer than 5 percent of all juvenile cases. A principal actor was to be the reporter, who, basically, would act in the role of a prosecutor. The reporter would be in a position to exercise discretion as to whether a case should be brought to the panel. As to qualifications for this post, the committee had little to say other than that a "legal qualification" was important (pars. 96–102). The term was perhaps deliberately left ambiguous.

The second major change proposed by the committee was the establishment of "social education" departments in the local authorities. The guiding concept would be the re-education and training of the wayward youth. Ongoing supervision of juvenile probationers and child care services would be transferred to the social education departments, effectively stripping the existing probation staff of its responsibility for juveniles and placing child care under educational domination.

In proposing a "social education" approach to the treatment of delinquency, the Kilbrandon Committee was following the prevailing outlook in Scotland. Child rearing was viewed in educational terms—education defined in a traditional and authoritative sense. Social work's philosophy and methods were as yet little understood—and in truth, the practice of social work in Scotland was generally far less sophisticated than that associated with modern professional social work. At that time there was, relatively, but a handful of trained workers in Scottish local authorities. For those who dreamed of building up social work services in Scotland, the Kilbrandon proposals posed a major threat.

"A Slap in the Face."   In the immediate aftermath of the release of the Kilbrandon Report in the spring of 1964, there was little reaction from social workers, who either had not read it or failed to grasp its implications. A few months later, however, Judith Hart, the new Under Secretary of State for Scotland, ignited the powder in a speech to psychiatric social workers. She spelled out the meaning of Kilbrandon for social workers, then left the meeting without waiting for their reaction. Megan Browne, the most respected figure at the gathering, jumped to her feet. "I must speak before I explode," she recalls saying. The Kilbrandon proposals would be devastating for social work in Scotland, she told her colleagues. Others picked up the theme, turning the meeting into an uproar.

Hart did not learn of the reaction until later, but she got the message. Successive encounters with members of the Association of Child Care Officers (ACCO) and other social service groups made it very clear that she had touched a raw nerve. There are even indications that the politically canny Hart, who was not enamored of the Kilbrandon Report, may have hoped for the reaction she got. In fact, she actively encouraged social workers to get involved in the political arena and let their voices be heard on policy. For many social workers, it was an unaccustomed role they were being asked to play; Kilbrandon was to be the catalyst that would mobilize them. It was, in the words of one social work leader, a slap in the face.

The Scottish Regional Committee of the Institute of Medical Social Workers (IMSW) declared that "educationists have not taken any lead in giving home and family circumstances the importance due to them." They urged, as an alternative to the social education departments, that family services be provided by departments of social work, incorporating all social work specialties (Campbell 1978, pp. 31–32).

The psychiatric social workers and child care officers made similar recommendations. The Scottish Branch of ACCO also criticized the existing fragmentation of services as a waste of resources. The new departments should be staffed by generically trained social workers, they said (ibid.). This theme—of common social work skills cutting across specialized settings—had been sounded in the influential Younghusband Report (Great Britain 1959) and was underscored by the movement by social workers toward a single professional association.

In their written comments on the Kilbrandon Report, the social work organizations were careful to salute the committee's work as dynamic, logical, and clear; their tone was on the whole more moderate than were the private conversations among social workers. They embraced the major recommendation, the juvenile panels, with enthusiasm. It is paradoxical that the social workers, who were fearful of an erosion of quality service if the "educationists" took over, and concerned generally about raising professional standards, had no difficulty with a proposal that crucial decisions regarding juvenile offenders be made by volunteers who would be essentially "a lay body . . . none [of whom] would be appointed by reason of any . . . specialist qualification, but simply on the basis of personal qualities" (p. 37).

However, the social workers urged training for such panel members. For example, ACCO said that "members of the panel and reporters should be required to attend a course of training" (Association of Child Care Officers, Scottish Region, n.d., p. 2). Nor was the criticism of the social education proposal unanimous among social workers. School social workers in Glasgow viewed it positively, presumably expecting that their service would come under the rubric of "social education."

The Scottish Branch of the National Association of Probation Officers (NAPO) took issue with "the implied criticism of the juvenile courts and services connected therewith" in the Kilbrandon Report. Understandably, NAPO opposed abolition of the courts in favor of the lay panels and urged instead that separate juvenile courts be set up throughout Scotland, similar to those already in existence in four jurisdictions (NAPO, Scottish Branch 1965). The probation officers were less united than the social workers, however; younger officers, those who had come into the system more recently, tended on the whole, to favor the reforms proposed by the Kilbrandon Committee. As a result, NAPO never put up very strong resistance to either the report or the subsequent white paper until it was too late to reverse the tide.

The Kilbrandon Committee effectively divided the potential critics of its work. The court reforms and juvenile panels, which posed a threat to the existing probation service, appealed to the social workers. To the NAPO members, the social education strategy—anathema to social work professionals—was of little moment. Long-term strains in the relationship between probation and social workers might have been exacerbated had it not been for a number of individuals with ties to both constituencies. A few people in the child care field had good relations with the younger probation officers, the ones who were least threatened by the Kilbrandon Report. This helped to blunt the reaction of the Scottish NAPO group to the juvenile panels.

The social education departments were a different matter. Social work professionals were determined to abort that particular scheme. They were aided in this effort by a number of forces. One was the forceful Judith Hart, a product of the London School of Economics and an active socialist in the Labour party. She was part of a group known as the "West Coast Mafia," centered in the Labour stronghold of Glasgow. Opinions as to her real interest in social work services vary, but she apparently sensed the potential for breaking new ground in Scotland, contrary to the standard pattern of following England and Wales in policy innovation. Hart's personality was an important factor in what transpired. Had Labour not turned out the Conservatives in the preceding election, bringing Hart into the Scottish Office, the Social Work (Scotland) Act would very likely never have happened.

The government waited for more than a year, while the momentum of reaction to the Kilbrandon Report built up, before making its formal response. In the interim, there were several developments that portended major changes in the ultimate policy.

On July 23, 1964, the Scottish Grand Committee—made up of Labour MPs from Scotland—reported to the House of Commons on the Kilbrandon Report (Great Britain 1964). In the debate that ensued, several major issues were aired. One of these was the question of the social education departments. Of this matter, Neil Carmichael, a Scottish MP and husband of social work leader Catherine Carmichael, said,

> The idea of a director of social education seems good, but if this were to be under the director of education while we still have the didactic attitude to learning which we still have in Scotland it would be quite disastrous. Our whole attitude to teaching in Scotland is not conducive to a proper integration of the problems in the family and in the school. . . . Many people with long experience of teaching . . . have admitted to me that it takes a long time to slough off the classroom attitude which is so prevalent in Scotland . . . and come to grips with the attitude which is necessary in successful work with individual delinquents. . . . The causes of delinquency are multifactoral and all studies have shown that they are dependent upon such factors as housing conditions, education opportunities, career opportunities, activity opportunities, . . . unemployment, and family relationships (pp. 76–77).

Carmichael then spoke of the need to combine all social services for "not just the individual, but the entire family." In so doing he was casting the problem which the Kilbrandon Committee had tackled in much broader terms than those of the report. It was a theme that other participants in the Commons debate picked up (ibid.).

The Scottish Education Department (SED), in whose bailiwick social work services fell, was also thinking along lines more comprehensive than those suggested by the Kilbrandon Report. In a draft letter to the Home Office in February 1965, the SED said, "A better description of what Ingleby, McBoyle,

Kilbrandon, Longford, etc., were all getting at . . . [is] a 'comprehensive social work service'" (Campbell 1978, p. 35). By March, the preference for comprehensive services was well established.

In June 1965, the Secretary of State for Scotland announced that the government had accepted the recommendation for juvenile panels, but because of the "interest shown" in the matching field organizations, that part of the proposals required further study. By responding separately to the two parts of the Kilbrandon scheme, the government now allowed the major focus of attention to become the nature and organization of social services in the field. This did not end the opposition to the court reforms by probation officers, but helped to weaken it.

It was determined that a white paper, officially spelling out the government's position, should be issued. Ordinarily, civil servants would have taken the responsibility for drafting such a document, drawing upon the Kilbrandon Report and the reactions to it. But these were no ordinary circumstances. Judith Hart was fully aware that it would be foolhardy to push ahead without more involvement of interested parties. So, in a break with the usual practice, she put together two working parties. One was a Joint Working Group of Local Authority Associations, which included representatives of local authority social work committees and civil servants. According to informants, the civil servants dominated this group, and little of importance came out of it. The second working group was the Kilbrandon Study Group, to be described in some detail presently. While the resulting white paper was ostensibly based on the deliberations in both bodies, it was the Kilbrandon Study Group that, in effect, produced the white paper.

The Kilbrandon Study Group. The use of outside advisers was itself a departure from convention. Judith Hart also refused to be restricted as to the participants in the study group. For representation from the civil service, she passed over the man who had expected to be appointed and, instead, chose Jimmy Johnston, a Scotsman who had worked his way up in the civil service and was viewed as having the instincts of a politician. A second civil servant was Andrew Rowe, who defied all stereotypes. He was not educated for the civil service, and he had spent some time teaching at Eton before entering the government. He later left government service to work full time for the Conservative party, where he was considered something of a maverick. An added plus for Rowe was that he had worked on probation issues, so would be sensitive to the concerns of probation officers. Both men had a kind of investment and enthusiasm that was atypical of civil service administrators.

For an outside adviser on the study group, Hart turned to Catherine Carmichael, a social work educator and the wife of Labour MP Neil Carmichael. Hart knew the Carmichaels socially; it seems clear that she wanted someone whom she knew and trusted, one who would also have the trust of the social work community. As a second adviser, Kay Carmichael suggested her old mentor, Megan Browne, a highly respected psychiatric social worker. Browne had been a member of the Probation Advisory Council. These two were prominent in Scottish social work circles but relatively unknown in England. Because Hart needed somebody with a larger reputation, Carmichael and Browne proposed none other than the Labour party's guru of social policy, Richard Titmuss, who promptly accepted. Thus the Kilbrandon Study Group was born, with Johnston and Rowe from the ranks of the civil service and Carmichael, Browne, and Titmuss as the outside advisers. While the two women played the more active advising role, Titmuss's involvement was far from token.

The composition of the study group assured from the beginning that the white paper would depart significantly from the Kilbrandon Report. Carmichael and Browne would insist on a reorientation of the field units from social education to social work. Carmichael and Titmuss had a strong "institutional," as opposed to clinical, orientation to human problems; and Titmuss's publicly stated bias was against a family service, narrowly conceived, in favor of a comprehensive approach to social services.

According to informants, the make-up of the study group raised some eyebrows and caused some outright criticism, but for other reasons: Scottish social work was being represented by two leaders of the Association of Psychiatric Social Workers (APSW). This meant that the largest contingent of social work personnel, the child care workers, were excluded, as were the medical social workers, a smaller but still significant constituency. The fact that psychiatric social work is the elite within the professional community, there as elsewhere, was an added irritant.

The psychiatric social work monopoly, however, appears to have been unintentional. Psychiatric social workers in Britain have a breadth of outlook quite different from the highly clinical emphasis in the United States. Probably as important in their selection was the fact that both Carmichael and Browne were prominent social work educators at the University of Edinburgh, and among the most visible element in the professional community in Scotland.

Judith Hart let Carmichael and Browne know that she visualized highly trained psychiatric and medical social workers assuming significant responsibility in the new social service system, and generally a very high quality of service. These were views with which they were fully in accord. Otherwise Hart did not involve herself directly in the work of the study group, except for an occasional "How are things coming?" when she ran into Carmichael socially. The study group invited comments and recommendations regarding the Kilbrandon Report. Carmichael and Browne have told the author that they were never aware of being subjected to significant pressure from the professional groups that had a stake in the outcome.

The collaboration with the civil servants, especially Johnston, was difficult at times for Carmichael and Browne. It is traditional for the administrative civil service to ask searching questions and to challenge various sets of assumptions. In fact, their special skill is in probing into matters with which they are only marginally acquainted, in order to get a grasp of the principal issues. This can be trying for professionals in a field as imprecise as social work. A special problem in the case of the Kilbrandon Study Group was that the professional advisers had only limited familiarity with public social service bureaucracies.

The model they continually sought to apply to social service delivery was that found in private, professionalized settings.

The civil servants, both new to the ways of social work, were dependent on the professionals for their information. Carmichael later told the author, "We were all very naive. We thought we were talking about social work. We should have been talking about the social services. We devised ideas appropriate for social work, not the social services."

A degree of frustration was inevitable, considering the political sensitivity of the subject matter and the fact that various interests would insist on having their input. Despite the frustrations, the Kilbrandon Study Group remained a cohesive and productive body. Its momentum was not seriously affected when Judith Hart left the Scottish Office toward the end of the group's deliberations. It was clear that a new policy thrust was in the making, one drastically different from the Kilbrandon Report.

The two groups set up by Hart—the Joint Working Group of Local Authority Associations and the Kilbrandon Study Group—worked independently of one another, so there was little opportunity for cross-fertilization. The advisers on the study group made repeated requests that the two groups come together. Eventually they did, late in the proceedings, but it was too late for the meeting to have any impact on what they were doing.

A White Paper with Green Edges. The use of white papers to clarify official government positions has been described in Chapter 1. An alternative device that allows the sitting government to advance a proposal without firm commitment is a *green paper,* which amounts to a probe, a set of proposals up for discussion. It is assumed that there will be maximum opportunity for the airing of different views regarding the green paper's contents. The green paper can either be liberally modified or withdrawn outright, if too much opposition comes to the surface.

Between these two types of documents lies a third sort of official statement of policy, one that is sufficiently tentative to allow a strategic retreat by the government without a loss of face. This is sometimes referred to as a "white paper with green edges." The document that emerged from the Kilbrandon Study Group on Scottish social services was such a paper. It was unusually tentative and general: "The proposals are presented as a basis for discussion with interested persons and organizations, with a view to comprehensive legislation when opportunity offers" (Great Britain 1966, p. v). In time, the generality and the tentativeness would come back to haunt the study group, for it allowed the government to adopt the new structure without committing itself to providing sufficient resources for the professionalized service that, to the social work professionals, was the heart of the scheme.

The white paper was a far cry from the original Kilbrandon Report, although politically it was important to present the new document as a direct outgrowth of the old. According to Catherine Carmichael, the real mission of the Kilbrandon Study Group had been, from the beginning, to look at the entire question of Scottish social services, not just the Kilbrandon Report. The problem of being freed up from the restricted purview of the Kilbrandon Committee, yet retaining the linkage with it, was handled by the study group thusly: "This paper puts forward proposals framed by the Government following the Report of the Committee on Children and Young Persons (Scotland) under the chairmanship of Lord Kilbrandon, which was published in April 1964" (Great Britain 1966).

The differences between the two documents were fundamental. The Kilbrandon Report's focus was on juvenile offenders, not even venturing into the area of child neglect. The white paper called for a comprehensive service system for a range of problems affecting persons of all ages. The Kilbrandon Report proposed ways of dealing with deviant behavior after the fact. The white paper went even beyond *prevention,* in a negative sense, to speak of positive *promotion* of human development. The Kilbrandon Report proposed a social education strategy, in field organizations dominated by a traditional educational philosophy. The white paper called for social work departments "based on the insights and skills of the profession of social work" (par. 10). The one major Kilbrandon proposal that was retained intact, the juvenile panels, instead of being the dominant focus of the new report, as it was of the old, occupied but a few pages at the end.

The white paper had thus changed Kilbrandon virtually beyond recognition without actually abandoning it. The outlook in the new statement was that of Richard Titmuss and the social work professionals on the study group. In short, a handful of strategically placed and determined individuals, with the support of a small and politically naive professional community, brought about a fundamental change in a major policy initiative. The question that lay ahead was whether the new thrust would survive the legislative process intact.

The Alignment of Forces. The issuance of the white paper made clearer the line-up of forces concerning the policy proposals. Allied with the social work organizations in favor of the plan was the Scottish Office, although it was no longer headed by Judith Hart. Richard Titmuss's not inconsiderable influence, both within the government and in the Labour party generally, was a major asset. Considering the decision-making process in British policy, these sources of support were vital to the success of the effort. Yet, the policy was a long way from being enacted. The white paper had intensified the opposition among the older group of probation officers, and now there appeared on the scene new and more formidable sources of resistance, namely medical officers of health and local authorities.

In each locality, the medical officer of health was the second most important government official, with responsibility for all health and welfare services. In British politics, the Society of Medical Officers of Health (SMOH) was known as a powerful organization that actively looked after its interests, although the lobby was less of a force in Scotland than in England. The Kilbrandon Report, which spoke of social education of juveniles under the direction of local education departments, was of peripheral interest to the medical officers. The white paper, however, called for a vastly expanded social work role, providing services for the total age span. In calling for the establishment of separate social work departments the white paper was proposing removal of a potentially very important program from the jurisdiction of the medical officers.

They were "furious," according to one well-placed informant, outraged that they had not been invited to meet with the Kilbrandon Study Group. The rejoinder was that for many years they had neglected social work services, and thus were a major reason for the sorry state of services in Scotland. Medical officers of health wrote critical statements regarding the white paper, saying that there was already movement afoot for combined social work and health centers, under the authority of the medical officers, and that a separate social work department would be "retrograde." It appeared to the social workers that the medical officers, having suddenly discovered that their neglected offspring was about to become a success, were making a belated effort to claim parental responsibility. But it was too late. The Scottish Office withstood the pressure from SMOH and refused to yield on the issue of the social work departments.

Another potentially powerful source of opposition was the constituency of sheriffs, who, along with the probation officers, objected to changes in the court system. They were never able to mount a significant challenge, however, particularly after the government announced in 1963 that it had accepted the proposal for juvenile panels. Furthermore, their position had been compromised from the beginning by the participation of several sheriffs on the Kilbrandon Committee.

A more serious threat to the aspirations of the social workers involved the issue of local autonomy. Fearing that placing a social work department in every locality would result in many operations too small to provide quality service, the professionals in the Kilbrandon Study Group pressed for regionalization as part of the package. This would have allowed a single social work department to serve a number of boroughs with better quality of service, and do so more efficiently. The larger boroughs, wanting to control their own operations, resisted the move. Looming in the background was the Wheatley Commission, which was due to issue a report on local government reorganization in Scotland in the not too distant future. Why do a partial reorganization now, it was argued, instead of waiting and doing a more adequate job later?

Despite the objections from within the study group, the white paper side-stepped the regionalization issue, saying simply that the social service reforms should not wait for Wheatley: "the Government decided to proceed at once with the review of the local authority social work services. Action which results from the review must clearly be compatible with the present organization of local government and must also be capable of adjustment to fit into the future pattern" (Great Britain 1966, par. 5).

Initially the Scottish Office had supported the social workers' position on regionalization, but eventually backed down in the face of strong pressure from Labour party MPs (Campbell 1978, p. 75). This did not end the fight, however. The social work organizations continued to lobby for regionalization during the campaign for enactment of the Social Work (Scotland) Act. But eventually they were forced to capitulate. In a letter to the Secretary of State for Scotland, dated July 26, 1967, four social work organizations proposed a number of compromises to placate the MPs from the large boroughs without losing the essence of the scheme. They included allowing services either to be based in large boroughs, exempting those with a population of more than sixty thousand, or be phased in gradually with a final deadline in the future (Davis 1967). A later statement by a working party for seven social work organizations said,

> Our view is that, much as we are disappointed at the inclusion of Large Burghs, reorganization must begin now. The experience gained by local authorities and their social work staffs will, by the time the Review on Local Government has reported, be considerable. The community will be familiar with the new pattern of social work, and social workers themselves will be adjusted to integration (Association of Child Care Officers, n.d.).

Somewhat surprising is the fact that in all the discussions about the white paper, the group that seems to have been least involved was the educators. Having been offered responsibility for an expanded program by the Kilbrandon Report, they showed none of the territoriality of the social workers in having it taken away from them. A number of informants suggested that the educators had little enthusiasm for taking on vast responsibilities for which they had little preparation. Once the notion of a comprehensive service for the total population had been established, it was beyond their realm. It must be remembered that education in Scotland was of a very traditional mold. Why then did the Kilbrandon Committee make such a decided thrust in that direction? The consensus among informants was that they acted out of a conviction based on prevailing assumptions in Scotland at the time, and not with regard to the vested interest of any group.

SOCIAL WORKERS IN THE POLITICAL ARENA

Dr. Gill Michael recalls her initiation into the Scottish social work community. A medical social worker by background, she became a field instructor at the University of Edinburgh in 1963. Having some spare time, she inquired about becoming active with the Scottish Branch of the Institute of Medical Social Workers (IMSW). She suddenly found herself not only an active member but the IMSW representative at the organizing meeting of the Standing Conference of Organizations of Social Workers (SCOSW)—the precursor to the British Association of Social Workers in Scotland. Such rapid propulsion of a newcomer into the center of professional affairs is an indication of the social work community's level of development at that time, just a year before the Kilbrandon Report appeared. Dr. Michael eventually became head of the Scottish branch of SCOSW.

Gill Michael arrived at a point when the Scottish social workers were just beginning to see themselves as a single professional group. The seeds for this development had been sown in 1959, with the Younghusband Report; it took the Kilbrandon Report to give the movement significant impetus. Prior to the formation of SCOSW, the Professional Caseworkers' Working Party had given evidence to the McBoyle Committee, and an ad hoc political group had been formed. Despite the fact that the members of these groups came from different social work organizations, they were essentially small knots of individuals who were personally committed to policy concerns. Moreover, such joint efforts tended to end up with rather diluted positions, in order not to offend any of the constituent groups. Meanwhile, the individual organizations also got involved in the political arena. The Association of Child Care Officers (ACCO) had a reputation for being especially active, though its former leader recalls that the members were preoccupied with "casework concerns."

The events in Scotland should not be considered in isolation from those in England. The parent associations of the Scottish social work units were giving encouragement to their collaboration; other forms of support varied from association to association. A major source of encouragement was the National Institute for Social Work Training (NISWT)* a London-based organization for professional development and training. Prominent persons associated with NISW journeyed to Scotland on several occasions to stimulate professional development and unity, and, as the implications of the Kilbrandon proposals became clear, participation in the policy process. There were those who viewed NISW as the major stimulus to the mobilization of Scottish social workers, but that does not do justice to the vitality of leadership within Scotland itself.

SCOSW consisted of eight organizations: ACCO; the National Association of Probation Officers (NAPO); IMSW; the Association of Psychiatric Social Workers (APSW); the Association of Social Workers (ASW); and Associations of Mental Welfare Workers, Moral Welfare Workers, and School Social Workers. Its primary *raison d'être* was not political action per se but the development of a unified social work profession in Britain. Following the release of the white paper on Scottish social services in 1966, the Scottish arm of SCOSW spun off a Parliamentary Action Group (PAG) to spearhead the drive for

*Later the term "Training" was dropped from the title and it became simply the National Institute for Social Work (NISW). It was and continues to be a major force in social work policy.

enactment of legislation. NAPO, whose relationship with the other organizations was always somewhat tenuous, opted out of this venture, as it later did regarding the formation of the British Association of Social Workers.

Even without the probation officers, PAG was beset by internal tension from the beginning. Not only were the respective organizations coming from different points with different priorities and some sensitivity about levels of training, but in the view of one of its leaders, there was competition for dominance among some of the organizational representatives. However, the members were able to resolve their differences sufficiently to act as a body on the Social Work (Scotland) Act. Vera Hiddleston, a veteran member of ACCO, was selected as PAG chairperson. Aside from the fact that ACCO had pioneered the idea of joint action in the first place and had a reputation of political activism, its membership consisted mainly of experienced but not trained social workers. Thus, it was not vulnerable to the elitism issue. An additional reason why Hiddleston was a happy choice was the fact that she had excellent ties with the more moderate elements in NAPO.

PAG wisely avoided simply becoming one more social work organization. In its public statements and communications with officials, the respective organizations were identified. Thus it was clear that a range of social work interest groups were pressing for the reforms. The major focus of the drive was the House of Commons in London. Despite the assured support of the government, there were several factors which made a concerted effort in the parliamentary arena imperative. With a heavy Labour majority in Commons, dissident Labour backbenchers would feel freer to vote against their party leadership than would have been true with a close split. Furthermore, one issue on which the government was rather equivocal was the matter of financial support for the reforms. Social workers were concerned that a new structure might be put in place without sufficient resources to mount the professional service they envisioned. As it turned out, this fear was well grounded. But PAG was also looking beyond enactment per se. A resounding vote in favor of the Social Work (Scotland) Act would send an important message to local authorities. Thus, the lobbying effort focused on MPs from all three major parties.

The tactics employed by PAG represent a wide range: news conferences and public meetings to drum up general support, direct contact with MPs by small delegations of two or three social workers, and calls to the rank and file to write to their own representatives in Parliament. For the first time, large numbers of social workers in Scotland were directly involved in politics.

The energy and enthusiasm of the social workers helped compensate for their lack of political sophistication. The following excerpt from the Newsletter of the Scottish Regional Committee of IMSW in August 1967, gives a sense of where some of the participants were, politically speaking:

> The difficulties and possible dangers of lobbying and our complete inexperience in this type of social action were recognized. However, after careful consideration of whether this was a wise and professional course of action, and whether it would be effective, the Regional Committee decided to support the proposal and nominated R as our delegate. The Institute General Purposes Committee approved of the decision, and agreed to pay R's expenses.
>
> On the 11th of July the delegates went to the House of Commons and had two meetings, one with fifteen Labour and two Liberal M.P.s, and one with seven Tory members.
>
> The delegates were impressed by their warm welcome, by the knowledge, interest and understanding of the M.P.s concerning the White Paper and the problems surrounding it, by the persistence of the questions posed by the M.P.s and their appreciation of the answers given by the delegates. They felt there was real communication of ideas, and that the M.P.s were enabled to see social workers as reasonable, knowledgeable and professional people, from whom they could seek further help and advice if need be.
>
> Having felt the responsibility which they carried

for the profession to be heavy and solemn, the delegates were delighted to find the occasion a happy and exciting one—exciting in that they felt 'involved in the democratic process' as R described it, and the incidental 'secondary gains' such as having drinks on the Terrace of the House and the opportunity of attending a debate in the House in the evening—made the day personally memorable for the delegates as well as historically significant for the profession in general and Scottish social work in particular (Institute of Medical Social Workers, Scottish Region 1967).

The rest of the article discusses the significance of the event as a demonstration of social workers' unity and their willingness to try to influence policy. Notably absent is any mention of the possible impact of the effort on policy.

It is hard to classify the social workers in political terms. At one end of the spectrum were the Carmichaels, experienced activists who understood how policy decisions are made. At the other end were those who were venturing into the political waters for the first time and for whom the act of involvement could almost be an end in itself. That the latter were more numerous than the former meant that widespread participation was unlikely for more than a relatively short time. Yet, with the government anxious to bring out a bill, time was on the side of the social workers.

Social workers who had participated in the campaign were asked how they would do things differently another time. There was general agreement that too much was left to chance and the total effort was too unorganized. One said, "Our innocence protected us," implying that if they had known then what they did afterward they might never have taken on the task. If she had it to do over again, there would be far more careful analysis of the political situation before venturing ahead. Under the press of necessity people learn fast: for instance, finding those with major influence, determining the proper spokesperson for a particular situation, and getting to the significant actors and briefing them.

LEARNING TO DEAL WITH CIVIL SERVANTS

An important area of learning for many social workers was how to work effectively with the civil service. A major factor in the relative speed with which social service reforms in Scotland moved toward enactment was the support they received from inside the government. Some English informants have gone so far as to attribute the success of the venture to the civil servants, with the social work associations playing a very minor role. But this seems an unfair judgment: Scottish civil servants themselves have attested to the great importance of the external support. There is no question that in virtually any political endeavor the working relationships of outside interest groups with opposite numbers inside the government can have a make-or-break quality.

There is frequently a basic mistrust of civil servants by those outside of government. The social work professionals in the Kilbrandon Study Group never got over their uneasiness about the intentions of the civil service members. Such mistrust sometimes led to problems. Gill Michael tells of the time when a delegation from SCOSW met with a group of civil servants. Some time after the meeting, she received a copy of the official minutes. As is the usual practice in the bureaucracy, they were a "laundered" version of what had actually transpired. She refused to accept them, whereupon she was severely chastized by an official who said, "If you're going to play that way you'll find that nobody's going to play with you!" After that SCOSW accepted the official minutes but kept its own minutes as a safeguard against having its position undercut.

Crucial to effective collaboration between those inside and outside of government is the kind of trust relationship that gets built up over time. While more intimate than a purely formal tie, it falls short of personal friendship. The parties to such a relationship are aware that they have different responsibilities and different constituencies. For example, there are times when it is not possible for a professional adviser within government to share all he or she knows about a given policy. The essential component is honesty between the parties.

The social workers found a "trusted professional" within

the Scottish Education Department in Marjorie McInnes. She was accepted as being thoroughly committed to the same goals as her fellow social workers, yet she also believed in abiding by the informal ground rules within the civil service, such as going through the proper channels in advancing one's interests.

It was in relation to this issue that the professionals within and outside of government found themselves at odds at one point. At about the same time that SCOSW came into being, the Scottish Education Department set up a Social Work Services Group, made up of administrators and professional advisers, in anticipation of the enactment of the Social Work (Scotland) Act. The professional advisers in the Social Work Services Group let it be known that SCOSW should deal with them and that they would, in turn, transmit their concerns to the administrators. SCOSW, however, was advised by a former civil servant that it should deal directly with the chief administrator in the Social Work Services Group, since he controlled the purse strings. They steadfastly insisted on this arrangement, over the objections of the professional advisers, and finally got their way on the matter.

It is not in the formal meetings with a chief administrator but in the ongoing, quasi-informal contacts with one's opposite number that one is in greatest danger of being compromised. Gill Michael, in her role as SCOSW chairperson, was particularly conscious of this problem. She sought to guard against it by planning with her associates for her meetings with Marjorie McInnes, and keeping them informed of what transpired.

Social workers rapidly discovered that good working relationships cannot be sustained unless one is able to use them to advance clearly articulated concerns and back up what one is saying. On one occasion SCOSW members sought and were granted a meeting with the Social Work Services Group, but it was on very short notice. Not having adequate time to prepare, they were ill equipped to respond when asked for their recommendations. Later they were taken to task by a professional adviser in the government who felt her own agenda had been undermined by their lack of preparedness. This is a particular hazard for an all-volunteer coalition that must reconcile internal differences in order to present a united position to officials. Good homework proved to be especially important as the social workers dealt directly with senior administrators in the civil service. Unlike professional social work advisers, administrators are least likely to be familiar with internally shared professional assumptions; and they are trained to ask searching questions.

THE ENACTMENT OF THE SOCIAL WORK (SCOTLAND) ACT

Time is a vital commodity in the parliamentary process. The crowded legislative agenda never has room enough for all items; sometimes even significant policy issues must be set aside. As a result, despite the government's firm support of the Social Work (Scotland) Act, action in Parliament was by no means assured. The fact of a crowded calendar led to shift of the action from the House of Commons to the House of Lords, where there was less pressure. This brought into play a different cast of characters in the legislative process from the one initially envisioned and forced a shift in the social workers' lobbying tactics.

At this point an old issue again came to the fore: financial resources to accomplish the reforms. Even in the white paper, the government had hedged on this question, to the distress of Carmichael and Browne. While asserting that a "major effort to attract, recruit and, when necessary, train staff is essential," the white paper then turned around to say,

> But however great the effort and however successful it may be in improving recruitment, there is unlikely to be a dramatic improvement in staffing in the next few years. One of the main reasons for reorganizing the services is to enable them to make a more rational and more effective deployment of staff. If this more effective deployment is achieved, it follows that the present staff will be able to provide a better service than now. Further improvements in the services can be expected to follow as additional staff are recruited and trained (Great Britain 1966, par. 6).

In the parliamentary debate, the implication was that there would be no significant new moneys, with the exception of a few hundred thousand pounds to cover the cost of hiring social work directors. The language of the Act as finally passed was permissive on the question of staff training: "The Secretary of State *may* provide courses of training. . . . The Secretary of State *may* make grants of such amounts, and subject to such conditions, as he may *with the consent of the Treasury* determine towards the expenses incurred by any body of persons in providing training as aforesaid" (Great Britain 1968b, sec. 9; italics added).

The white paper had called for a sweeping new conception of social services, a comprehensive array of supports which would be used in concert to aid families and individuals in need. Emergency financial assistance was seen as an integral part of this array. The conception was one of social work in its broadest sense. The Act translated this grand vision into something of a different order:

> It shall be the duty of every local authority to promote social welfare by making available advice, guidance, and assistance on such a scale as may be appropriate for their area, and in that behalf to make arrangements and to provide or secure the provision of such facilities . . . as they may consider suitable and adequate, and such assistance may be given to, or in respect of, the persons specified . . . in cash . . . (sec. 12).

This statement is a clear departure from the fragmented and delimited provisions for human welfare then in existence. It placed on local authorities major new responsibilities for their citizens of all ages. Having wallowed in the backwater of the social services and, in some minds, never left the nineteenth century, Scotland was suddenly being called on to embark on a bold initiative that, if fulfilled, would place it well in advance of the rest of the United Kingdom. To the social workers who had fought so long and hard for their image of a social service system, however, the Act was a disappointment. They had lost three battles: over regionalization, over sufficient specificity of language to assure fulfillment of the aims, and over the financial support to make the new scheme a reality.

Eleven years after the passage of the Social Work (Scotland) Act, various observers were asked what the long-term result had been—and was it worth the struggle? None had any question that the Act had been a major turning point in Scottish social welfare. Although the quality and extent of services had developed at very uneven rates in different localities and the financial assistance provisions had indeed been used more as emergency aid than part of a more comprehensive promotion of human welfare, a backward and impoverished social service system had been transformed into a modern, professional one. Since 1968, the proportion of trained social workers in the local authorities had gone from 30 percent to 90 percent. The western islands off Scotland, which then had no qualified social workers, now had twenty. Even the battle of regionalization had been "won" in the end, with the enactment of local government reorganization following the Wheatley Report. There was no question also that the active involvement of large numbers of Scottish social workers in the campaign had helped to transform them into an organized group with an ability to look to their interests in the political arena.

Scottish social workers had strong conviction about the need for social work principles to predominate in the provision of personal social services. They saw the original proposal for "social education" as a backward step which would be harmful to consumers. An expansion of services and of training in social work was consistent with this humanitarian concern. These developments would also involve a greater demand for what social workers had to offer and so served their proprietary interests, as well. The fact that there was no protest against turning parts of the "professional" responsibility of probation officers over to lay people without special qualifications suggests a degree of selectivity in the concern about raising professional standards of service. It was where the commitment to the public interest was concomitant with the vested interests of the social work community that the social workers became most active politically. It is, in fact, questionable how far the zeal for the public good would have carried a group of people in an arena where they had so little prior experience or enthusiasm.

5
The Local Authority Social Services Act

A BASIC CHARACTERISTIC OF SOCIAL LEGISLATION IN BOTH BRITAIN and the United States has been its piecemeal, pragmatic nature. The brand of socialism that took root in England in the nineteenth century was a far cry from the sweeping changes prescribed by Marx. Fabian socialism, for example, took its name from a Roman general best known for a cautious strategy of delay and avoidance of direct encounter. This symptom-specific orientation to reform is no more apparent than in relation to the personal social services.

Even during the postwar period of drastic economic and social innovation in Britain, as Handler (1973) points out, "state coercive intervention was restricted to rather narrowly defined, fairly extreme situations—violations of law, truancy, 'beyond control' and neglect." Handler views this reluctance as based on a positive view of those in need and contrasts it with a later tendency for the state to intrude more actively in family life. The delimited nature of state intervention is a more pervasive pattern than he suggests, however, and seems to be part of a deep-rooted commitment to individual and family privacy. Regardless of whether the state's intervention has been in the form of intrusion or bounty, it has resulted in problem-related increments in the state's activity, without a comprehensive family policy or children's policy.

Over the years, a contrapuntal theme to this piecemeal approach has been the call for a more rational and orderly system of personal social services. Beginning in the 1860s, the Charity Organization Society sought to counter the fragmentation of private philanthropy (Younghusband 1964). The specialization integration issue split the Royal Commission on the Poor Laws of 1905–1909 (Hall 1976). The commission majority held that the specialist "is too apt to see only what interests him in the first instance and to disregard wider issues," and criticized separation of services that "must result in a multiplication of inquiries and visitations, causing annoyance and waste of time and money" (Hall 1976, p. 2). These are issues that have been raised by integration proponents ever since.

The proliferation of personal social service programs after World War II gave new impetus to the call for services integration. For example, within a single year, 1948, Parliament enacted the Children Act, the National Health Service Act, and the National Assistance Act, each providing for personal social services under different auspices at the local level (Handler 1973, pp. 24–32). In response to the apparent disarray, a number of committee reports called for a more coherent system for delivering services. Said the influential Younghusband Committee (1959), "The existing sectionalization of these services no longer makes sense administratively, in economy, or from the point of view of social work" (par. 553).

Each emerging social service program gave birth to its own cadre of workers and its own administrative organization. In England and Wales, the problem was further complicated by the fact that several ministries of the central government were involved. Inevitably, common sets of group interests began to form around each of these entities, laying the foundation for resistance to later attempts to break up the special domains. The Younghusband Committee noted with concern "a tendency in some areas for new specialisms to emerge with their own intense loyalties" (par. 553).

The issue of social service organization became entwined with another, even more urgent, concern: child delinquency and neglect. The traumatic experiences of children during the war and the rising rate of juvenile offenses afterward spurred a great deal of public interest in these problems. The Children Act of 1948 stressed prevention and the desirability of keeping children in their own homes. It was a natural step to move from that position to the need to intervene with "problem" families (Handler 1973). From the government's standpoint, the fact that substitute care was more expensive was an added inducement to emphasize preventive work (Campbell 1978, p. 16). As the focus shifted to work with the total family, it became clear that fragmented, uncoordinated services would make that difficult. Donnison articulated this connection between family intervention and the need to reorganize services in a book entitled *The Neglected Child and the Social Services* (1954).

In 1956, the Ingleby Committee was appointed to examine ways of preventing juvenile delinquency. Its charge was directed mainly to the administration of juvenile justice, with secondary attention given to preventive work with families. The composition of the committee—mainly judges and lawyers—further encouraged attention to the justice system. Despite the fact the the Ingleby Report concentrated on flaws in juvenile justice administration, the recommendations were aimed primarily at preventive intervention with families. It may be that the committee shied away from juvenile justice reform because of the strong resistance that could be expected from the courts and police. The Ingleby Committee reiterated the theme of better coordination of the personal social services. The resulting Children and Young Persons Act of 1963 laid the foundation for an integrated family service.

In 1964, the Labour party saw crime as an issue with which it could challenge the Tory government. A party committee headed by Lord Longford produced a report entitled *Crime: A Challenge to Us All*. As if in anticipation of the Seebohm Committee, the Longford Report called for establishment of a high-powered panel to review the existing structure of services and propose changes. In addition, it added impetus to the establishment of an integrated family service. When Labour took over the reins the next fall, seven members of the Longford Committee moved into influential positions in the government, helping to assure action on its recommendations (Hall 1976, pp. 19–20).

SHAPING THE ISSUES
When Labour came to power in October 1964, the need for better integration of personal social services at the local level was no longer at issue. The question became, rather, what kind of integration was desirable. The logic of the preceding committee reports and legislation seemed to push in the direction of a preventive family service. Such a direction would be consistent, not only with the prevailing concern about child behavior and neglect, but also with what was historically a central mission of the emerging social work profession, the enhancement of family life. Powerful political interests, however, were now about to intervene to dispute that logical argument.

We have seen in the preceding chapter how the initiative was seized in Scotland by Under Secretary of State Judith Hart, together with an aroused social work community, to alter the direction of policy there. The situation was far more complex as concerned England and Wales, yet many of the same underlying dynamics were present.

In the case of England and Wales, a basic question was jurisdiction. Whereas a single department was concerned in the case of Scotland, several departments could claim a voice in social service policy for England and Wales. None of the departments was willing to yield control to anybody else.

Since children and youth services were of particular interest, there was a case to be made for developing an integrated family service under the department that then had major responsibility for children and youth, the Home Office. In fact, officials there moved ahead to translate the Longford Report into policy. However, the Ministry of Health was also a major center of social services policy, as were the Ministry of Housing and Local Government, and the Ministry of Education. We have noted previously the abhorrence of British governments of public fights, in contrast to the readiness of American cabinet members and other top officials to air their dirty linen in press leaks and public statements. The infighting is there, in the British instance, but it is carried out more quietly and circumspectly. In the case of services for children and youth, the upshot was that the Home Office was induced to hold off on its plans, and the locus of planning shifted to an interdepartmental Cabinet committee on social services (Hall 1976, pp. 21–22).

One minister whose domain would be significantly affected by Home Office pre-emption of social services planning was Richard H. S. Crossman, the Minister of Housing and Local Government. A stalwart of the socialist wing of the Labour party and former assistant editor of the *New Statesman,* Crossman had close personal ties with a number of leading intellectuals, including Richard Titmuss. Titmuss opposed the idea of a family service strategy, preferring a more comprehensive approach to deal with a wide range of problems affecting people of different ages and conditions. It will be recalled that he promoted the same kind of scope for Scotland as a member of the Kilbrandon Study Group. Thus, Titmuss's opposition to a narrow family service concept was consonant with Crossman's wish that the Home Office not dominate the social service planning. A number of leaders in the social service field agreed with the more comprehensive approach (Hall 1976, pp. 21–22).

A major center of the opposition to a family service was the National Institute for Social Work Training. Following the Younghusband Report (1959), which called for a major investment in training of social service personnel, the Institute was established to undertake a variety of educational and research activities. Since then it has provided full-scale training programs; short-term workshops and seminars; consultation to social agencies; research; publications on staff development, human behavior, practice, and social change; and a program for visiting scholars from other countries. In a country where university-based social work training was still relatively rare, the Institute was a dominant influence in the social services.

Several key persons connected with the Institute voiced

their concern about the rapid movement by the Home Office toward development of a family service department (Hall 1976, p. 22). The argument was set forth publicly by Richard Titmuss in a speech at a health conference in the spring of 1965. He saw the proposed departments as essentially extensions of the existing children's departments in the local authorities "to which would be transferred certain other responsibilities." He linked the proposal to "our historical preoccupation with social pathology in the form of (what have been called) 'multi-problem families'" (Titmuss 1968, pp. 88–89).

A second issue raised by Titmuss was that of comprehensiveness. The family-centered focus would exclude many kinds of social needs from the purview of the "integrated" departments. He raised a third concern that had special meaning to social work professionals: that of professional unity. Describing his more comprehensive vision of services integration, Titmuss declared,

> For social workers, this larger structure should help to break down artificial and irrelevant specialized loyalties. In the future, social workers must be seen (and must be helped to see themselves) as workers in a unified organization of services and not as the servant of any one discipline with a separate and fragmented organizational structure (pp. 88–89).

Titmuss spoke at a time when social work professionals were in the midst of forming a single organization out of seven existing professional associations; and among those who responded to his call was David Jones, chairman of the Standing Conference of Organizations of Social Workers. Titmuss's speech was a masterful summation of three issues particularly salient to the social service professionals identified with the Labour government: the pathology orientation implicit in the family-centered approach, the lack of comprehensiveness and general timidity of that approach, and the implications for the drive for a unified profession. To these issues must be added the aforementioned territorial concerns of the respective government departments. Together they spelled trouble for the family-centered proposal emanating from the Home Office.

The small group that then met with Titmuss to pursue the points he had made in his speech was dominated by people associated with the NISW. According to David Jones, executive director of the Institute, it was a matter of coincidence that the organization was so heavily represented—as it was later in the Seebohm Committee. Although there is no evidence suggesting a deliberate attempt to dictate social service policy, there clearly was a relatively small group of influential persons who had well-established ties to one another and to the Labour government, a group that had a common view of the direction in which policy should go. They included members and nonmembers of the social work profession.

David Jones drafted a memorandum in the group's behalf calling for an inquiry into the integration of services in the local authorities. It was approved and sent to the pertinent ministers. The proposal got an immediate and positive response from Richard Crossman, for whom it provided a means of holding the Home Office at bay. Other ministers also reacted positively. But a characteristic approach to delicate matters in British governments is delay, as a means of settling differences quietly and bringing dissidents along, thus presenting a united front. It took several months to put together a committee of inquiry. Once formed, the committee extended its deliberations over an eighteen-month period, and the government did not actually present a bill to Parliament for another eighteen months after that (Hall 1976, pp. 140–41).

THE SEEBOHM COMMITTEE

Hall comments on the great care with which the membership of the Committee on Local Authority and Allied Personal Social Services (the Seebohm Committee) was chosen. She says that "the ministers involved were anxious to see that their interests were sympathetically recognized" (1976, p. 29). It may be more precise to say that they were anxious to avoid people hostile to their interests. A minor distinction, perhaps, but it suggests a basically defensive posture in the respective departments. Yet, however cautious, the process was far from failsafe, from the ministers' viewpoints. One civil servant who was consulted on the selections recalls, for instance, that medical professionals in the Ministry of Health were notably uninterested in the make-up of the Seebohm Committee, apparently unaware of its potential importance. As a result, only one member of the medical profession, Professor J. N. Morris, ended up on the committee, and he was not representative of the predominant outlook of the doctors.

The selection process was described by one participant as a "blackballing system," in which those with too controversial or too defined a position were eliminated along the way. One casualty of this approach was Richard Titmuss, who was too clearly identified with a particular model of social services. He was able, however, to get a younger colleague at the London School of Economics, Roy Parker, onto the committee. Titmuss was one of the first persons consulted by the committee members after its inquiry began. In the view of some observers, he hovered in the background throughout the deliberations, a kind of *éminence grise*. His connection to Richard Crossman was not unimportant to the committee's interests. Surprisingly, little use seems to have been made of the work of the Kilbrandon Study Group, in which Titmuss had been actively involved in Scotland, although the basic subject matter was the same. Some observers have attributed this to a general myopia among English professionals when it comes to possible contributions to social policy from across the northern border.

The circle of social welfare leaders identified with the National Institute was amply represented on the Seebohm Committee. Its head, *Frederic Seebohm,* later Lord Seebohm, was chairman of the Institute, as well as a trustee of the influential Joseph Rowntree Memorial Trust. *Robin Huws Jones,* who became a central figure on the committee, was principal of the Institute. Another committee member was *Lady James of Rusholme,* the wife of the Institute's president. *Peter Leonard,* one of the two professional social workers on the committee, later joined the staff of the Institute (Hall 1976, p. 31).

In addition to these and the aforementioned *Morris* and *Parker,* there were three other members of the committee: *Baroness Serota,* a former member of the Longford Committee and active in London local government and the children's services field; *Michael Simson,* secretary of the National Corporation for the Care of Old People; and *Sir Charles Barrat* and *W. N. Lane,* both identified with local government outside of London. While Baroness Serota had experience and interest in both local government and services to children, it was probably the latter connection which led to her selection.

The Internal Dynamics of the Seebohm Committee. The nature of the Seebohm Committee's internal workings is by no means simple. Different members of the committee and those who viewed it from outside have come away with different impressions about the patterns of influence within it. Unlike their American counterpart, committees such as this do not have access to professional staffs to carry the major load of research and writing. Thus committee members are required to invest a maximum amount of time and energy in committee work. In short order the members of Seebohm Committee became a close-knit, working body. With the exception of Lane, they attended sessions regularly.

Lord Seebohm left no doubt that he was the chairperson of the committee in every sense of the word. His "right hand man," in the words of one informant, was Robin Huws Jones. An energetic man with highly tuned political antennae, Huws Jones had a long history of leadership in the social services. Before becoming principal of the National Institute for Social Work Training he was director of social science courses at University College of Swansea. He had served as vice chairman of the Younghusband Committee in the late 1950s. He was a member of the small group that urged the establishment of a committee of inquiry following Richard Titmuss's 1965 speech, as was Professor Morris, a personal friend. These two had ready access to the Minister of Health, Kenneth Robinson.

Professor Morris's strategic importance, as the representative from the medical profession, naturally made him an important member of the committee. There was a high degree of interaction between him, Lord Seebohm and Huws Jones. Despite Professor Morris's position in the pecking order within the committee, however, he was not able to prevail on the key issue of whether doctors or social workers were to be the dominant professional influence in mental health services. One observer saw him as something of a maverick on the committee, though this view is not universally shared. According to some observers, M. R. F. Simson, secretary of the National Corporation for the Care of Older People, was a fourth member of this "inner circle."

A second subgroup in the committee was composed of Baroness Serota, Lady James of Rusholme, and Peter Leonard, a social work educator. They appear to have had less influence within the committee than the first group.

Meanwhile, quite separate from the others were Lane and Barratt, the two local authority representatives. Like Morris, they tended to be one-issue people. Also like Morris, they were strategically important to the ultimate success of the committee. Apparently, little effort was made to appease them or accommodate their views, but their concerns were taken into account in another way: according to one member of the committee, the rhetoric in the Seebohm Report was consciously geared to local authority audiences. In view of these divisions within the committee, it is striking they were able to reach consensus and issue a report without any minority addenda.

Roy Parker played an interesting role in the committee. Despite the fact that he was previously unknown to this group and thus outside the "old boy network," Parker appears to have been one of the more influential members. His connection with Richard Titmuss seems to have been a less important factor in his standing in the committee than his ability to make an important contribution to its work. His skill in developing cogent arguments and committing them to paper was recognized as a major asset; its importance was enhanced by the fact that the Seebohm Committee's ultimate impact on policy, like that of other government committees and commissions, was dependent upon its ability to make a persuasive case for its recommendations. At the time of the committee's meetings, British policy was still less influenced by scientific studies and hard data than by effective rhetoric (Klein 1976).

Parker had a second important asset: time. He was on sabbatical leave from the London School of Economics during the 1966–67 academic year (Hall 1976, p. 39). Particularly in view of the lack of professional staff resources for bodies such as the Seebohm Committee, this is a major consideration. Parker thus presents an interesting picture of the individual who, in a sense, earned his spurs by his distinctive contribution to a policy group, not primarily on the basis of past relationships with influentials. The factors on which his influence rested—expertise and time—are ones we shall see again and again in social service politics. Many organizations have dramatically increased their impact on policy at the point that they have been able to hire professional staff who can then devote full time to the minutiae of the governmental process.

Paradoxically, Baroness Serota became most important to the Seebohm Committee after she left it. She was appointed Minister of State for Health in 1968. As one of Richard Crossman's chief subordinates, she was thus in a position to carry her influence to the very core of the policy-making process. This she did most effectively.

Robin Huws Jones's chief contribution to the success of the Seebohm Committee was internal. It frequently fell to him to resolve differences which cropped up between committee factions. A number of observers have commented on this as a special talent of Jones. The tradition of policy making in Britain is predominantly consensual. The Seebohm Committee needed to come out with a unified report if it hoped to overcome formidable opposition and persuade a government that was only marginally interested to carry its recommendations forward.

The fact that consensus was finally achieved and a single report issued is a tribute to Huws Jones's skill as a conciliator as well as Lord Seebohm's leadership. Along the way there were sharp differences which threatened to split the committee. Huws Jones's personal friendship with Professor Morris, a dissident on certain issues, probably did much to keep the group together. For Morris, at least, there were costs associated with the consensus. Some elements in the medical community, who had looked upon him as their spokesman on the committee, were said to have ended up viewing him as a traitor to his professional colleagues. Another committee member who raised provocative issues was W. E. Lane, who spoke in behalf of local authority interests. It was these two sets of interests—the doctors and the local authorities—that were to provide the most serious opposition to enactment of the policies proposed in the Seebohm Report.

Social Work Input to the Committee. It appears that the social work professionals on the Seebohm Committee were not subjected to pressure by their colleagues. This may strike American readers as unusual, but it is consistent with a British view of the proper functioning of such bodies. Direct pressure on their members is considered in a way not unlike direct pressure on judges regarding cases they are hearing. Committee members should be free to look at issues "objectively."

The Seebohm Committee was set up at a time of intense activity directed toward the development of a single social work professional organization. Instead of uniting disparate social work groups, as had been the case with the Kilbrandon Committee in Scotland, the Seebohm Committee was a potentially divisive element. With probation excluded from the Committee's charge, that matter was not at issue. But for the other constituents of the Standing Conference of Organizations of Social Workers (SCOSW), the issue of social service reorganization presented problems. It should be remembered in this regard that the main impetus for reform was coming, not from the social work professionals per se, but rather from a group which cut across several disciplines concerned with the social services.

The social work group whose views seemed most consonant with those of the Seebohm Committee majority was the Institute of Medical Social Workers (IMSW). In evidence prepared for the Committee, IMSW declared,

> We think that radical changes can only be accomplished satisfactorily by establishing a new Social Service Department. . . . We envisage the new department as covering all services at present established

within existing Children's and Welfare Departments and such personal welfare services as may exist in Education and Housing departments. From the Medical Officer of Health would be transferred the social work services of mental health, of care and after-care of the ill, disabled and people otherwise at risk, and some services relating to domiciliary and daily care for special groups (Institute of Medical Social Workers 1966, pp. 4–5).

A major bone of contention for some groups was the concept of a generalist social worker, who would deal with all types of situations. The Association of Psychiatric Social Workers (APSW), for instance, asserted that "it is neither possible nor desirable for one person to be familiar with all aspects of legislation and administrative detail in relation to the many problems which affect clients" (Hall 1976, p. 51). The psychiatric social workers, all of whom had advanced training, saw professional standards being undermined by a policy that would throw all local authority social service workers into one bin.

The policy thrust being pursued by the Seebohm Committee presented special problems for child care workers. The succession of acts dealing with children and youth since 1948 had created a large cadre of workers, under the aegis of the Home Office, whose careers were built on the notions of child protection and family rehabilitation. The family-centered approach put forth in the Longford Report was consistent with the vital interests of these workers. The child care field, however, was far from unanimous on the subject. Among those who had urged a committee of inquiry—and challenged the family service focus—following Titmuss's 1965 speech, was at least one person identified with child care (Hall 1976, p. 23 n.). There were also elements in this field who were in the vanguard of the drive for a unified social work professional organization and firmly committed to the establishment of comprehensive social service departments.

As a way out of the dilemma, the major child care workers' organizations—the Association of Child Care Officers (ACCO), and the Association of Children's Officers (ACO)—proposed a phased reorganization, with the first phase involving children's services only. It was clearly a compromise position, one that left no one entirely satisfied (Hall 1976, pp. 49–50). But, in terms of getting the Seebohm Report acted upon, the strategy of compromise worked. In fact it was ACCO that took the initiative in the subsequent campaign for enactment of the reforms.

The evidence submitted to the committee by the child care officers and other social workers has been criticized for its vagueness and lack of supporting data. To some extent, the same thing can be said of most evidence submitted to panels of this kind. Even the material supplied by government departments, particularly the Ministry of Health, was criticized on similar grounds. Certainly the Seebohm Committee's own approach to its task encouraged subjectivity. But a specific factor in the weakness of the evidence from the social workers was the problem of reconciling internal differences, while trying to make a significant contribution to the policy debate. The tendency for political considerations to take priority over technical ones was true not only of the social workers; it characterized the whole process of developing the policy on social services from beginning to end.

The Seebohm Proposals. The Seebohm Report, issued in July 1968, was basically a rhetorical document. Its arguments were grounded on untested assumptions and lacked empirical support, a fact that critics readily pointed out (see Sinfield 1970; Smith 1971; and Townsend 1970). Even in the interpretation of its charge, the committee had taken major liberties. It will be recalled that those who agitated for a committee of inquiry wanted to drop the family service concept in favor of a comprehensive approach to social service reorganization. The charge to the committee, however, was "to consider what changes are desirable to secure an effective family service" (Great Britain 1968a, par. 1), a necessary concession to the Home Office. The committee handled this problem by simply redefining "family" as including "childless couples and individuals without any close relatives: in other words, everybody" (par. 32).

In contrast, the exclusion of probation services from the committee's task was readily accepted. This had already been agreed upon as too controversial an area by the group that had called for the inquiry in the first place. Other questions of just how comprehensive were the proposed social service departments to be were not so easily resolved. A particularly contentious area, both within the committee and in external pressure groups, was mental health. This is the question on which Professor Morris was seen as particularly adamant. It was to become a major arena of combat between the social workers and medical officers of health, who, understandably, did not want to give up control over a significant piece of their domain (Hall 1976, pp. 104–106).

The committee proposed a model of service delivery in which unified social service departments would include the functions of existing children's and welfare services, plus certain functions of health, education, and housing departments. The consolidation of functions was seen as encouraging greater use of services and also attracting more resources, including personnel (pars. 139–51). The committee envisioned services as being delivered through area offices which would encompass populations of from fifty thousand to one hundred thousand. Teams of ten to twelve social workers would staff the program. Maximum authority would be delegated to the area offices (pars. 583–92).

The committee put forth a major argument for use of social service generalists in the area offices, asserting that "a family or individual in need of social care should, as far as possible, be served by a single social worker . . . since the basic aim of a social service department is to attempt to meet all the social needs of the family or individual together as a whole" (par. 516). The committee argued, further, that

> Narrow specialization can have a detrimental effect on professional judgment. For example, in work with grossly disturbed and socially inadequate families specialization can . . . adversely influence the assessment which workers make of the level at which such families can function, for the workers concerned may have little contact with other families who are functioning

at a considerably higher level under similar environmental circumstances (par. 518).

It was an argument that seemed to be drawn from the same
"family pathology" orientation which the committee leadership
was bent on countering in the first place. Contrary to an im-
pression which has grown up among some American observers—that the Seebohm Committee was out to eliminate specialization entirely—the report makes clear that there is still a
place for the specialist. However, decisions to enlist the help of
specialized services would lie primarily with the generalist who
had first contact with the consumer (par. 519).

A section of the report which received relatively little attention in the ensuing debate was chapter 16, entitled, "The Community." In words reminiscent of the social promotion concept
enunciated in the Social Work (Scotland) Act, the proposals
were seen

> as embodying a wider conception of social service,
> directed to the well-being of the whole of the com-
> munity and not only of social casualties, and seeing the
> community it serves as the basis of its authority, re-
> sources and effectiveness. Such a conception spells, we
> hope, the death-knell of the Poor Law legacy and
> the socially divisive attitudes and practices which
> stemmed from it (par. 474).

The report then goes on to lay out specific tasks for the
social service departments. They include community development, stimulation of citizen participation, and encouragement
of volunteers and voluntary organizations (pars. 480–500).
Speaking at a gathering of American social workers several
years later, Lord Seebohm referred to the chapter on the community as "perhaps one of the most important chapters in the
whole Report" (1974, p. 71). But at the time the Seebohm Report was issued, the attention of social workers and others was
on matters of more immediate vital interest to them. One of
these was training.

Considering the central role, both in the Seebohm Committee and in the agitation which led to its establishment, of

persons connected with the National Institute for Social Work Training, a major interest in training was to be expected. Of the non-Institute people on the committee, three—Morris, Parker, and Leonard—were involved in higher education, two in the social service field. Outside the committee, training requirements were of concern to various social work groups because of the threat of exclusion of those without the proper credentials. The issue was especially problematical to SCOSW, whose constituent organizations spanned the psychiatric social workers, all of whom had advanced training, and other groups most of whose members had no special training (Hall 1976, p. 50).

The report emphasized the need to train all staff, not only senior staff or those with professional qualifications. Especially important were social work personnel. For these the training should be in generic skills, in line with the proposed service delivery model. The report spoke for training outside of universities as well as inside and decried the sharp demarcation that seemed to exist between workers with these two kinds of preparation. Instead, universities should extend their services beyond their own walls and support various forms of preparation, including in-service training of social service staffs. There should be training for research, as well as practice (pars. 568–80). To a large extent, the kind of training program envisioned was one in which an organization like the National Institute for Social Work Training would be especially qualified to take a leadership role. There is no implication of a conscious attempt to fashion the training proposals on the basis of the Institute's experience. The more plausible explanation for this thrust in the Seebohm Report is that this was the training experience with which the committee leadership was particularly familiar.

POLITICAL STRATEGIES: THE INSIDE ROUTE

Having managed to alter the basic thrust of social services reorganization policy, from one oriented toward family pathology to a positive and comprehensive concept of service provision, the reformers now faced the task of translating the Seebohm proposals into law. It was an awesome task indeed, considering that they were working against a crowded policy agenda, an unenthusiastic government (Hall 1976, p. 82), strong criticism from a significant faction in Labour's left wing, and the active opposition of powerful lobbies. The major parties all endorsed social service reorganization, but in this instance party endorsement would mean little.

Within the government, the proposals were in danger of falling victim to an intense political struggle between Home Secretary James Callaghan and Secretary of State for Social Services Richard Crossman. Neither one was willing to give up control over services then under his jurisdiction. Once they reached a compromise—as one informant put it, "in order not to cross swords in public" for fear of embarrassing the government—Crossman became the pivotal person regarding the proposed reforms.

Crossman was not greatly impressed with the results of the Seebohm Committee's eighteen-month labors (Hall 1976, pp. 82–83). But then, he is said to have had little interest in social services generally, being more concerned with health policy. Still, a basic rationale for the formation of the Department of Health and Social Security which he oversaw was the amalgamation of functions. In his diary,* he quotes the following exchange with Prime Minister Harold Wilson regarding the Seebohm proposals:

> he said in his own Harold fashion, "Well, you ought to get what you want but we can't push it too hard."
>
> "Well, if unifying the social services isn't in the right what on earth am I at a merged Ministry for?" I replied very indignantly (Crossman 1977, p. 142).

In Crossman's world, political considerations loomed particularly large—those and personal relationships with key individuals. None of the members of the Seebohm Committee were among his personal acquaintances at the time the Committee

---

*The material in Crossman's diaries, while a rich source of detailed information regarding the period, should be viewed with some caution. In the words of one informant, they were seen as "colorful but highly subjective." The writer has used them primarily where Crossman's views, however subjective, were pertinent.

was deliberating. But the Seebohm Committee had one advocate who was a close friend of Crossman: Richard Titmuss. Crossman wrote in the spring of 1968, "I have also got out of Titmuss a list of the important social welfare people I should know" (p. 35). It was Titmuss who introduced Crossman to Professor Morris: "On this occasion [July 11, 1968], Richard Titmuss had brought along his friend Professor Morris" (p. 131). It is clear that Titmuss was a major factor in keeping the Seebohm proposals in front of Crossman and in getting them on the government's legislative agenda. Another was Baroness Serota.

Upon her appointment as Baroness-in-Waiting, she had to resign from the Seebohm Committee. In a major stroke of luck for the social service reformers, she was appointed as Minister of State for Health the following year. Crossman later told an interviewer that at the time of her appointment he was unaware that she had served on the Seebohm Committee (Hall 1976, p. 92). This is disputed by his diary:

> I had come to the conclusion that Bea Serota, who is so thoroughly competent and who was a Home Office nominee to the Seebohm Commission [sic], would do me a world of good by coming to our side in the battle against the Home Office on the implementation of the Seebohm Report (Crossman 1977, p. 378).

Observers both within and outside the government have credited Baroness Serota with a central role in promoting the Seebohm proposals within the government. In the view of at least one informant, the secretary of state essentially turned social services policy over to her, but she believes that he was vitally interested in the problem.

Crossman's diary is replete with references to informal social gatherings involving persons both inside and outside the government. It seems clear that a certain amount of state business was strongly influenced if not actually conducted on such occasions. Those who met the secretary over lunch or dinner had an important means of access to him. Baroness Serota, Professor Morris, and, of course, Richard Titmuss were all included in this inner circle at the time that the Seebohm reforms were being promoted. Such informal channels were used, not only to promote ideas with senior government officials, but also to cushion the impact of adverse recommendations. For instance, during the Seebohm Committee's deliberations, such channels were sometimes used to alert ministers to what was being proposed, in order that they not be taken by surprise by the report's contents.

Civil servants with an interest in social service policy had to act more circumspectly in advancing their ideas. Only by religiously observing the established channels of communication could they hope to maintain their credibility. In the Ministry of Health, where there was considerable support for the Seebohm plan, social work professionals had to work through the civil service administrators in feeding in their ideas. Baroness Serota's arrival on the scene was said by one informant to have strengthened the position of these professionals within the ministry.

The government's response to the Seebohm Report was strongly influenced by what else was happening at the time. Proponents of a particular policy often forget that theirs is not the only concern with which officials are dealing, and a proposal may be side-tracked, not because it lacks merit but simply because other measures take priority. The Seebohm Report came onto the agenda at the same time as two other major issues: reform of the National Health Service and local government reorganization. It so happened that these three questions presented the government with an awkward problem which came close to scuttling the Seebohm recommendations.

The Report of the Royal Commission on Local Government (Maud Report), which called for a basic overhaul in local authorities, was issued in June 1969, some eight months after it was due. Meanwhile, a bill for redrawing the boundaries of parliamentary districts was waiting in the wings. According to an all-party agreement in 1958, the lines of the districts were to be revised at periodic intervals to reflect population changes. Convinced that such a redrawing at this time would cost the Labour party too many seats in Commons, the Wilson government postponed action, on the rationale that redistricting should wait upon the basic local government reforms contained in the Maud Report (Crossman 1977, p. 506 n.).

Meanwhile, government policy on the National Health Service (NHS) reorganization was being held up, also for political reasons. If it was necessary to delay action on NHS and local government reform, why was it all right to move ahead with Seebohm, which had major implications for both NHS policy and the powers of the local authorities? In September 1969, Crossman wrote,

> to make anything of Seebohm we shall have legislation next session. Otherwise Medical Officers of Health will retain their power to take over integrated services, which will mean the death of Seebohm's essential principle that personal social services should also be brought together under a single Director. . . . On the other hand, I can't agree to legislate on Seebohm without simultaneous declaration of the independence of the Health Service, which will be pre-judging an essential part of the Maud Report (p. 634).

After lengthy delays, the problem was resolved when it was decided to move ahead with health policy without regard to the Maud Report, early in February 1970. Ten days later the Local Authority Social Services Bill, implementing the Seebohm recommendations, was published (pp. 801, 815).

Of the three kinds of reform being considered—social services, National Health Service, and local government—only the first, that based on the Seebohm Report, became law before the Labour government was defeated in June 1970. No doubt the fact that it was the least controversial of the three was a major contributing factor. It was one of the few legislative achievements on the domestic side with which the Wilson government could go to the electorate. But the Seebohm proposals also entailed political risks, so it is doubtful that they would have been enacted without external pressure.

POLITICAL STRATEGIES: THE OUTSIDE ROUTE
The story of the efforts to implement the Seebohm proposals within the government is a story of key individuals, working in

small meetings and private discussions. In the public arena, however, the active efforts of many persons were necessary. The social workers who sought to promote these proposals were not working in a vacuum. Ranged against them were powerful interest groups, including the medical profession, significant elements among the local authorities and the National Union of Teachers (NUT). These were groups which more than once had been able to force a government turn-around on policy. Their failure to seriously impede the momentum behind enactment of the Seebohm proposals is one of the more interesting aspects of the whole case.

Hall (1976) comments on the contrast between the social workers' David and the British Medical Association's (BMA) Goliath. The social workers were politically unsophisticated and were just in the process of trying to come together as a professional community. The BMA had for years been influential regarding health policies and had close ties with the Ministry of Health. Why the apparently greater success of social workers in promoting their interests? Hall sees a major factor in the way the two professional groups used their potential power: "an examination of the strategies of the two groups suggests that social workers took the personal social services much more seriously than the medical profession and mobilized their resources much earlier and more effectively" (p. 58).

It is important to recognize certain characteristics of the BMA that distinguish it from the monolithic American Medical Association (AMA). It is possible to identify three major constituencies within the medical profession in Britain: general practitioners, the dominant group in the BMA; specialists, who are organized in a number of Royal Colleges; and local authority public health physicians who make up the Society of Medical Officers of Health (SMOH). Frequently issues which are most salient to one of these groups are much less so to the other two. On occasions, the Government has been able to play one of these factions off against another (Eckstein 1960).

The doctors whose vital interests were most seriously affected by the Seebohm proposals were the medical officers of health, who would stand to lose control over a significant part of their operations. But while they were important officials in the local authorities, as a group they were second-class citizens within the medical community. At the time, the main elements in BMA were much more concerned about the impact of the NHS reorganization than changes in the organization of social services. BMA knew the make-up of the Seebohm Committee, knew that the lone medical man on it was not a reliable spokesman for the interests of the medical establishment, and gave both written and oral evidence to the committee. Thus, the explanation for BMA's belated and weak intervention seems less a matter of being outfoxed by the social workers than simply one of its priorities lying elsewhere.

Concessions to other interest groups are evident in the differences between the Seebohm proposals and the Local Authority Social Services Act (LASSA) itself. Educational interests wanted to keep school social services in local education departments, so the Seebohm recommendation that school social services come under the Social Service Departments was scrapped. Likewise, a proposal to include public housing social services was dropped from the bill.

The position of the local authority associations regarding the Seebohm Report was mixed. They counseled delay, on grounds that the reform in the single area of social services should await a clear policy on the more general reorganization of local government. The reshuffling of responsibilities among local officials—which the Seebohm Report called for in certain areas—posed a threat to existing vested interests in local authorities. But the overriding issue for them was autonomy, freedom from central government control. Anything that smacked of a mandatory scheme could expect opposition from the local authorities. Yet in one respect the autonomy issue worked to the advantage of the Seebohm lobby. In called for the removal of certain functions from National Health Service control and their location in the local social service departments, the social service reformers were allied with the wish to preserve local autonomy (Hall 1976, pp. 54–55, 68–69, 100).

In the end, the local authority forces lost out on the question of control over selection of the director of social services. The bill which was finally enacted stated:

> (3) The Secretary of State may make regulations prescribing the qualifications requisite for a person's appointment as a local authority's director of social services.

> (4) Until the first coming into force of regulations made under subsection (3) above, a local authority shall not appoint, nor concur in the appointment of, a director of social services except after consultation with the Secretary of State; and . . . he may give directions prohibiting his appointment (Great Britain 1970, sec. 6).

While losing out on the question of control over the social service director's position, the local authorities still retained considerable autonomy. The vagueness of the resulting legislation would allow them wide latitude in the implementation of the reforms. From the beginning, the local government faction had been viewed by the reformers as a major target group.

A more serious threat to the Seebohm principles came from individual local authorities, many of which simply began to institute their own social service reorganizations. These frequently followed lines that had been explicitly rejected by the Seebohm Committee. For instance, a number of authorities created combined health and social service departments with the medical officer of health at the head (White 1969).

Some of the opposition to enactment of a Local Authorities Social Services bill arose, not from vested self-interest, but from those who felt that the action would prevent the adoption of more radical reforms. The Child Poverty Action Group had submitted written evidence to the Seebohm Committee, but its counsel was not sought at any point in the deliberations. Peter Townsend, the leader of this group and editor of a major critique of Seebohm (1970), was said by one informant to have tried to have the Seebohm Report shelved and to have sought to enlist the aid of the doctors, who had their own reasons for opposing it. The counter-campaign from the left, however, was never able to generate widespread public support for its position, a necessity in any such "outsider" strategy.

It was clearly the social workers who spearheaded the campaign for the enactment of the Local Authority Social Services bill. Under the leadership of the Standing Conference of Organizations of Social Workers (SCOSW) a Seebohm Implementation Action Group (SIAG) came into being. About seventeen organizations were represented. In addition to social work professional groups it included client-serving and public interest organizations. Foundation money was obtained to support the campaign, but this went mainly for publications. It was primarily a volunteer effort. In the words of the campaign chairman, D. T. White,

> The work was undertaken in a voluntary capacity by various people. . . . The only paid staff involved were the staff of the professional associations of social workers. . . . This was largely confined to . . . the General Secretary of the Association of Child Care Officers, . . . which was more politically active than any of the other professional associations of social workers. The Joseph Rowntree Memorial Trust did give us some money for the expenses of the campaign largely related to publication costs of various leaflets and booklets which were prepared (White 1979).

With the Association of Child Care Officers (ACCO) playing a central role—White had previously been its president—the SIAG sought maximum involvement of social workers. A pamphlet of "Speakers Notes" was distributed to all social workers in participating organizations, along with draft letters for them to follow in writing to their own Members of Parliament. Local meetings of social workers with the MPs were used to help open doors with government officials.

It is not surprising that ACCO was the organization that took much of the initiative in these efforts. As had been the case in Scotland, it was more politically active and sophisticated than most social work organizations. The fact that the majority of those involved were less experienced was both an advantage and a disadvantage in White's view:

For most social workers this was the first time that they had asked to be involved in political activity and there was a considerable amount of reluctance at the beginning to undertake the tasks which their colleagues in the leadership of SIAG asked them to do. . . . Large numbers did participate and . . . were extremely effective, largely because they were not sophisticated in their approach and . . . they were seen by the Members of Parliament to be concerned for their clients and not for themselves. . . . This had a very considerable impact on ordinary Members of Parliament and Members of the House of Lords, who were also included in our campaign (1979).

However, one civil servant, who identified strongly with the social workers, saw the early efforts not only as "extremely naive," but also somewhat self-defeating. In this person's estimation, the delegations who made visits to government officials early in the campaign "presented a purely professional case. They were not cutting any ice. They were able people but they talked about things the ministers were not interested in. They were professionally oriented and didn't know political techniques. They were just not well organized."

This informant saw things change as the social workers gained experience. It is, of course, impossible to generalize about "the social workers." There were among them some politically sophisticated individuals. And to some extent, their energy and enthusiasm offset their naiveté, as had been true in Scotland.

The major targets of the campaign were of two sorts. One was the MPs. The focus was on all parties. In some ways, Labour was less enthusiastic than the other parties, since for certain elements in the party cash assistance was more important than personal social services. Furthermore, Conservative MPs were freer to prod the Labour government in parliamentary debate when it dragged its heels on the Seebohm proposals. As it turned out, the bill passed just before the Conservatives came to power, so their support was crucial to successful implementation of the policy.

The other major target was the general public. The release of the Seebohm Report had been well orchestrated in the news media. A major story appeared in the July 24, 1968, issue of the *Times of London,* along with positive editorial comment (1968a, 1968b). The strategy behind the public campaign was that this would embarrass the government into action, since it needed to show that it was moving along in the right direction. There is consensus among informed observers that the campaign had the desired effect and made it difficult for the government to continue to procrastinate.

LASSA was finally approved at the last possible moment, for Parliament was dissolved the same day, May 29, 1970. While the incoming Conservative government might have carried through with such legislation, the process would have been dragged out even further, and the resulting law would have been substantially different. As the bill had moved into its parliamentary phase, its reception had been lackadaisical rather than contentious, and the movement toward enactment had the aura of anticlimax. This takes away none of the importance of the Act nor the impressiveness of the social service professionals' achievement.

LASSA was not so much a blueprint for reform as a framework within which reform could take place. The most dramatic impact was on volume of demand for personal social services. Speaking of the effects of LASSA, nine years after its passage, David Jones said it had created "almost more of a demand for services than the system can handle" (*Washington Report* 1979; Seebohm 1974, p. 75; and Goldberg 1978). This has had the unfortunate effect of swamping some agencies and pressing staff to deal with crises at the expense of preventive work. As of this writing, the issue of specialized versus generic services, so central to the Seebohm proposals, appears far from settled. The trend, according to Jones, has been toward the emergence of new specialties (for instance, intake and referral and inter-agency liaison) and generally increasing specialization.

As was true in Scotland, the reforms in theory went further than the reforms in practice. The price of acceptance by the local authorities had been a relatively permissive approach to implementation. Thus, the investment in personal social services, while significantly higher than before, did not live up to the expectations of the architects of the scheme. In particular, the quality of staff recruited was less than what had been envisioned. Between 1972 and 1974, by far the greatest increase in staff was in welfare assistants, who, for the most part, received little special training (Hall 1976, p. 123). Thus, despite the mandate that all local authorities provide the comprehensive social service program, the adequacy with which this was done was very uneven (*Washington Report* 1979).

The contention between medical and social work interests appears to be far from over. The problem is aggravated by the structure of financing. The National Health Service is nationally administered and funded; local authority social services, including some forms of residential care, are, in part, funded locally. Decisions on care of chronic patients tend to be made on the basis of where the financial burden will fall rather than the best interests of the patient (Schneiderman 1978).

The persons interviewed for this study were in basic agreement that LASSA had been a major step forward; and, as a result, personal social services were better, on balance, in terms of quantity, scope, and quality. As one informant put it, "it would be impossible to go back to what we had before."

SOCIAL WORK PROFESSIONALS IN THE POLITICAL ARENA

As was true in Scotland, the achievements of the social work professionals in promoting their interests in the political arena was the result of a combination of efforts by a relatively sophisticated elite and a politically inexperienced rank and file. Coming at a time when the social work community was coming together in professional unity, the experience helped to speed the process of amalgamation and increase the sense of professionhood.

The sets of interests at work were more complex than in the case of Scotland, where a smaller social work community had more in common to begin with. The issue of family pathology versus comprehensive services for all cut one way for child care workers and another for other workers. The issue of generalist versus specialist was particularly controversial among social workers with the highest levels of professional training.

By the time the Seebohm proposals had moved from the status of a committee report to legislative package, the bulk of the social work community had become convinced that its collective interests lay with speedy and positive action. Especially as the issue of medical domination of social services came to the fore, social workers found a common focus around which to rally. At that point they found it most compatible with both their view of human welfare and their own interests as a professional community to support integrated personal social services organized on the basis of the main skills to be employed, that is, social work skills (Hall 1976, pp. 104–106).

6
The Aborted Reform:
The Allied Services Act

THERE IS NO GREATER CONTRAST BETWEEN THE BRITISH AND American systems of policy making than in the ability or inability of the executive arm of government to carry out its stated objectives. The failure of the Allied Services Act in the United States to become law is an excellent case in point. For a comparable situation in Britain, one would have to imagine that a particular policy had been called for in the Queen's speech, that the Secretary of State for Social Services had made a major public commitment to its enactment, and that it was defeated in three successive tries in Parliament, without even getting so far as a floor vote. At the very least, such a state of affairs would occasion a major crisis, and, very likely, a call for a vote of no confidence in the government.

The fate of the Allied Services Act constituted no crisis for the Nixon and Ford administrations. The act's chief protagonist, HEW Secretary Elliot Richardson, went on to be Secretary of Defense, and then Attorney General under Nixon. Richardson, a Republican, later served in the administration of Jimmy Carter, a Democrat, as ambassador-at-large.

We have followed two case histories in which social workers were in the vanguard of the fight for social service reorganization. The problem was defined in terms of both consumer welfare and the vital interests of the social service professionals. On the surface, the Allied Services Act (ASA), first introduced in Congress in 1972, seemed to represent a similar set of concerns for American social service professionals. It, too, would promote the integration of specialized services at the local level—in the characteristically American way of leaving initiative to the states.

American social workers and others, however, saw in the Allied Services concept the potential for hurting consumers' interests as much as helping them. More important was the general apathy toward the bill among the professionals, who did not view it as serving their own interests. The main opposition came from service specialists, who saw it as hurting both their target clientele and themselves. Thus occurred the paradox of American social workers, who praised the services integration movement in Britain, but abandoned the concept in their own backyard.

This may not be as contradictory as it sounds. At the time of the Seebohm Report and the development of the Local Authority Social Services Act, social services integration was basically an abstraction for Americans, one that was enjoying a certain vogue in professional circles. Later, as Seebohm-in-operation revealed some problems not anticipated with Seebohm-in-theory, and the demonstration projects in the United States did not live up to their high promise, the skepticism about the integration concept grew. As a result, what had once been looked upon as inherently sound began to be looked on as inherently questionable (see Austin 1978; Morris and Hirsch-Lescohier 1977; Morris 1974).

SERVICES INTEGRATION IN THE UNITED STATES

The notion of consolidating specialized providers of social services into an integrated whole has roots in the United States that run back over a hundred years. This history has been marked by a recurrent pattern of rapidly proliferating agencies followed by attempts to develop an orderly system out of them. The central problematical issue overhanging the process has been that of the independence of the individual service provider.

In the 1870s, Americans responded to widespread unemployment accompanying a severe depression with an outpouring of the kind of impulsive generosity for which they are famous. The resultant crazy quilt of charities caused concern among philanthropists that many truly needy persons would go unaided, while others might make a profitable business of working several charities at once. London's Charity Organization Society (COS), established in the previous decade, served as the model for American cities.

An initial attempt to set up a New York COS was abandoned when several influential charities refused to go along with the idea of a central registry of persons receiving public and voluntary relief (Watson 1922, p. 177). The first successful COS in the United States, that founded in Buffalo in 1877, felt constrained to assure its member agencies that it was not out to destroy their individuality or abridge their operations (p. 182). Twenty-two "considerations" were appended to its bylaws. Of the twenty-two, one was felt so important as to warrant being italicized. It stated, *"The Charity Organization Society does not interfere in any way with any existing Society cooperating with it. Each retains its autonomy intact; its rules, funds, modes of operation and all that gives it individuality"* (Gurteen 1882, p. 245).

At the time of these early attempts, "charity" was a relatively undifferentiated concept, with no clear demarcation made between the functions of almsgiving, moral uplift, and child protection. In the early years of the twentieth century, the dawning sense of professionalism in social services was accompanied by increasing specialization. A newly emerging instrument for integrating services was the community welfare council, or council of social agencies. The first of these was established in Pittsburgh in 1908 (Tropman 1971, p. 151). The impetus for service coordination came from the professionals. Paralleling this was a concern among large donors about multiple appeals for funds.

As in the previous instance, the push for integration followed a period of rapid growth in services of all kinds—a result of both the aforementioned specialization and the reform movements which began at the end of the nineteenth century. The patterns of operation that developed in the community welfare councils varied from community to community. In some instances, they had a role in setting budget allocations to agencies under the united fund-raising system, but they tended to act with great restraint regarding most aspects of agencies' operations. This resulted in an image of councils as relatively weak elements in the social services arena.

Although originally based exclusively in the voluntary sector of social welfare, councils in recent years have been involved increasingly in the public sector, directing as much as 50 percent of their efforts to the latter (Tropman 1971 p. 152). This movement has been accompanied by an increased reliance of voluntary agencies on public funds. The extent to which community welfare councils have been able to integrate services has depended mainly on their ability to influence the flow of funds to member agencies. In many instances, they have acted more as coordinators of separate entities.

So far we have talked about drives for services integration which followed rapid expansions in social programs. In the 1950s, there was a new rise in interest in integration, but this was less in response to an expansion than to a growing sense that social problems such as family breakdown and juvenile delinquency were increasing despite a substantial social services outlay. The finding that small percentages of families were using a disproportionate amount of services (Buell 1952) reinforced this concern. Rather than considering the possibility that the services themselves were ineffectual, professionals tended to focus either on inadequacies in the clients or the malcoordination of services. A number of reports focused on gaps in service, fragmentation, and duplication of effort (ibid.; Allport 1955; Virtue 1952; Wilensky and Lebeaux 1958, pp. 247–65).

Few major innovations toward social services integration came out of this period. Such devices as case conferences among professionals in different agencies dealing with the same "multi-problem" family, and the social service exchange, an outgrowth of the old COS central registry, had been used for years. A family-centered project in St. Paul, Minnesota, sought to reduce fragmentation and duplication by having agencies agree upon a single worker in one of them to handle a given family (Wilensky and Lebeaux, p. 261). Spurred by an upsurge in juvenile delinquency, a variety of multi-service projects were launched during this same era; but these tended to be separate and time-limited operations that were added to the existing complex of social agencies rather than integrating them (Kahn 1976, p. 29).

The large-scale movement of government into the personal social services that occurred in the 1960s shared several characteristics with the earlier expansions of private philanthropy in the United States: ad hoc accretion of special-focus programs with little basis in empirically demonstrated need, and even less regard for what already existed; a growing concern about fragmentation, duplication, and waste; and resistance of newly established centers of special interest to being regimented. Strong in the conviction that social services could solve human problems if they were administered in the right quantities and in concert, planners focused on integration at the direct delivery level (Kahn 1976).

One such effort was the Neighborhood Services Program (NSP), which was launched in 1966 under the joint sponsorship of the Department of Housing and Urban Development, HEW, the Department of Labor, and the Office of Economic Opportunity. The mechanism for integration was the multi-service center, which was designed to provide for a range of human needs at the neighborhood level (Perlman and Jones 1967; Newman 1968).

This effort was later superseded by the more ambitious Model Cities program, initiated in 1967. This, too, sought to integrate services at the delivery level. However, as has frequently happened with federal initiatives, the demand for a share in the funds rapidly outstripped the resources (Bernard 1975). With one hundred fifty cities participating, Model Cities could not deliver on its promise.

By the time Richard Nixon entered the White House in

1969, many doubts were being expressed about the existing social service efforts. There were those, for instance, who had begun to question the efficacy of the social service strategy for solving human problems altogether (Moynihan 1972). Even among some social service advocates, there was concern as to whether integration could take place at the delivery level unless it also occurred further up the line, at the organizational level. For the new administration, a major concern was the apparent lack of control over spending for services.

THE NEW FEDERALISM

Following his election in November 1968, President-elect Richard Nixon told a newsman that he saw his chief job as being foreign policy. Let the Cabinet deal with "the humdrum of domestic affairs," he said, adding,

> I've always thought this country could run itself domestically without a President. . . . All you need is a competent Cabinet to run the country at home. You need a President for foreign policy; no Secretary of State is really important; the President makes foreign policy (Evans and Novak 1971, p. 11).

Nixon was soon disabused of the notion that he could turn domestic affairs over to his Cabinet chiefs while he operated on the grander scene of international diplomacy. His problem was compounded by his Cabinet selections. Following the time-honored rules of American politics, Nixon's choices of department heads had been guided largely by political considerations. This placed such strong-minded ex-governors as George Romney, Walter Hickel, and John Volpe in charge of key domestic sectors (ibid., p. 52). If the president was to wrest control over domestic policy from the federal bureaucracy, he would have to take a direct hand in the proceedings.

In its first year, the Nixon administration came forth with several domestic initiatives but the signals were confusing. The president who had campaigned against the growing welfare burden and in favor of a strong role of states offered a welfare reform package that would both add appreciably to the public assistance rolls and move toward uniform national standards. (In all, a coherent philosophy of government was lacking.)

In January 1970, presidential speechwriter William Safire circulated among administration colleagues a document entitled "New Federalist Paper No. 1," over the pseudonym of *Publius*. The President was said to have had a hand in writing it. Its message was as follows:

> A sea-change in the approach to the limitation of centralized power—part of what is "new" in the new Federalism—is that *"States' rights" have now become rights of first refusal*. Local authority will now regain the right to Federal financial help; but it will not regain the right it once held to neglect the needs of its citizens. States' rights are now more accurately described as States' duties; that is a fundamental change in Federalism, removing its great fault without undermining its essential local-first character (*Publius*, 1972, p. 95).

Such an activist and positive construction on states' rights was soon challenged by presidential assistant Tom Huston, who, under the pen name of *Cato* wrote his own position paper entitled, "Federalism: Old and New, or, The Pretensions of the New Publius Exposed." In it he called for a more faithful adherence to the constitutional principle of dispersion of powers among the several states (p. 96). Eventually a total of four such papers was produced in this in-house debate. Out of the exchange emerged what was to become the theme of Nixon domestic policy during the remainder of his stay in the White House, the New Federalism.

The essence of New Federalism was the belief in maximum control over government activity at the state and local levels, but not at the expense of national goals. As "Paper No. 3," by Richard Nathan of the Office of Management and Budget (*Althusius*), declared, federal responsibility should be reserved for areas where state control was not feasible, but in these areas federal initiative was right and proper. Thus, the Family Assistance Plan was a proper exercise of the federal prerogative, because the welfare of a child should not depend on the state that child happened to live in. The Office of Economic Opportunity should not simply be dismantled but should be redirected. Since pollution problems knew no state boundaries, and many were beyond the capacity of a single state to deal with, environmental policy was an appropriate area for federal intervention (pp. 132–37).

One of the appeals held out by the proponents of New Federalism was the reduction, not only of federal power but also federal spending. So it was natural for attention to turn to such "big spenders" as HEW, HUD, and the Manpower Administration in the Department of Labor. Of these, HEW was the ideal target, since it symbolized rapid and uncontrolled growth and social service policies which had failed to deal effectively with poverty and social unrest.

HARNESSING THE WELFARE ESTABLISHMENT

To bring the sprawling HEW empire under control, Nixon turned to his longtime friend, Robert Finch. In many ways Finch was the obvious selection for the spot. Since the two had met in 1946, when Nixon was a freshman congressman, and Finch the staff aide to another California representative, there had been no more constant friend and confidant. He was Nixon's campaign manager in the 1960 race against John F. Kennedy; then, against others' advice, he took on the same role in the luckless gubernatorial campaign of 1962. In 1966, Finch demonstrated his political ability when he scored the biggest electoral triumph in California history as the running mate of gubernatorial candidate Ronald Reagan (White 1969).

When Nixon ran for president in 1968, he urged Finch to join him on the ticket, but Finch refused. He could be more help, he asserted, as simply a friend and adviser. When Nixon and his close advisers were still anguishing over the vice presidential slot in the midst of the Republican convention, Finch was again the overwhelming choice, far preferable to Spiro Agnew. Again he refused.

Finch had other attributes that made him appropriate for HEW Secretary. He was "the liberal" in the inner circle. When he ran with Reagan in 1966, he openly parted company with him, taking a distinctly more liberal stand. Nor was this a contrivance to garner votes. According to Theodore White, Finch was authentically committed to the poor (his family had suffered severe economic adversity), to minorities (he had developed compassion while living in a racially mixed area and had sensed the serious implications of the Watts rioting before others had), and to adequate health care (he had watched his father die from the slow ravages of cancer; pp. 140–41). Here, then, was a trusted friend, a proven political asset, and a genuine liberal—a man who could help balance off the conservatives with whom Nixon had surrounded himself.

Finch lacked two important attributes: knowledge of the intricacies of welfare policy and knowledge of Washington. Either one has proven damaging to HEW secretaries; in combination they were devastating. His virtues may have contributed to his undoing, in that he brought other liberals into key positions in HEW, possibly weakening the confidence of the White House in his judgment. Finch's problem was sometimes viewed as indecisiveness, as, for example, when he selected Dr. John Knowles, a Boston physician, as Assistant Secretary for Health, then backed off under pressure (Evans and Novak 1971, p. 64). This is a common diagnosis for liberals who initially take a forward position and then find themselves becoming isolated.

Finch seems to have underestimated the problems in simply managing the huge welfare bureaucracy. Holdovers from the Johnson days were not about to make it easy for the Nixon crowd. Having had no knowledge of welfare matters and a political career limited to California, he was extremely dependent on the bureaucrats. His dealings with Congress were particularly humiliating. For instance, he was no match for Ways and Means Committee Chairman Wilbur Mills, who knew, perhaps, more about welfare policy than anyone else in Washington and delighted in lecturing the administration on its intricacies. Finch, the close confidant of Nixon, thus watched his influence ebb, and he finally requested that he be relieved of his duties.

ENTER ELLIOT RICHARDSON

It is hard to imagine any greater contrast than that between the shaggy Finch, the Westerner who had come up the hard way, and the urbane aristocrat from Boston who succeeded him, Elliot L. Richardson. The new HEW secretary could draw upon previous experience in Washington, first as Senator Leverett Saltonstall's legislative aide, and then as HEW Assistant Secretary for Legislation in the Eisenhower administration. When tapped by Nixon for the HEW secretaryship, he was serving as Under Secretary of State. He was more circumspect than his predecessor about expressing his liberalism, an important consideration during the uneasy years of Nixon's first term.

This was not a man to be badgered in Ways and Means Committee hearings. During his confirmation hearing, Richardson was told by Senator Russell Long, the powerful Chairman of the Senate Finance Committee, "I do not see how a man can ever know what is going on, much less run that department the way that we would like to have a federal agency administered." Without hesitation Richardson answered by saying he was a man "who measures his satisfactions by the scale of the possible" (*National Journal* 1973). At a news conference he was asked about his plans for HEW. His calm response was that of a seasoned politico: "I am not in a position to give answers to questions about HEW. I don't have any anyway. I haven't had time to become familiar with the department" (Lyons 1970, p. 44). Despite the disclaimer Richardson did have ideas—one was to avoid mistakes he had observed during his earlier stint in HEW.

His passion was for orderly administration. On one occasion White House staffer William Safire (1975) noted some of Richardson's doodling: a strong, neat complex of interwoven geometric shapes—"powerful abstractions" (p. 200). The doodles bespoke a strong will and a tidy mind. At the State Department, his chief contribution had been to unsnarl internal lines of communication, not raise issues of foreign policy; and he had supreme confidence in the possibility of solving any problem if one used the right techniques (Lydon 1970). Within six months of having taken the helm at HEW, he was reported to be firmly in charge of the vast operation. More remarkable still was his apparent ability to do this while winning the loyalty and respect of his employees, including many liberals who had opposed his predecessor (Delaney 1970).

Richardson played by the rules of the game, and he expected others to do so, as well. When Nixon vetoed a bill for hospital construction without informing his HEW Secretary, in whose bailiwick it belonged, the reaction was swift and intense. Richardson was "flabbergasted and angry when he learned of the veto not from the White House but from a news ticker," reported journalists Evan and Novak (1971, p. 126); and he took the issue directly to Nixon adviser John Erlichman. The HEW secretary could also stand on principle when it would have been easier to duck sensitive issues. For instance, he took an activist approach to implementation of a Supreme Court decision upholding compulsory busing for school integration and got Attorney General John Mitchell to go along with him (p. 399).

In December 1971, six months after his arrival at HEW, Richardson assembled several hundred HEW employees and delivered an address he later referred to as "my Castro speech":

> [I]t contained all the things I would have liked to say to my 110,000 fellow workers if only I could have rounded them up in some great plaza and harangued them, like Fidel Castro, for three or four hours (1976, p. 127n.).

The speech was expanded and published in the form of a booklet for internal consumption, under the title, *Responsibility and Responsiveness: The HEW Potential for the Seventies* (1972). Here Richardson, who did the actual drafting, summarized his philosophy of the federal government's role in welfare and laid out a program to implement the philosophy. It was a strong appeal for rationality in governmental planning: "To be sure, values, feelings, and attitudes will always, as they should, play a large role in the final choice, but the effort to improve our analysis of the issues cannot help but increase the likelihood that the resulting decision will be sound" (p. 6).

Richardson was particularly critical of "overlap, waste, duplication, jurisdictional jealousies, [and] persistence in outmoded methods" (p. 8). Multiplicities of categorical grant-in-aid programs and specialized agencies spawned by the government, together with conflicting federal guidelines, were destroying the effectiveness of HEW's efforts, he said. The solution did not simply mean cleaning up the federal government's act, but dispersing more control of programs to the states and localities.

Richardson cited four main avenues by which HEW hoped to translate philosophy into action: reduction of red tape in federal assistance to states, consolidation of specialized grant programs, services integration at the state and local levels, and decentralization of decision-making authority. The speech might well have been delivered by Richard Nixon. But while it was highly compatible with the New Federalism, it had its roots at least partly in Richardson's earlier experience in Massachusetts.

As Lieutenant Governor of the Bay State from 1965 to 1966, Richardson sought special responsibility for instituting administrative reforms in the state's health and welfare programs (Lydon 1970). In his words, "I became increasingly disturbed by the tendency to lose sight of the whole person—to subdivide a person's problems and parcel them out to a host of different agencies" (1976, p. 180).

When Richardson tried to develop a Massachusetts plan for Medicaid that would cut across jurisdictional lines of the welfare and public health establishments, he ran into resistance from officials of HEW. He also sought to advance his ideas for services integration through national legislation. He got three friendly senators (none, incidentally, from his home state of Massachusetts) to introduce his Community Services Act. He also wrote to state human services administrators around the country promoting the plan, and several offered to testify at hearings on the bill. Then something happened which was to become a hallmark of Richardson's career: in the midst of the campaign for human services reform he moved to a new job, that of Massachusetts attorney general, and the campaign foundered.

Now, in his "Castro" speech, Richardson expanded on his vision of social services integration. One could not, he said, blame fragmentation entirely on the policies and procedures of the federal government, and it could not be overcome solely by federal action:

Local agencies tend to be fully as jealous in protecting their own turf as any federal entity. Professional disciplines do not lose their guild-mindedness at the local level. As a consequence, an individual in need is all too often forced to go from agency to agency, none of which is capable of dealing with him as a whole person (p. 20).

Richardson's answer to the problem was consistent with his administrative bent: better coordination of local operations, joint planning by service providers, and the creation of comprehensive systems. He then outlined two strategies through which the federal government could help combat the problem. One was research and demonstration projects for testing out the feasibility of services integration. The other was new federal legislation, then being developed by HEW, that would

help local service providers break down the categories that slice the individual into segments, bridge the barriers between the helping professions and build an integrated approach to the goal of reducing dependency. . . . [The legislation] will also widen the flexibility of Federal support for States and localities through provisions for transfers of Federal funds between programs, waivers of inconsistent Federal program requirements, and limited funding for planning and administrative costs. . . . It would not pay for additional programs, but underwrite the administrative costs of improving the system (p. 21).

This was to become the Allied Services Act. On its face it was an innocuous bill to provide a more rational service delivery system at the local level and prevent "hardening of the categories" from causing fragmentation, duplication, and inaccessibility of services. Consistent with the New Federalism, it increased the power of decision at state and local levels. Amid the rising anger over the "free-spending" ways of Washington, Allied Services would cost a pittance to administer. Moreover, its chief protagonist was perhaps the first man ever to bring the unruly HEW into line, one whose "basic training" in Washington years before had been in the delicate area of congressional relations. All in all, Allied Services would seem to have been a shoo-in. But its champions had overlooked two key factors: one was the general lack of interest among social workers and other liberals; the other was the fierce opposition of specialized agencies which feared that their bailiwicks were to be invaded.

There was something of a contradiction in Richardson's version of the New Federalism. On the one hand he sought tight administrative organization and accountability. On the other, there was a naive faith that state government would act in a rational and responsible manner, despite the poor record of many states in the past. Richardson could not assume that most states would have either the resources or inclination to provide the kind of administrative and technical enlightment he had known in Massachusetts. The contradiction was inherent in many aspects of the New Federalism (see Newman and Turem 1974).

THE ALLIED SERVICES ACT

Soon after he came to HEW, Richardson assembled a departmental task force to work on legislation to carry out his ideas. Even among those assigned to flesh out the proposal, enthusiasm varied greatly. Said Richard Verville, who had worked under Richardson in Massachusetts, "It was an assignment, but I was also personally interested." For others, it was "Elliot's thing," something that came with the job, but not a source of real excitement. One aide privately termed it "a bunch of s—." Richardson was neither aware of these attitudes nor of the fact that they were shared by some of the people he relied on most heavily to carry his ideas forward.

It struck Richardson at the time that it was taking his staff an unusually long time to come up with a bill. In retrospect, he thinks there may have been reservations that were not being expressed openly. In actuality, there was an active process of trying to come up with a viable piece of legislation. Informal soundings with congressional staff members soon alerted the HEW task force to the fact that the proposal would have a lot of trouble. It is the opinion of a number of former HEW officials that none of this was shared directly with Richardson.

The bill which emerged from the task force faithfully reflected the Secretary's philosophy of social services. It embraced many of the points in the Castro I speech. Described by Richardson as a "bottoms up" approach to social service reform, the bill was to provide for federal assistance to states willing to

> establish coterminous sub-State boundaries for HEW programs, develop comprehensive, goal-oriented State service plans for four or more major HEW grant-in-aid programs, and designate local units of general purpose government to assess local service needs and develop local plans for integrating and rationalizing the service delivery system (Richardson 1973, p. 26).

Two-year planning grants, three-year administrative start-up grants, and provision of comprehensive support systems such as information, referral, and transportation would become available to states. Then, the most innovative features of the bill: states would be authorized to transfer up to 25 percent of federal funds from one program to another; and HEW requirements found to impede services integration could be waived (p. 26).

The bill was a pale shadow of the measures enacted in Britain for the reform of the personal social services in Scotland, England, and Wales, although it had the same general objective: services integration at the local level. A permissive invitation to states to participate, it offered limited financial incentives for doing so. It was a tentative and modest step in the direction of social service reform, and it generated little enthusiasm outside of the secretary and a small circle of his subordinates.

On a number of occasions Elliot Richardson alluded to a cartoon by Oliphant which had appeared in the Denver *Post* at the time of his appointment to HEW. It showed the secretary's office "filled with sniggling, smirking coffee drinkers clustered around the secretary's chair. The caption was, 'Come in, sir, we represent the thousands on your staff. You will find us petty, uncooperative, devious, unreliable, and thoroughly bureaucratic'" (p. 5). Richardson denied that he had found this to be true, but it must have been a disappointment to find that his own enthusiasm for Allied Services was not widely shared by his staff. More than outright opposition or even lack of personal interest in the concept was the conviction among many of those around Richardson that Allied Services would never get anywhere in Congress. According to a former HEW official,

> A few of us took it very seriously at the time. I knew it would not go through. I offered ideas on various pieces in order to muffle some of the overreaction of [outside] constituencies for which I had responsibility. I knew from the reactions I was getting that it couldn't go anywhere. I didn't tell Richardson that. I don't know whether other people did or not.

1972: A Limited Effort Yields a Limited Response. On May 18, 1972, President Nixon sent the Allied Services bill to Congress with a thousand-word message urging its enactment. In the House, it was first assigned to the Ways and Means Committee. That committee discussed it several times, but held no hearings and essentially sat on it. Then in an unusual move, Chairman Wilbur Mills asked the House leadership to reassign the bill to the Education and Labor Committee. It was subsequently buried. Behind the apparent snafu, there were forces at work that were more obvious in later attempts to enact the Allied Services bill. Elliot Richardson correctly saw the nation's governors as a natural constituency for the proposal. It was they who had the most to gain from it politically, for with it they would have substantial control over the flow of federal social services funds within their states. Historically, categorical funding formulas, which direct federal assistance to specified state agencies, have given the directors of those agencies a great deal of independence from control by the governor's office.

In looking to the governors as a major source of support, Richardson was banking on a group that ostensibly had political clout but, in reality, was of only limited value in influencing Congress. At the time, partisan, sectional, and other schisms had prevented the governors from becoming a strong force on the national scene. It was the specialized agencies in the states that had developed close ties with congressional committees and the HEW bureaucracy over the years. Furthermore, governors were often holding office in preparation for election to other posts, while the agency heads were careerists with a vested interest in their operations. Thus, they and their professional employees had both a greater stake and greater longevity in their current posts.

Richardson says candidly that he underestimated the opposition to Allied Services. This may explain the belatedness of his own direct involvement in lobbying efforts. For example, it was not until November 1972, six months after the bill had been sent to Congress, that he got to carry the message to the nation's governors, a constituency on which he counted for support. In part, he was bouyed by his firm belief in the rightness of the proposal and the certainty that no right-thinking person could have serious objections to it. In part, he may have been misled by the failure of subordinates to share with him their own pessimism about the bill's chances. As a general philosophy, he says, he believes in expending only the resources necessary to accomplish a given task. His estimate of the required resources for passage of the Allied Services bill was off by a wide margin.

Richardson's apparent misreading of the congressional reaction to Allied Services is somewhat mystifying. He was not new to the ways of Congress, having specialized in congressional relations in his earlier stint in HEW in the late 1950s, and being a personal friend of many of its members. He also demonstrated on other occasions an ability to think in political terms— for example, in advising President Nixon on federal social service expenditures (see Chapter 7). Allied Services was not the only instance where he was unprepared for the congressional opposition to his ideas (see Richardson 1976, p. 206).

All this soon became moot, however. Shortly after the November 1972 elections Allied Services lost its chief proponent: Elliot Richardson became Secretary of Defense. He says he would have preferred to stay on at HEW. Does he think that would have improved the chances of Allied Services in subsequent efforts to enact it? Yes. As it turned out, Richardson's successor at HEW, Caspar Weinberger, was also a supporter of the Allied Services concept, although his interest related more to fiscal control than the plight of the consumer. Frank Carlucci, a man whom Weinberger brought with him from the Office of Management and Budget (OMB), was particularly taken with the idea, and became the main mover in later attempts to enact the bill.

The Politics of Services Integration.   The 1972 bill never got far enough to become a major focus of conflict between supporters and opponents, but various interest groups were put on notice by its introduction. Professionals in the fields of aging, mental health, and rehabilitation were among those who saw a threat to their special funding arrangements and autonomy within the states if Allied Services were enacted. An example of how they responded is seen in the experience of the National Rehabilitation Association (NRA) and its executive director, E. B. Whitten.

The first instance of federal aid to social services—for populations other than those viewed as special federal charges, such as Indians, ex-slaves, and war veterans—was in the field of vocational rehabilitation. In the early 1920s, the concept of rehabilitation of physically disabled veterans was extended to include disabled nonveterans (Wilcox 1969, p. 324). In a country obsessed with a fear of dependency and government intervention, what could be more truly American than helping those who were unemployed "through no fault of their own" to reenter the work force? Federal grants-in-aid supported state-operated rehabilitation programs; and so began the development of a cadre of professional helpers whose careers depended on federal subsidization of their state agencies. Rehabilitation programs found particularly fertile soil in the South, where other kinds of social welfare tended to be viewed with suspicion.

E. B. Whitten began his career in rehabilitation in his home state of Mississippi. In 1946, he became state rehabilitation director. His work led quite naturally to his becoming active in the National Rehabilitation Association. The NRA was finding it increasingly important to stay close to developments in

Washington, and in 1948 it asked Whitten to establish an office in the nation's capital. Thus, while other social service associations continued to operate out of national offices in New York, Chicago, and Columbus, Ohio, NRA became part of the Washington scene. Whitten, as a full-time, paid representative, was able to develop personal ties with a wide range of people on Capitol Hill and in the administration. Especially important in the complex policy arena, he was around to find out what was happening to various pieces of legislation and administrative regulations. When Elliot Richardson began his relatively brief experience of handling congressional relations for HEW, Whitten had been at it for ten years already. Backing him up was a cadre of supporters in every state who had close ties with their own congressional delegations.

To the first Nixon administration, casting about for ways to "turn welfare into workfare"—that is, get people off of public assistance and into regular employment—rehabilitation presented an attractive model for going about it. Here was a program already in place in every state—a program which had demonstrated that it could bring in nonproductive people and produce work-ready people. Why not broaden it to include those other nonproductive people filling up the welfare rolls? The result was that the Rehabilitation Services Administration (RSA) began in 1971 to work with people other than those usually thought of as physically disabled—delinquents, alcoholics, and drug abusers. These latter groups came under a term coined in the bureaucracy: "behavioral disorders." Theoretically, it could be broadened to include any number of nontraditionally handicapped persons: those coming out of prison and those on welfare, for instance.

But in an administration keyed to cutting federal costs, this trend could mean only one thing: more places to put a shrinking supply of money, with the result of a diluted program for those groups to which RSA had traditionally been committed. Furthermore, rehabilitation professionals had always prided themselves on not being associated with the welfare stigma; they worked with the "deserving" poor. Accordingly, NRA and allied groups sought help from friends in Congress. Congress responded by inserting in vocational rehabilitation legislation in 1972 a prohibition against allowing "behavioral disorders" to serve as a basis for inclusion in rehab programs.

When the Allied Services Act came along, it looked to Whitten and his associates like one more attempt by the Nixon administration to whittle away at their hard-won gains in the rehabilitation field. The crux of the problem was the provision allowing governors to transfer up to 25 percent of federal funds among programs. Theoretically, rehabilitation programs could be the beneficiary of such shifts, but the professionals in the field were convinced otherwise.

Outside pressure groups normally have most of their dealings with specific agencies or congressional committees. In the House of Representatives, rehabilitation matters generally find their way to the Committee on Education and Labor; and within that the Select Subcommittee on Education, whose chairman in the early 1970s was John Brademas. As far as is known, Brademas's district in Indiana does not have an unusually large quota of physically handicapped persons. Yet, over the years, he has had a special interest in rehabilitation and related matters. Brademas is also a Democrat; according to some informants, he was not about to give the Nixon administration unnecessary help in enacting its program. Partisan political considerations, however, do not appear to have been paramount, since he has also opposed reform attempts by the Democrats. Brademas allowed his name to be added to those of the sponsors of the Allied Services bill, but he was clearly not its champion.

Both the majority and minority contingents of a congressional committee have paid staff whose positions are not covered by civil service protection; they are thus dependent on their politically-attuned mentors. Predictably, they try to anticipate and reflect the outlook of committee leadership. Conversely, committee members are dependent on staff for information; more than technical background data, they also look for guidance on what is good or bad legislation. The first time around, the word on Allied Services was "bad." Accordingly, when the bill came into the jurisdiction of Education and Labor, it was soon clear that it would go no place.

There was no active lobbying by Whitten or others. They knew they did not need to worry about it. Allied Services 1972 was killed by a set of shared attitudes among people used to working closely together.

The bill presented something of a dilemma for one individual in HEW. This was Edward Newman, the commissioner of RSA. As the chief officer in rehabilitation matters, he was expected to look after the interests of the handicapped and programs in their behalf. He also had developed close working ties with Whitten and the staff of the Committee on Education and Labor. But he had worked with Richardson in Massachusetts and felt a strong loyalty to his boss. He became aware from his outside contacts that Allied Services in its original form was doomed. Within HEW, he suggested changes to meet the criticism. But all of this was to be of no avail. Too many parties had too much to lose.

1974: Strike Two.   It is one of those political ironies that the most serious and best executed campaign for ASA came in 1974, after its author and strongest champion, Elliot Richardson, had left the government; when the Nixon administration was in disarray; and when the social service professionals were rapidly mastering the art of coalition politics. The 1974 version of the bill had minor differences from its predecessor. Instead of proposing merely to help states and localities to "coordinate their various programs and resources available to provide human services," the new bill sought to help "develop, demonstrate, and evaluate means of improving the utilization and effectiveness of human services through integrated planning, management, and delivery." It was more specifically aimed at economic self-sufficiency as an ultimate goal, in keeping with a growing emphasis of the federal government's approach to social services.

The specifics of the bill were little changed from the 1972 version, except that now 30 percent of funds, instead of 25 percent, could be transfered from one program to another. Thus, the challenge to the defenders of categorical programs was even more serious. Possibly the proponents of ASA thought this would give them more room for maneuver if they were forced to compromise later. Again, the bill went to Education and Labor, with Brademas as a cosponsor of the bill, but he gave no indication that he was any more enamored of it than before.

The supporters of Allied Services were better organized this time. One of the persons who had worked on the 1972 bill in HEW, Christopher Cross, had by now moved over to the minority staff of the House Educational and Labor Committee. Whereas the earlier bill had never gotten to the hearing stage, Cross and others were determined to get hearings scheduled on its successor. Little encouragement, however, came from the committee staff. A fellow minority staffer recalls, "I didn't think it was good legislation. Chris and I did not see eye to eye on it. I thought it was better for him to handle it, since he was an advocate. Conceptually there was nothing wrong with it, but it just wasn't [politically feasible]."

By working through the ranking minority (Republican) member of the Select Subcommittee on Education, Albert Quie of Minnesota, and the majority chief counsel, Jack Duncan, the proponents were able to prevail upon Brademas to schedule hearings. Meanwhile, Cross, together with HEW staff members, sought to line up support. Their best response was from representatives of general government at the state and county level, but the support was by no means unanimous. The National Governor's Conference, the National Association of Counties, and several governors, including Georgia Governor Jimmy Carter, were among those who backed the proposal.

The main opposition came from those in the specialized social service fields: mental health and mental retardation, physically disabled, and the blind. Having been alerted to the hearings, E. B. Whitten wrote asking for the opportunity to testify. It was clear that those opposed to the legislation were in communication with one another, although the channels were less clear. Other interests had specific concerns, which they voiced without opposing the concept outright.

Unfortunately for the 1974 bill, it was the Nixon administration that came to be identified more and more as the supportive constituency. The state and local general government forces were less than solidly identified with Allied Services, largely because it offered no major infusion of money, only the opportunity to shift around what was already in the pot. By 1974, the states and localities were lining up against the Nixon administration over its attempts to restrict the flow of social service funds. This fight over funding restrictions had thrust Allied Services into the background. Governors, who were looked to as the main counterforce against the specialized professional interests, were preoccupied with what to them was a much more salient fight. The National Governors' Conference and the National Association of Counties did offer testimony in behalf of Allied Services in the 1974 hearings, but their lack of enthusiasm was clear.

The main support for Allied Services in the hearings came from those without a political constituency: HEW Under Secretary Frank Carlucci and former Secretary Elliot Richardson, by then a fellow at the Woodrow Wilson International Center for Scholars. Much of Carlucci's time was spent dealing with questions that had been raised and offering changes to deal with the objections; but none of these were related directly to the crucial issue of transfers of funds from one program to another.

As against the mixed support for the bill, much of which was combined with objections to specific items in the proposal, there was strong opposition from those identified with categorical services. The lead-off witness on the first day of hearings was Whitten, the bill's main foe. He complained that his organization, NRA, had not been consulted in advance in the formulation of the measure. He also drew a distinction between "service integration," which he said he favored, and "administrative integration," which he said was in the Allied Services proposal. His essential concern was that specialized agencies should be free to collaborate without being brought into a single organization (U.S. Congress, House, Committee on Education and Labor 1974, pp. 9–25).

Also speaking or submitting written statements to the subcommittee in opposition to the bill were spokespersons for a regional medical program, the American Social Health Association, the National Education Association, the American Foundation for the Blind, and the National Association for Retarded Citizens. In one way or another all focused on the threat that Allied Services posed to the ability to plan or provide services for designated populations and through designated institutions, that is, the categorical funding pattern. The one exception to this solid position was the testimony of the National Association of State Mental Health Directors, which supported the Allied Services concept. The opponents were joined by the major voice of organized labor, the AFL-CIO, which also spoke in behalf of categorical funding of social services (ibid.). In so doing, it was protecting the interests of the many unionized employees in specialized agencies.

The questioning of witnesses by Subcommittee Chairman Brademas tended to confirm the view that he was not sympathetic to the bill. In particular, he questioned whether the local demonstrations of services integration around the country had shown the beneficial results claimed for it. Despite his cosponsorship of the bill, it was clear where he stood. As chairman of the Select Committee he could keep the bill from being acted upon. Once again, the Allied Services bill died in committee.

The Social Workers' Dilemma. One organization asked to react to Allied Services 1974 was the National Association of Social Workers (NASW). In 1972, there had been internal memos indicating that NASW should consider taking a position, but there were other priorities at the time. This time, a school social worker from Gary, Indiana, Walter Rogers, testified on NASW's behalf. The statement was equivocal.

The equivocation was not a simple reflection of indecisiveness on the part of NASW. By 1974, NASW had been in existence for nearly twenty years, the result of a merger of specialized organizations not unlike that which led to the formation of the British Association of Social Workers. In the interim, it had developed a highly professional lobbying arm headed by Glenn Allison, a former California social worker. He had been brought on staff in 1971, at the time of a major shake-up in NASW's leadership. Perceiving correctly that the social workers lacked two essential ingredients for influencing social policy decisions—political muscle and a major research capability—Allison and his associates sought to borrow both from groups who had them. In the process, he built up an extensive web of relationships with administration officials, congressional staff, and other outside interest groups.

NASW had maximized the impact of its limited resources by engaging in coalition politics and presenting testimony in congressional hearings on carefully selected issues. The coalition strategy had its costs, for it meant NASW often had to avoid taking a strong stand on one issue for fear of jeopardizing its outside linkages. One such instance had been the decision not to take a position in the 1972 presidential race between Nixon and liberal Democrat George McGovern, despite efforts of rank and file social workers to get NASW to back McGovern.

In the case of Allied Services, significant elements in the NASW leadership urged an outright rejection of the bill, as a thinly veiled attempt by the Nixon administration to cut back on social services. Aside from the maintenance of good relations with HEW officials, NASW had to consider its own membership. There were social workers on both sides of the issue. The final result of these deliberations was the testimony Rogers presented before the Select Subcommittee on Education. It endorsed the general concept at a time of shrinking funds but questioned whether greater coordination of social services would be effective.

On the issue of threats to specialized programs, the NASW statement urged "safeguards to ensure that categorical funding boundaries will not be arbitrarily disregarded and that parties who might be adversely affected by fund transfers are duly notified and are given adequate opportunity to voice their objections and to appeal unfavorable local and state decisions" (U.S. Congress, House, Committe on Education and Labor 1974, p. 43). NASW, like other liberal groups, mistrusted the motives of an administration bent on curtailing social welfare costs.

1975: Strike Three and Out. It is not unusual for a bill, having been killed in the legislative process, to keep surfacing—sometimes with a different name and selected concessions in order to blunt criticism and win a few more adherents. In the case of Allied Services, HEW decided to come back the next year after it died in committee. The new bill labored under several burdens: Congress was flexing its muscles more boldly in the wake of the Nixon resignation; and an alliance of governors and social service professionals had forced the administration to accept a major compromise on the question of social service funding. The bill was also saddled with a name that in the past had failed to generate much excitement and was associated with past defeats. A congressional staff member has said of Allied Services: "It was improperly named. 'Allied Services' didn't mean anything. That hurt because people didn't understand it."

The sponsors had made some major modifications in hopes of winning new supporters, but the name made it easy to stereotype the new bill as a carbon copy of its predecessors. One important change was in the controversial fund transfer provision. Thirty percent of federal assistance could still be shifted among programs in a state, but, "25 of the 30 percent which may be transferred must be among programs directed at essentially the same target population or for cooperative efforts to integrate administrative support services for programs included in the plan" (U.S., Congress, House 1975, p. 5).

While the concession would not calm the fears of specialized agencies and special interest organizations, it robbed their claim that needy populations might be neglected of much of its force. HEW issued publicity material explaining the new bill and sought to recruit additional support. Proponents were able to find more than thirty cosponsors for the bill in Congress.

Congressional committees had been the graveyard for previous Allied Services bills, along with countless other measures; and the committee structure now posed a new challenge to the latest Allied Services proposal. Under new rules, several House committees could claim jurisdiction over the same measure. The House parliamentarian advised the proponents that the bill could go to as many as six committees. By eliminating references to food and housing in the text of the bill, they had been able to eliminate two additional committees. Sending a measure to so many committees promised to tie it up almost indefinitely and almost certainly assure its demise. On the other hand, to obtain exclusive jurisdiction in the Education and Labor Committee would throw it right back into the lap of the unfriendly Brademas.

In an effort to get around these obstacles, HEW Secretary Caspar Weinberger brought Republican members of a number of committees together with Republican House leader John Rhodes to map strategy. It was agreed that Rhodes would ask the speaker of the House to establish an ad hoc committee made up of members of all the relevant standing committees. Rhodes's effort was rebuffed by House Speaker Carl Albert; according to one informant, this may well have been because of negative experiences with such ad hoc committees in the past.

This left the two unattractive options of placing the bill at the mercy of six different committees, or trying to stay with Education and Labor. The latter strategy was decided upon, and the next step was to sit with Brademas and try to determine what he wanted. It was obvious that without his acquiescence, still another Allied Services bill was headed for oblivion. The contacts with Brademas were largely inconclusive. After six weeks of such efforts, supporters decided to go ahead anyway. With the cooperation of House Education and Labor Committee Chairman Carl Perkins, primary referral was made to that committee. If it survived there, it would then go to Ways and Means, Interstate and Foreign Commerce, and possibly Government Operations. While the gantlet was more than challenging, it appeared to be the only viable strategy.

In 1976, Albert Quie, the ranking minority member of the Education and Labor Committee, was still trying to get hearings on the Allied Services bill. Chairman Carl Perkins agreed they should be held after a number of other measures were disposed of, but the hearings never took place. Once again the patient died of neglect.

The 1975 Allied Services bill came at a time when other

major issues were crowding it into the background. Its foes were as well organized as before and had demonstrated their ability to wield considerable influence in the political arena. It still lacked the ability to mobilize a significant constituency in its behalf.

But ideas die hard. As of the spring of 1977, officials in the Office of the Assistant Secretary for Planning and Evaluation, HEW, were still trying to figure out what had gone wrong and were still speaking hopefully of a new attempt to launch an Allied Services bill, although possibly under a different name (Marcus 1977). The new Democratic president, Jimmy Carter, who was a firm advocate of services integration, had written in support of a previous Allied Services bill, and he pointed with pride at the record of his own efforts as governor of Georgia to integrate human services. At the time, Carter was still enjoying his brief honeymoon with Congress. Enough, perhaps, to keep the spark alive, but the HEW officials were receiving little encouragement regarding Allied Services. It appeared that events had passed it by.

CONCLUSION

The Allied Services Act was the victim of both action and inaction. The action was by groups concerned mainly with specialized social services and the potential loss of categorical federal financial support. The cadres of paid professionals, the ones most attuned to the funding issues and with vital career interests, as well as social concerns at stake, were able to communicate with constituencies made up of the people who benefited from the existing array of services and their families. Beyond these stood elements in the general population who had natural sympathy for persons afflicted with physical disabilities, and who could, if necessary, be enlisted in support. As it turned out, the professionals needed little of this larger support; they could utilize their existing networks of relationships with lawmakers to squelch the Allied Services Act. Their influence did not lie in their political muscle nor the threat of retribution at the polls for those who defied them; John Brademas could have allowed the Allied Services bill to go to the House floor without any fear of retaliation. Instead, Whitten and his fellow professionals had become an essential component of the legislative process. They had the intimate knowledge of their respective fields that could help a Brademas stay on top of the issues; and in Congress knowledge is a vital commodity.

By keeping a low profile on Allied Services and failing to generate excitement about it, the administration had little with which to counter the professionals' built-in advantage. A different kind of bill, one offering additional funds to the states or promising dramatic changes, might have mobilized the governors and others in general government at the state and local levels to become more directly involved. If that had happened, it is likely that the social service professionals would have sought more actively to draw upon their client constituencies and possible public sympathy.

The Allied Services Act was also killed by inaction. There were social service professionals who had spoken admiringly of services integration as an abstract concept, but who never became actively involved in trying to promote the piece of legislation whose basic purpose was services integration. One may, with Alfred Kahn, see a degree of faddism in this process (Kahn 1976). Today's panacea becomes tomorrow's source of disillusionment. Such a fate has befallen school desegregation and the separation of money payments from personal social services in public assistance. Even the personal social services, as such, have gone through similar fluctuations in popularity.

The social workers' lack of enthusiasm for the Allied Services bill may have been based on a miscalculation. As we have seen, services integration in Britain was accompanied by a dramatic surge in demand for services. The incentive in the Allied Service bill, while a far weaker stimulus, could have prompted some states and localities to integrate services. The experience in some services integration projects in the United States suggests that, just as in Britain, an appreciable increase in demand could have resulted (United Services Agency Evaluation Project 1977). This is conjecture, to be sure; but in a period when social workers were becoming alarmed by a decline in funding and in apparent lack of appreciation of their contribution by the general public, it is possible that Allied Services could have helped to promote a growth phase in the field.

7
The Battle over
Social Service Funding

THE ALLIED SERVICES ACT WAS NOT A POLICY SCHEME TO FIRE THE imagination. One of its greatest enemies was apathy on the part of its potential supporters. The issues surrounding it were complex and, to all except the service specialists who feared an erosion of their special relationship to the federal government, rather nebulous. But when the Nixon administration and congressional conservatives threatened a massive assault on social service funding, social service professionals were confronted with a palpable threat. The problem affected both public and voluntary agencies providing a wide range of services. It thus was the occasion for a major mobilization of these interests. They realized that they were fighting, if not a threat to their very existence, at least a severe curtailment of their programs and, ultimately, of demand for their services.

PERSONAL SOCIAL SERVICES:
A NEW FEDERAL RESPONSIBILITY
The same concerns about family breakdown and child neglect that emerged in postwar Britain were also evident in the United

States in the late 1940s and 1950s. In the fifties they were compounded by an association in the public mind between poverty and personal failure. The natural target of much of the concern was the public assistance program that seemed to combine both problems, Aid to Dependent Children (ADC). This was established as one of four categories of financial aid in the Social Security Act of 1935. Unlike the social insurance provisions of the 1935 act, public assistance is means tested; that is, persons are required to demonstrate that they lack the means for self-support in order to qualify for aid. The other three categories were Old Age Assistance, Aid to the Blind, and Aid to the Permanently and Totally Disabled. While recipients of all such aid bore a stigma, the greatest public onus was on families receiving ADC.

Even in the depths of the Depression of the 1930s, when ADC was created, recipients of public assistance were stigmatized. But it was in the relative affluence of the postwar years, when the assumption was that "anybody can find a job who wants one," that recipients of Aid to Dependent Children felt the full force of public resentment. Greatly intensifying the reaction was the belief that the ADC caseload was predominantly black; thus, attitudes of racism comingled with the general sentiments about the poor. In actuality, blacks were in the minority in the ranks of ADC recipients, but they were the most visible part, since they were the largest group in large urban areas. And it was true that, in proportion to their numbers in the total population, their rate of participation was much greater than that of whites. Neglected by the public critics was the fact that blacks also had the worst educational and employment opportunities.

During the 1950s, under the permissive Eisenhower administration, several states asserted their right to impose restrictions on ADC programs within their borders. States often skated close to the line of noncompliance with federal requirements, secure in the knowledge that the federal government was unlikely to disqualify them from receiving federal matching funds. In one memorable case, Indiana launched a program to publicize the names of relief recipients, in outright violation of the federal statute which required confidentiality; it then got its influential senator, William Jenner, to persuade his congressional colleagues to change the federal law for federal funds so that the state would not be disqualified (Indianapolis Chapter, AASW, 1952). Elsewhere, "suitable home" provisions were used as a thinly veiled means of removing thousands of families from the ADC rolls. In Newburgh, New York, a punitive thirteen-point code aimed at the city's needy became the national symbol of efforts to "do something" about the rising cost of public welfare (Axinn and Levin 1975, p. 236).

There was another, more benign reaction to the problem of economic dependency, but one which nonetheless was consistent with the assumption that the poor were poor because of their own failings. This was the belief that it was not willful violation of society's norms that brought mothers and children into the ADC caseload, but rather their emotional and cultural deprivation. Thus, the term "hard core" or "multi-problem" was used to describe families that were (1) poor, (2) black, and (3) on public assistance (Wilensky and Lebeaux 1958, pp. 169–174). Liberal stalwarts like economist John Kenneth Galbraith were in tune with the belief that direct intervention on a one-by-one basis with those experiencing poverty could effectively deal with the problem (Handler 1973, p. 116).

This perception of the issue found wide support in the body politic. Especially as it concerned families with young children, it fit in with enlightened child welfare philosophy that preferred "rescue" activity with the child in his own home rather than removal to substitute care. For moderates it was a welcome alternative to the punitive policies then being put forth. Conservatives such as Louisiana Senator Russell Long were willing to try rehabilitation as a way of getting people off of the welfare rolls. These sentiments coalesced around the view that financial aid was not enough but needed to be augmented by personal social services (Handler 1973, pp. 117–16).

By 1956, ADC had become Aid to *Families with* Dependent Children (AFDC) underscoring the goal of family rehabilitation. Amendments to the Social Security Act authorized services "to help maintain and strengthen family life and to help

. . . parents and relatives [charged with the care of children on AFDC] to attain the maximum self-support and personal independence consistent with the maintenance of continuing parental care and protection" (U.S. Congress 1956).

Although no funds were appropriated to support this objective, the new language represented something of a land-mark, since it involved the federal government directly in the provision of personal social services. Up to that time, the federal government's role had been limited to consultation and other nonfinancial support of child welfare services in the states but no federal subsidy. It was not until 1962 that federal funds were appropriated for grants-in-aid to states for personal social ser-vices, and the service provisions in the Social Security Act were broadened to include persons not currently receiving public assistance. The philosophy underlying the 1962 Public Welfare Amendments was summed up in President John F. Kennedy's message to Congress, in which they were proposed:

> merely responding with a relief check to complicated social or personal problems . . . is not likely to provide a lasting solution. Such a check must be supplemented, or in some cases made unnecessary, by positive ser-vices and solutions. . . . Public welfare, in short, must be more than a salvage operation. . . . Its emphasis must be directed increasingly toward prevention and rehabilitation (Kennedy 1962).

The real focus of the 1962 Amendments was the family with children, on AFDC or in danger of entering the rolls. As time went on, however, their interpretation became broadened to provide support for a range of personal social services to families who were self-supporting, and thus, only remotely re-lated to AFDC. In order to induce states to develop such ser-vices, the Amendments called for a reimbursement formula of 75 percent federal funds to 25 percent state funds.

Social Service Expenditures Out of Control.   Buried in the language of the 1962 Amendments lay a ticking time bomb. In calling for the use of community resources to meet specialized problems, Congress made provision for purchase of services from other public agencies. At first little use was made of this provision. Mott (1976) attributes this to the failure of HEW to exercise leadership in helping states mount new programs. States were slow to pick up on the implications of an open-ended (that is, without fixed cut-off), 75-25 funding formula for services offered through a variety of public delivery systems (p. 3).

In 1967, the Social Security Act was again amended to promote work by welfare recipients; for AFDC families, child care provisions were now mandated in order to free parents to work. At the same time, the definition of what constituted "social services," for purposes of federal reimbursement to states, was greatly expanded. Expanded also was the definition of persons eligible for such benefits. These changes came at a time when the political climate was shifting. No longer was the need for financial support necessarily related to family malfunctioning. In this way, personal social services became administratively disengaged from the dispensing of financial assistance in HEW, and similar guidelines were sent out to the states (Axinn and Levin 1975, p. 252).

National policy was thus moving in conflicting directions. On the one hand, there was greater emphasis on inducing welfare recipients to become self-supporting. On the other, personal social services were less and less tied to the notion of getting people off the welfare roles.

During this period, federal expenditures under the 75-25 funding formula moved upward at an increasing rate. Then, as states became fully aware of the bonanza, federal spending suddenly lurched upward at a dizzying pace. In four fiscal years, 1963 through 1966, the average annual increase in federal social service outlays to states under the public assistance titles of the Social Security Act was 22.7 percent. In the four fiscal years 1969 through 1972, the annual average rise was 70.2 percent, with the last year alone registering a 130.8 percent increase (based on Mott 1976, p. 9). With actual state claims of 1.7 billion dollars in Fiscal Year (FY) 1972, the states were due to dip into the federal treasury to the tune of some 4.7 billion dollars the following year, or an annual rate of increase of more than 175 percent (Iglehart 1972).

The repercussions were political as well as economic. It was claimed that states were shifting some of their nonwelfare burdens onto the federal government, under the loose language of the Social Security amendments. Brookings Institution economist Martha Derthick (1975) has charged that Illinois, in particular, used the social service money to substitute for state funds in order to deal with a one hundred forty million dollar deficit caused by rising public assistance rolls; and she saw decisions in HEW being made under political pressure from above (pp. 44–51). Edward Weaver, former director of the Illinois Department of Public Aid and now executive director of the American Public Welfare Association, hotly denies this interpretation. But in the atmosphere of the early 1970s, the critics were listened to more than the defenders. No matter the extent to which the state budget offices were responsible for the increase, politically the escalation was associated with "big government," burgeoning public assistance rolls, the manifest failure of social services to solve the problem of poverty, and the racially tinged upheaval in American cities.

These themes were already well established in the public mind by the time Richard Nixon made his second bid for the presidency in 1968. Having been edged out by John F. Kennedy in 1960, and then defeated in the race for governor of California two years later, Nixon had appeared to be politically washed up. However, he sensed the shifting mood of the country as the spirit of the sixties wound down; his moderate conservatism was a political philosophy whose time had come.

The Ceiling on Social Service Spending. It is ironic that the greatest escalation in federal assistance to state and local social service programs should have occurred under a Republican president dedicated to bringing the welfare state under control. Nixon was caught in the same web that had ensnared others who called for "fiscal responsibility"—the uncontrollability of a large share of the federal budget. Once an "open-ended" program was in place, there was nothing to do but keep paying all claims which met the formula, or revise the whole program.

According to informants who were close to the situation, HEW officials had created part of the problem by encouraging states to use the 75-25 funding arrangement to finance operations whose "social services" rationale was tenuous to say the least. By calling prison guards "rehabilitation specialists," Illinois was able to unload onto the federal government part of its regular correctional costs. Likewise, New York renamed people in the education system with social service titles. California was particularly creative in finding ways to use the federal matching dollars for its basic operations.

By 1972, states which had been less alert to the opportunities were beginning to line up; the lid threatened to blow off completely. Not that 4.7 billion dollars, the amount projected for 1973, was necessarily an unreasonable sum for the national government to be spending for state-based programs for human services. As of the early 1970s, the United States trailed most European countries in the percentage of its gross national product expended on social welfare. Nonetheless, the rapidity of the escalation, which had been entirely unexpected, and the fact that the rise in spending was not accompanied by a comparable rise in the quality or quantity of social services constituted a major crisis.

As early as 1970, fiscal conservatives tried to put a cap on the open-ended social service formula. A new section proposed for the Social Security Act would have included such a ceiling, but it failed to get much support. Then the Comptroller of HEW suggested a ceiling on each state's social service allotment in 1971 equal to 110 percent of its 1970 share. This was rejected as unfair to states which had only recently begun to tap into the federal funds. It was pointed out that to freeze the states on the basis of current amounts would leave California with more than one-third of the total funds.

In June 1972, HEW Secretary Elliot Richardson sent President Nixon a memo containing four alternative means of plugging the financial drain: (1) an "expansion-of-effort" restriction, in which states would have to spend more if they were to get more federal dollars; (2) a combination of the expansion-of-effort restriction plus a reduction in the scope of services already being subsidized by federal funds; (3) a phased introduction of restrictive regulations that would have the indirect effect of curtailing the federal outlays; or (4) federal action limited to a requirement that states develop a planning and accounting mechanism, in effect leaving the open-ended formula intact (Iglehart 1972, p. 1301).

In the election year atmosphere of 1972, the president chose the fourth option as the one least likely to ruffle state feathers; the administration would wait until after the election, then slap on restrictions via the HEW regulations. If there was to be an immediate closing of the open end, it would be the Democratic party–controlled Congress that would have to take the political heat for doing it. It was the Senate, where members' six-year terms made them less vulnerable to pressure, that responded to the challenge. The Senate Appropriations Committee imposed a 2.5-billion-dollar ceiling on the social service spending, and the full Senate refused to remove it. In the House-Senate conference established to iron out the differences in the two houses' versions of the HEW appropriation bill, the senators thus stood for the ceiling. However, House conferees, led by House Appropriations Committee Chairman George Mahon of Texas, were adamant in refusing to go along with the ceiling. They finally prevailed, with the result that the social service bonanza remained.

Back of the refusal of Congress to put a ceiling on social service financing was active lobbying by governors, state welfare directors, county officials, and social work professionals. The large states which had already been exploiting the federal assistance would face a fiscal crisis of mammoth proportions if a major source of revenue for existing programs were suddenly to shrink. It was not that the federal government was threatening to reduce total social service spending; with many additional states wanting in, the large states might stand to get a smaller share of the total pie. At least as compelling was the argument of the states which had not benefited from the federal money up to now: Why should they be deprived of the kind of aid the other states had already been getting just because up to now they had not been asking for it? It was inequitable, they said. One such state was Texas, the home state of House Appropriations Committee Chairman Mahon.

One must look beyond such rational arguments for an understanding of what was operating to avert the spending ceiling. A key actor in the proceedings was Pennsylvania Congressman Dan Flood. Over the years, Flood had been able to use his position as chairman of the House Appropriations Subcommittee on Labor and Health, Education, and Welfare both to enhance his influence in Congress and channel generous amounts of federal aid into his home district. His repeated re-election to his House seat was a foregone conclusion, even in the face of a major scandal involving influence peddling.

He was, in short, a formidable force. He was also a colorful and dramatic figure who had been an actor before becoming a politician. It was Flood's style, as well as his position as Appropriations Subcommittee Chairman, that helped him sway the Senate-House Conference Committee on the social services spending ceiling. According to one conference participant, "Flood was so strong in favor of removing the ceiling that the other sub-committee members were virtually silent on the question, even those who favored the ceiling" (Inglehart 1972, p. 1302).

By being conciliatory on all other matters, the House conferees were able to stand firm on removal of the ceiling. The conference report, and thus the final congressional action on the appropriation bill, included no cap on social service spending. The ball was now back in the president's court. He decided to accept the challenge. He vetoed the Labor-HEW money bill, citing as a major reason the fact that Congress had not attached a ceiling on social service financing. The veto was sustained (Mott 1976, p. 11).

Meanwhile, efforts continued in the Senate. Senators, because they stand for re-election every six years, are under less constant pressure to please the voters than members of the House of Representatives, whose tenure is up for challenge every two years. Consequently, the fear of retaliation at the polls for cutting back on services was less serious to many senators. Some, such as Louisiana's Russell Long, have a secure hold on their seats. Long, as chairman of the influential Finance Committee, had consistently tried to cut down on welfare programs of all kinds. He sought a bill to which the social service money ceiling might be attached as a rider. In the Senate, unlike the House, amendments can have only limited substantive relationship to the bills to which they are added; a rider is such an amendment. For a time, the administration's bill for reforming public assistance, H.R. 1, looked like a suitable vehicle; but, as its fortunes began to fade, Long and others looked for an alternative bill. They finally settled on revenue sharing.

As part of the New Federalism, the Nixon administration had been promoting grants to states with a minimum of restrictive conditions on their use. This device, which came to be known as revenue sharing, had actually been proposed as far back as the early 1960s, in the Democratic administration of John F. Kennedy. In the fall of 1972, work was nearing completion on the Revenue Sharing Act, which would provide several billions in federal aid to the states with minimal strings attached. Long reasoned that this would be an excellent bill to which to attach the social service money ceiling: "You have something that [the states] want and that's a good time to raise the question. Trying to pass it out in and of itself is tough. . . . They would line up in solid opposition to a ceiling and try to keep it from passing" (*National Journal* 1972, p. 1562).

Long, however, was not satisfied with merely curbing further expansions of social service funding; he wanted to cut it back sharply. He got the Senate Finance Committee to call for a repeal of all social service funding, with the exception of child care and family planning, which were estimated to cost 600 million dollars. To make this politically acceptable to the states, the committee agreed to add 1 billion dollars a year to the unrestricted revenue sharing money.

Long controlled the Finance Committee but not the total Senate. The committee's proposal thus went through some intricate legislative maneuvering on the floor, as opponents of the cuts in spending tried to protect the funding. In the process, the

600-million-dollar estimate for child care and family planning became a definite figure.

In the end, Long prevailed in the Senate, thanks to his mastery of the parliamentary process and the fact that many senators voted without full realization of what was going on. As a result, the Senate version of the Revenue Sharing Bill now contained a rider that limited child care and family planning subsidies to 600 million dollars and wiped out all other funding earmarked specifically for social services (*National Journal* 1972 p. 1564). If the move was to be stopped, it would have to happen in the House-Senate conference on the Revenue Sharing Act.

The social service advocates were by this time reconciled to the fact that some kind of ceiling would be imposed. The real question was how much. In the Senate they had argued for a 3.6-billion-dollar cut-off. That clearly was going to be too high. They banked on the House conferees, who were proving more responsive to their pleas. At a break in the proceedings three governors—Carter of Georgia, Hall of Oklahoma, and Mandel of Maryland—approached Representative Wilbur Mills, the powerful chairman of the House Ways and Means Committee. According to an informant, it had been determined in advance that with a 2.5-billion-dollar ceiling, Mills's home state of Arkansas would lose no social service money. That was the appeal they made to Mills: Go for the 2.5 billion dollars, which will not hurt programs then in existence in Arkansas. The strategy worked.

In conference, when Mills supported the 2.5-billion-dollar ceiling, the majority of conferees agreed. Mills also favored limiting services to current welfare recipients, as opposed to the existing language, which included potential and past recipients. In the conference committee a requirement was added, to the effect that 90 percent of the federal social service funds should be earmarked for services to current recipients, with the exception of work-related child care, family planning, and services for the retarded. Again the governors and welfare professionals went to work, and, as a result, were able to get the exemptions to the 90 percent rule expanded to include services to narcotic addicts, alcoholics, and children in foster care (*National Journal* 1972).

There were further efforts to protect the states with the largest investment in the federally subsidized services from losing any money they currently were getting; but the conference came out with a strict population basis for apportionment. As a result, twenty-three states would be held to a level below that which they had projected for FY 1973. But changes were already underway in the states, in reaction to the uncertainty and in anticipation of severe restrictions on their social programs. As one observer put it, nobody wanted to open a new day care center and then find it had to be scrapped a year later. Consequently, the claims of states, rather than rising toward the magic figure of 2.5 billion dollars, actually declined slightly in each of the succeeding three years. It would be only after new legislation placed a solid foundation under federal funding of state social service programs that the state claims would begin to rise again (O'Donnell 1978). In October 1972, the Revenue Sharing Act became law, and with it the 2.5-billion-dollar ceiling on federal subsidies for personal social services under the 75-25 formula.

The social service forces could look on the outcome as a partial victory. Although they had once hoped to escape without any kind of cap on the federal aid, they had then faced a bleak prospect of a 600-million-dollar ceiling on child care and family planning, and no other federal funds earmarked for general social services. While theoretically social services might receive some of the general revenue sharing money, the prospects of getting a substantial slice of this were slight. The 2.5-billion-dollar ceiling was to be only the beginning. Already moves were underway to curtail even further the federal financing of personal social services.

The fight over the limitation on social service funding was one more step in a realignment of interests that was to spell trouble for the Nixon administration. After his election in 1968, Nixon had set out to woo the nation's governors, and for a time the strategy paid off. Revenue sharing was to provide the financial underpinning of the alliance. The governors had a key role in helping push through the Revenue Sharing Act of 1972. Their order of priorities was different from that attributed to them by the administration, as the fight over the social service ceiling made clear. As between freedom from federal interference and the lure of federal funds, the governors' primary concern was with the latter. When Senator Long held out the bait of another billion in unrestricted revenue sharing money in exchange for a curb on social service funds, he found little interest on the part of the state chief executives. They were more interested in the total size of the pot than their autonomy in spending it. In time, the whole revenue sharing scheme became less attractive, as governors began to see it primarily as a device for cutting the federal budget (Iglehart et al., 1973).

In addition, by the early 1970s a new breed of governor was beginning to emerge on the scene. Far from being antagonistic to social service programs, many had strong loyalty to them. Some had themselves been social service professionals in their earlier careers. The heads of the human resources agencies, the umbrella-like integrated systems, were frequently recruited from categorical programs, and thus these program interests had a direct line to the governor's office.

THE PROFESSIONAL ASSOCIATIONS

In view of the great amounts of social service money at stake, one might have expected an all-out fight against the spending ceiling by social service professional organizations. But the response was limited. The main brunt of the battle was borne by the American Public Welfare Association (APWA), working through its constituent body, the National Association of State Public Welfare Administrators. For example, the only testimony offered against spending curbs at hearings before a subcommittee of the Joint Economic Committee in September 1972, came from welfare commissioners of six states (U.S., Congress, House, Subcommittee on Fiscal Policy 1972).

The National Association of Social Workers (NASW), which had as big a stake in social service funding as any professional body, found itself in an ambiguous position on the issue. By 1972, the "social services" money was going for many state functions that were clearly not social services, as well as for bona fide social programs (Derthick 1975). In the words of NASW lobbyist Glenn Allison, "We couldn't defend a completely open-ended appropriation. People *were* abusing it. If we'd held out against any ceiling, that could have blown the whole thing." Instead, NASW and others sought a delay in the closing of the open end until the next fiscal year. NASW did not get into the fight over what the eventual ceiling should be, since "nobody knew what was legitimate."

In essence, the social work professionals lacked a clear signal as to the implications for their clients. They thus were in a weak position to rally their forces against the spending ceiling. There was also the belief among some professionals that outright opposition was sure to lose; the social workers could not afford too many losses if they were to establish political credibility. Better, it was said, to pick a battle where the odds were not so heavily on the other side. That battle was not long in coming.

The Administration Seizes the Initiative. Soon after his landslide re-election victory in November 1972, President Nixon carried out a major shake-up of HEW. The new secretary was Caspar Weinberger, who as head of the powerful Office of Management and Budget (OMB) had already sought to rein in the sprawling HEW bureaucracy and the programs it had created over the previous decade. Weinberger shared several characteristics with the man he succeeded, Elliot Richardson. Both were highly competent and felt comfortable with the world of ideas. Both had been editors of the Harvard Law Review, and both were less interested in the nature and scope of social programs than the efficiency with which they were run. There the parallels stopped. Richardson was more familiar with the substance of welfare policy, and, according to those who worked with both, more "people oriented." To Weinberger, if the law called for a certain emphasis, then it was important that program operations reflect that emphasis. In his concern for the prudent use of resources, it was possible for him to lose sight of the underlying purpose of a program. Ideologically a devout fiscal conservative, he had earned his spurs in California in the administration of Governor Ronald Reagan.

Weinberger brought with him from OMB men who shared his philosophy. Among them was a fellow ex-Californian, James Dwight, who was put in charge of the Social and Rehabilitation Service (SRS), the unit which oversaw welfare operations. Dwight—who has been described by social service advocates as bad-tempered, humorless, and lacking in political finesse—made clear his distaste for social workers and their programs. When invited to a meeting of the American Public Welfare Association (APWA), he flatly refused to attend. When a delegation of social service representatives came to his office to discuss their concerns, he pointedly stared at a clock at the other end of the room and abruptly stopped the session at the end of the allotted hour.

The changing climate had been signaled prior to the shake-up. In December, Dwight's predecessor, John Twiname, issued a memo to HEW's ten regional offices, spelling out guidelines for allocation of social service funds to states, under the 2.5-billion-dollar ceiling and new restrictions voted by Congress. It stood in sharp contrast to an earlier memo to the regions, in June 1971, which had seemed to encourage an expansive orientation to services (Derthick 1975, p. 54). While ostensibly a straightforward reflection of congressional intent, the new memo was looked upon as being more limiting than necessary. It was met by a storm of complaints by the states. With billions of dollars in federal subsidies at stake, some states instituted law suits challenging HEW's interpretation of the law. Around this time the Community Services Administration (CSA) of HEW drafted new regulations, to cover the changes in the social services funding provisions in the law. These, too, were met by strongly negative comments from the states.

In mid-January, outgoing HEW Under Secretary John Veneman told a conference of state legislators that new regulations that were forthcoming would sharply limit the eligibility of nonrecipients of public assistance for federally-aided social services (Mott 1976, p. 27). Congress had already made an initial move in this direction; in establishing the 2.5-billion-dollar ceiling it also ordered that 90 percent of the services, with a number of specific exceptions, be earmarked for those on public assistance. But Veneman was more specific. Previously, persons who had been on assistance within the previous two years and those anticipated to be likely assistance recipients within the next five years were eligible for social services. Since it was impossible to say whether a person would need financial aid some years in the future, it was an extremely permissive requirement. Now, said Veneman, what had been figured in years, in terms of former or anticipated welfare status, would be in months (ibid.).

In February, the new regulations were issued. They were the work of James Dwight, but they reflected the "new look" in the Nixon administration. In the months to come, Dwight would bear the onus for the overkill that united the social service professionals, the governors, and key congressional leaders against the administration. He was a convenient scapegoat, though he did not seem to mind the role of the social services' chief antagonist in the least. The tone of the administration's orientation to social work was summed up by top White House aide John Ehrlichman, who told a reporter that social workers idled by federal cutbacks "will have to find honest labor somewhere else" (*Wall Street Journal* 1973).

The new social service regulations were even more restrictive than had been anticipated. Services were to be geared, directly or indirectly, to the single aim of making welfare recipients self-supporting. The number of services was also sharply curtailed. Aside from current recipients of financial assistance, the only persons to receive services would be those who had left the rolls within the past three months or who were expected to need assistance in the next six months (*Federal Register* 1973). The language went far beyond the restrictions that Congress had imposed in the Revenue Sharing Act of 1972 (90 percent of services for financial aid for recipients, with several kinds of services exempted from even this limitation).

When proposed rules appear in the Federal Register, interested parties have ninety days in which to comment on them before they take on the binding force of law. In this case, HEW was inundated with more than two hundred thousand negative comments (Havemann 1974, p. 1840). The outpouring, rather than giving Dwight and others pause to reconsider the policy, appears to have reinforced a belief that they were under siege from hostile forces; they were convinced that the overwhelming electoral victory in November had been, among other things, a mandate to carry out the purge of social services. They dug in their heels. Delegations which sought to talk with HEW officials were given the cold shoulder.

For their part, the social service advocates were girding for a bitter fight to save federally funded social services. Caught in the middle, with less and less ground to stand on, were HEW officials who felt Dwight had overreached himself. Barred by departmental edict from communicating with the social service advocates—something akin to consorting with the enemy, apparently—they could do little but bide their time and hope for a relaxation of HEW's adamant stance.

The Social Services Coalition.   It was not in the nature of the National Association of Social Workers (NASW) to take tough or controversial positions on policy issues. Its reluctance to be drawn into the 1972 presidential election campaign had stemmed largely from its concern about alienating the Nixon administration in behalf of what it viewed as a lost cause, the candidacy of Democrat George McGovern. The same concern had limited its response to the proposed ceiling on social service spending. But now the hardnosed and provocative tactics of the administration left it no choice but to fight.

The idea of forming a coalition of social service interests was not a new one. Some years before, Glenn Allison's predecessor as NASW lobbyist had been part of a loose affiliation of social welfare representatives, but this had become dormant. Allison now took the initiative in reactivating an expanded version of the original coalition in what was to become known simply as the Social Services Coalition (SSC). In addition to the public welfare people who had predominated before, the SSC included representatives of national voluntary agencies, community action projects, and labor unions. The group was also well connected, politically, through the participation of the chief lobbyist of the National Governors' Conference (NGC),

Allen Jensen; Senator Mondale's aide, Bertram Carp; and a member of Michigan Congressman Don Fraser's staff.

It is worth noting how the list of SSC invitees was developed. Allison invited a number of persons he had known previously. Jensen recruited some fellow Iowans who were now based in Washington. Their personal trust in Jensen was important to their willingness to participate in the SSC. The selection was a considered process but also an informal one; it was important that people knew with whom they were dealing, so earlier personal ties were important. The fact that Allison and Jensen had known and worked with one another previously was crucial, for they were the principal leaders of the coalition from the outset.

Allison played the role of facilitator. By nature noncombative and consensus-oriented, he maintained a neutral stance as between the diverse interests within the SSC. When work had to be done in subcommittees, it was he who helped organize them and then played broker among them. Initially the adamant stance of the administration and the desperate nature of the battle against the regulations made unity an easy matter. But as time wore on and the focus shifted from stopping regulations to fashioning legislation, the internal cohesion was severely tested. Much of the credit for avoiding a break-up at such points goes to Allison.

Taggart (1977) surveyed a majority of SSC members regarding influence within the group. They were asked both how much political power the different members represented and how influential they were in affecting SSC decisions. Allison, as NASW representative, was rated low in political power, in relation to other members; and yet, he was seen as being one of the two most influential members. One way in which he gained such influence was by refusing to exercise it in behalf of any special agenda of his own. He was thus functional to the group in helping it work toward the goals shared by the majority.

A factor that freed Allison to be broader in his perspective than other coalition members was that the stake of his constituency, professional social workers, in the continuation of social services was more general than that of many of the groups represented. It mattered little whether the threatened field was aging, child welfare, or mental health; all were relevant to the people from whom Allison derived his base of support. In the eyes of Mary Logan of the AFL-CIO, the concern was also broad: the bread and butter issue of jobs, especially in the public social service sector. For Jensen, the budgetary problems of the states were paramount. Some SSC members were only peripherally involved—for them, it was enough to play a watchdog role, close enough to the action to make sure the SSC did nothing adverse to their interests but no closer.

To many SSC members, the test of its efficacy was how it affected the interests of their special constituencies. For some this was really the only issue, and they were willing to risk a break-up of the group in pursuing their particular concerns. One special interest representative who did not follow this pattern was Elizabeth Boggs, of the National Association for Retarded Citizens. She saw the broader implications of the issue of the regulations, so had a stake in keeping the SSC functioning. She also had an important contact within HEW, Suzanne Woolsey. In time, this would be a major asset for the coalition.

The position of Allen Jensen of the NGC in the SSC was at times a difficult one. As interest turned to legislation, a new issue arose: the extent to which states should be bound by national standards. The majority of governors—and therefore the dominant sentiment within NGC—favored maximum state autonomy. This was not Jensen's personal leaning, but he could not openly challenge it. Many members of the SSC were just as strongly committed to national standards. Jensen, with one foot in each group, would find himself in an increasingly tenuous position in succeeding months, suspected by both camps of being too friendly to the other. It was Allison who would have the major role in supporting Jensen within the SSC. In the early days of the SSC, however, such issues were still in the offing. The basic preoccupation of all parties was the battle over the HEW regulations.

THE BATTLE OF THE REGS

Confident that it was in a politically unassailable position, the HEW leadership refused to consider significant modifications in its controversial social service regulations. Statements by the congressional leaders on welfare matters, Chairman Long of the Senate Finance Committee and Chairman Wilbur Mills of the House Ways and Means Committee, had led Dwight and others to believe that Congress would go along with the tight eligibility requirements for receipt of social services. As had Elliot Richardson before, they underestimated the power of social service advocates to influence congressional thinking.

One resource available to the SSC members was their respective constituencies in their parent organizations. There began a massive effort to mobilize these broader constituencies in opposition to the regulations. This was a significant factor in generating two hundred thousand adverse written comments to HEW. Such large-scale reactions rarely if ever occur spontaneously. In this case the outpouring of critical comments was a direct result of well-organized movements across the country: social service professionals and the client populations who had a stake in the continuation of service programs, working together at the state and local levels.

In March, a task force of the National Governors' Conference issued a report criticizing the regulations and calling for the use of a social service eligibility standard based on income rather than public assistance status. Members of the task force met with HEW Under Secretary Frank Carlucci, another man recruited from OMB by Weinberger. He was less curt than Dwight but made no commitments of any kind (Mott 1976, p. 28). The day after the NGC task force report, thirty senators cosponsored legislation seeking to limit sharply the changes in the regulations then in force. There followed a number of legislative initiatives to nullify the impact of the HEW draft regulations.

On May 1, HEW made clear that it would not be swayed from its course. The regulations were reissued virtually unchanged, in what was presumably to be their final form. The only concession was a slight softening of the income restrictions on eligibility of nonrecipients of welfare. The regulations were scheduled to go into effect on July 1 (*Federal Register* 1973b). By moving ahead in this way, the administration had placed on its critics the burden of responding to its initiative. Unless action were taken soon, the new policy would be a *fait accompli*.

The critics' options were severely limited. Congress could not rewrite the regulations; that was an administration perogative. And two months was hardly time to prepare and pass an entirely new social service funding bill—especially since the president was likely to veto such a bill, forcing further delays in an attempt to override. There was one other recourse: to delay implementation of the regulations. This was the tactic seized upon by the congressional opponents. The initiative came from an unlikely source: Chairman Russell Long of the Senate Finance Committee, a longtime foe of the expanding social service programs. It had been questions from Long during an earlier hearing that had led James Dwight to believe that the senator supported stringent limits on social service eligibility for nonwelfare recipients. But the make-up of Long's committee had shifted with the reorganization of the Senate in January. Moderates and liberals like Walter Mondale of Minnesota, Mike Gravel of Alaska, and Robert Packwood of Oregon had replaced some of the arch-conservatives on the committee. Being politically astute, Long knew that he could best retain his strong control by being willing to bend at the appropriate time.

Leaders of the Social Services Coalition had asked one of its members, Bert Carp, to try to get the support of his boss, Senator Mondale, for new legislation which would annul the HEW regulations entirely. The result was that the Finance Committee scheduled hearings on the regulations. With Chairman Long declaring, "We don't want to cut off low-income persons from day care, family planning, or other services they need to stay off welfare," the committee heard a steady stream of witnesses describe the dire consequences of implementation of the regulations. Long then used the device of a rider to the Debt Ceiling bill to delay implementation until the following January. In the final version of the bill, the deadline was November 1, 1973 (Mott 1976, pp. 32–33).

The social service advocates had gained time in which to maneuver. There would be one more attempt by HEW to head off the opposition by putting out regulations with cosmetic changes, but this too would be rejected (Mott 1976, p. 35). The delaying tactics were used once again by Congress, pushing the deadline back to January 1975. With this kind of breathing room the climate surrounding the social services issue began to shift. Now, instead of merely defensive warfare against the regulations, the social service forces were in a position to take the offensive with new social service legislation. This would move the center of action away from HEW, where the antagonists were in command, and over to Congress, where the external interest groups had a greater opportunity to influence decisions. In time HEW officials would acknowledge the new status quo and agree to negotiate with the opposition.

A First Try at Legislation. When NASW had first been approached regarding the Allied Services Act, it had been too preoccupied with other matters to respond. In particular, it was working on its own social services bill. Aside from its potential impact on national policy, the NASW bill had one side-benefit for the membership: tangible evidence that it had "arrived" in the arena where policy decisions were made. The result was a piece of draft legislation which included the following provisions:

1. Federal funding for state social service programs meeting certain standards. Within these standards a state would have maximum leeway in developing its own social service package.

2. A set of four goals to which state social service programs were to be directed. These were the same as the ones contained in a Goal Oriented Social Services (GOSS) system that had been developed in HEW's Community Services Administration. These goals included self-support, self-care, community-based care, and institutional care.

3. Eligibility for services based on income, without reference to public assistance status.

The threat of the HEW regulations prompted other efforts to frame new social service legislation. A subcommittee of the Social Services Coalition came up with a set of ten principles, to serve as the basis either for revising the regulations or formulating new legislation. These placed greater emphasis on federal standards and requirements for state programs than did the

NASW bill. Mandated services were listed, and states were not to use federal funds to refinance programs they were already carrying on. The principles also called for flexibility in determination of who was eligible for services. Day care, home health, and other programs for highly vulnerable populations should meet national standards. The principle of fair hearings to handle recipients' complaints was also included (NASW 1973).

A much more limited set of principles emanated from the Annual Meeting of NGC. It supported the use of income as the primary determinant of eligibility for services and the inclusion of former and potential welfare recipients and called for a broad definition of acceptable services (Mott 1976, p. 32). It departed from the SSC statement by mentioning neither mandatory services nor national standards of service performance. This difference between the NGC and the SSC—the question of how much latitude states should be allowed—became a central issue, one that not only threatened the alliance between the two groups, but created dissension within the Social Services Coalition, as well.

Jensen of the NGC staff now became a central actor in moving the issue toward resolution. In August he met with the directors of the state human resource administrations at the Minneapolis airport. To each he handed a notebook laying out the alternative forms that legislation might take. The directors went back to their respective states to confer with their governors. The fifty state chief executives then participated in three regional meetings under NGC auspices. Finally, the governors came together nationally. Out of this process came elements of a social services bill that emphasized state autonomy. Meanwhile, Jensen was involved with SSC members in a parallel effort. Aware of the potential conflict in the way the two groups were moving, he sought to modify the stands of both.

A specific issue was that of mandated services, which some but not all SSC members were pushing. A way around this problem was to specify a list of services, but leave these optional with the states. Such a list appeared in the bill that Senator Mondale submitted, along with a number of cosponsors, in October. This bill also contained a requirement that states not use social service funds to refinance existing programs, the so-called "maintenance of effort" clause. There were strong sentiments within the NGC for a straight-out revenue sharing bill with minimal strings attached to the federal financial aid. Jensen fought for adherence to the principles established earlier by the SSC and NGC, arguing that it was important to continue to work closely with the coalition.

The Mondale bill looked very promising for a time, but it eventually ran afoul of a series of amendments tacked on by Senator Long. He had been unhappy with the list of optional services and the maintenance of effort provision in the bill and had tried unsuccessfully to rally the governors behind a revenue sharing alternative. What then emerged from the Senate Finance Committee was legislation containing many of the principles which had been included in Mondale's bill. It also carried with it Long's amendments designed to force absent parents of children on AFDC to provide financial support. The House refused to back the legislation, reportedly because of the Long amendments (Mott 1976, pp. 37–38).

A Break in the Impasse with HEW.   Working within HEW were a number of officials who were uncomfortable with the obdurate stance the department had taken regarding the regulations, but they felt their hands were tied. Some of them had close ties with members of the Social Services Coalition. While the people outside were drafting legislation, the HEW staff members had to content themselves with doing issue papers which were for internal consumption only.

It was John Young, commissioner for the Community Services Administration (CSA), who finally made a breakthrough. Young was a systems man, and he readily admitted to not knowing anything about social services. However, he was open and willing to learn, and he soon gained the trust of his fellow HEW staffers. He became something of a buffer between the abrasive Dwight and other members of the department. Because of the strictures against involvement with "the enemy," it was with considerable risk that Young made contact with Allen Jensen in the spring of 1974. He had to do so in a careful and low-keyed manner. As one informant recalls, "he didn't exactly hide the fact, but he didn't advertise it, either."

Young took along his aide, Mike Suzuki, to the first meeting with Jensen. Suzuki, a social worker, had been hired by HEW after his pro–social service outlook had created problems for him in California's welfare system. He was one of the people in HEW who felt constrained by the department's adamant stance on the regulations and its orders against communicating with the social service advocates. The meeting was exploratory, with everyone being somewhat guarded. A second meeting with Jensen involved other HEW "liberals"—Assistant Secretary for Planning and Evaluation William Morrill, who had been urging greater leeway for states than would have been allowed by the proposed regulations; and his assistant, Suzanne Woolsey, who had ties with at least one member of the Social Services Coalition.

The HEW representatives got the go-ahead to continue. It was feared that if HEW kept up the wall any longer it would simply be walling itself in, while others went ahead and made policy. As for Jensen, he got a mixed reaction from his constituencies. It was hard for them to believe that HEW was at last open to a true give-and-take. But everyone was sufficiently interested in breaking the impasse—including House Ways and Means Committee Chairman Al Ullman, who had been prodding NGC to get together with HEW people—that the negotiations went ahead.

The initial negotiations were between NGC representatives and members of the HEW staff. Consorting with the enemy was still a sufficiently sensitive issue on all sides that, despite the fact that a majority of the participants were Washington-based, they decided to meet at Chicago's O'Hare Airport. This remained the meeting place after that, and the group which met became known as "the Chicago Fifteen."

Jensen made it a point to keep the Social Services Coalition informed of these developments. Soon their uneasiness about where he and NGC were headed was intensified by the private negotiations between NGC and HEW representatives. As a result, Jensen brought Glenn Allison in on the subsequent meetings of the Chicago Fifteen. This helped to prevent the resulting policy from becoming a simple trade-off between HEW's wish to restrict eligibility for services and the wish of some governors for maximum freedom for each state to chart its own course. Another SSC member who was brought into the negotiations was Bert Carp, Senator Mondale's staff assistant, and a member of the House Ways and Means Committee staff was kept informed of developments (Havemann 1974, p. 1842).

Allison took advantage of the new climate of conciliation to propose some elements that might be included in a social services bill. For these he went back, not to the SSC list of ten principles, but to the original bill that NASW had developed. In its permissiveness regarding state initiative, it was closer to the views of NGC than were the SSC principles, which stressed mandated services, national standards and maintenance of effort. Members of the Chicago Fifteen were responsive to the content of what Allison proposed, and many of these elements found their way into the final legislation.

Development of Title XX. Out of the Chicago Fifteen meetings came a new legislative proposal. It reflected the contributions from a number of sources—NASW, SSC, NGC representatives, and HEW staff members. It contained a set of goals to which services were to be directed. They included self-support; self-maintenance; prevention of unnecessary institutionalization; and for those for whom institutionalization was necessary, adequate care. A fifth goal, protection of children and adults in danger of abuse or neglect, was later added.

On the matter of eligibility, the result was a compromise. Income would be the basic determinant of eligibility for services (that is, persons below a given income level would be eligible), but a designated proportion of the funds would be for services to persons receiving public assistance. There would be no mandated services, but some services were explicitly excluded from federal matching funds. Two other issues especially important to members of the SSC were left up in the air: standards for day care services and the principle that federal funds should not be used to refinance existing state programs (Havemann 1974, p. 1842).

Jensen had selected governors whom he felt were "responsible," that is, oriented to adequate services, to represent NGC at the negotiations. He banked on their being able to persuade their colleagues to go along with the plan. But when they broached the proposed legislation to a meeting of the governors in Seattle in June, they were met with a revolt from the revenue-sharing "hard liners." They had to settle for a simple majority in favor of the plan, which would put them in a weak position in further negotiations (Mott 1976, p. 43). Jensen's position had been undercut by the response from the governors; he had to worry about his future relationship to NGC, for his image as one who could "deliver" NGC in the future had been weakened. At this point he moved off center stage.

The proposal which now proceeded toward congressional action bore the imprint of both the NGC and the SSC. These two groups had been instrumental in forcing a reprieve from HEW's restrictive regulations and developing a more positive social service policy. But it was not they who would engage in the hard bargaining that would produce a bill. In the words of one informant, "the mechanics took over." By "mechanics," he meant people more interested in the nuts and bolts of policy, the specifics of legislation, than in its underlying philosophy. They included HEW staff members and representatives of the National Association of State Public Welfare Administrators, the group that had spearheaded the fight against the 2.5-billion-dollar ceiling but had been on the sidelines during the most recent stages of the battle over social service spending.

The bill that finally went into the congressional hopper in October 1974 included the five service goals; the principle of eligibility for services based on income, with half of the funding earmarked for services to current public assistance recipients; a listing of activities that would not be eligible for funding, and thus, by implication, the acceptance of any other services through which states would seek to achieve the goals; a requirement that states make public their service plans in advance of implementation and invite comments from the public; and strict standards for day care programs receiving such funds (Havemann 1974, pp. 1842–1844).

After the months of wrangling over issues large and small, the congressional action seemed almost an anticlimax. Ten weeks after it was submitted in the House of Representatives it was ratified—with no major changes by either House of Congress. It was signed into law by the President on January 4, 1975 (Mott 1976, p. 45). The battle over social service funding was over. It was only a battle; the basic struggle continues today.

ASSESSING THE ROLE OF SOCIAL WORKERS

With one exception, all informants who were interviewed by the writer concurred in the judgment that the Social Services Coalition had an important impact on the policy that finally emerged. Specifically mentioned as contributions from the SSC members were the fifth goal—dealing with services to those in institutions—and day care standards. The list of optional services that was attached would probably not have been included without pressure from SSC, according to one observer. On a less tangible level, it was suggested that the presence of the SSC gave important leverage to both Jensen in the NGC and the more liberal members of the HEW staff. NASW, which had initiated the coming together of the SSC, had also contributed content from its own earlier social services bill to the formulation of what was to become Title XX.

Glenn Allison of NASW played a pivotal role, not only in helping to get the SSC off the ground, but in keeping it together when its internal unity was threatened. He also helped maintain the linkage with Allen Jensen and, thus, with the NGC. The SSC constituent organizations might conceivably have made the same kind of headway working on their own, but this is questionable. Social services and the professionals who staffed them were sufficiently controversial in the early 1970s that it might have been easy for the administration and congressional conservatives to exploit their differences and thus keep them off balance. Unfortunately, there is no way of empirically verifying such conjectures.

If the role of the social work professionals is to be criticized in relation to the battle over social service funding, it may be around their hesitancy to jump more actively into the fray at an earlier point, for example, when a ceiling was being placed on financial assistance to state social service programs. There are also those who believe that the SSC settled for too little. As one informant put it, not without bitterness,

> What we ended up with was a revenue sharing bill. . . . The states could do little more than refinance existing services. But what money they had available they didn't use for new services. . . . It was a mistake to be neutral [speaking of the NASW role]. . . . We're paying for it now.

Certainly, the American social work associations were more hesitant to get into the political fight than their British counterparts, and they were primarily responding to the initiative of others rather than actively pursuing their own objectives. In assessing the differences, however, one must keep in mind the different social and political contexts within which they operated.

8
Dilemmas of Professional Self-Interest

WE NOW EXAMINE TWO CASES THAT DEAL, NOT WITH POLICIES governing personal social services per se, but with matters of direct concern to the social workers who staffed the services. In the United States, the issue of licensure was framed in legislative terms, as social workers in the most of the fifty states sought licensing acts in their respective jurisdictions. The other case involves a widespread series of strikes by unionized social workers in Britain in 1978 and 1979. As we shall see, both public interest and self-interest considerations were present, although the self-interest end appeared to dominate in both instances.

THE NALGO STRIKES
The successful enactment of the Local Authority Social Services Act and the launching of a unified professional association may have seemed to usher in something of a Golden Age for British social work. If so, the gold soon lost much of its luster. A rapid expansion of social services after the act was passed filled up the ranks with workers who had only the slightest identification with the social work profession. Indeed, the rapid growth of the

social service work force was not accompanied by an expansion of membership in the British Association of Social Workers (BASW); membership actually declined at one point.

In this way, the unity that had been forged in the heat of the battle for social service reform eroded sharply in succeeding years. For many workers, the point of identification was not a professional association but rather a trade union. By far the largest and most powerful union to which local authority social workers belonged was the National and Local Government Officers' Association (NALGO). Of its total membership of seven hundred ten thousand in 1978, only twenty-five thousand were social workers (Healy 1978a). The National Union of Social Workers (NUSW) numbered only in the hundreds.

Trade unions were still alien for many professional social workers and offended their sense of social mission. Said one letter writer to the BASW journal, *Social Work Today,* in the early stages of wide-spread strikes by social workers in 1978,

> The present situation over the social workers' "walk out" leaves me speechless and shocked at such an action. Have these good people stopped to think who the poor souls are who will suffer most at a time like this? . . . Are these really the people who have chosen a profession looking after the troubled and needy ones in our society today? . . . Where are the "*carers*" of our society today? (1978a, p. 8).

Such sentiments became less and less popular among social workers, however, as increasing pressure for cuts in government social programs during the 1970s threatened their careers. A string of Conservative victories in local council elections in 1977 and early 1978 further heightened the social workers' sense of apprehension (*Times of London* 1977; Warman 1978). When the feared cutbacks became reality, the attitude among social workers hardened further.

The issues that began to emerge in the deteriorating relations between local authorities and their social work staffs were complex. At first, the social workers focused on the cuts in service. NALGO called for a ban on overtime work by its members, as a way of protesting against the cuts and dramatizing their impact on consumers of services (*Times of London* 1977). When some locals refused to go along with the overtime ban, NALGO switched tactics and called for a one day strike in its 1200 branches (Thomas 1977).

Complicating the situation was the fact that salary levels for social workers, unlike those of many local authority employees, were set nationally by the National Joint Council for Administrative, Professions, Technical, and Clerical Staff in Local Government (NJC). Thus, as the *Times* editorialized at one point, workers "handling vicious young thugs in the deprived and decaying areas of the inner cities" were paid at the same level as those serving grateful elderly clients "in a pleasant village in Cornwall" (*Times of London* 1978). In June 1977, NALGO's Annual General Meeting passed a resolution calling for the abolition of the national salary grading, and allowing local branches to bargain with their respective employers (Wilton 1978d).

Meanwhile, NALGO social workers in London's Lambeth District presented a claim to the local council asking for improvements in the grading of positions. In the ensuing impasse, which went on for months, NALGO threatened strike action but seemed hesitant to carry it out. In March 1978, a settlement averted the strike. The following month, social workers in the Southwark District demanded changes in the grading of positions. The refusal of the local council to negotiate brought to a head the issue of local versus regional or national collective bargaining (Wilton 1978d).

NALGO leadership was reluctant to force the issue but was being pressured by social work militants in the units based in local authority departments. At the NALGO Annual General Meeting in June, a year of apparent foot dragging brought a storm of protest from local units. Goaded by the rank and file, the leaders agreed to strike action in support of the regrading claims of social workers in three districts. An additional cause of dissension was the belief among some social workers that they and their colleagues were being used by NALGO leadership to obtain local bargaining rights for other local government employees (Pryce 1978b, p. 12).

In the weeks following the annual meeting, a series of local union claims, backed by limited job actions, evoked a stiffening of the stance of management. Local councils were consistently refusing to get involved in negotiations with their social workers. They were backed up by the National Joint Council (NJC), which flatly rejected a bid by NALGO leaders for the right of local branches to bargain independently. Thus evolved "the issue" that was soon to dominate a lengthy and bitter strike in fourteen social service departments around the country (Wilton 1978d). It was an issue that, while meaningful to the participants, was hard to interpret to the social work community, let alone the general public. It appeared that the local councils were prepared to allow the strikes to occur.

A complicating factor was the presence of "post entry closed shops" in some locals. Analogous to union shops in the United States, these require new employees to enroll in the union. Social workers who wished to defy the strike orders risked not only informal pressure from their fellow workers but disciplinary action and even loss of their jobs. This was a highly controversial issue that caused further divisions among the social workers (Drucker 1980).

The Strikes Pose a Dilemma for Social Workers. In mid-August, the social workers in two NALGO locals, in Southwark and Newcastle, went out on strike. They were joined a week later by workers in Tower Hamlets. Management presented a united front. The secretary for the management side in NJC urged local authorities to stand fast against local negotiations. His offer to bargain on the grading issue with NALGO on a national level made the union's position more ambiguous in the public's eyes (Drucker 1980).

As opposed to the unity among management, the picture on the union side was one of disarray and dissension. Because the action was among specific locals against their respective authorities, many NALGO social workers were not directly involved. There was also an atmosphere of distrust of the NALGO national leadership on the part of the social workers, a small minority in the total membership.

BASW now entered the fray directly. One month after the

first locals went off the job, it voted to form its own union, expressing disappointment in NALGO and declaring that social workers were better able to decide what was good for social workers. The vote at BASW's Annual General Meeting was 63 percent in favor of the move, an action that "brought most of the eight hundred delegates to their feet cheering" (Healy 1978b). NALGO promptly retaliated by ousting BASW from its Joint Consultative Committee, an advisory body of some sixty professional associations. The action moved BASW General Secretary Chris Andrews to say, "I'm sorry that NALGO has taken this line. It is, however, a predictable response. I can understand NALGO's concern that over 60 percent of the votes at the AGM were a clear vote of no confidence in them as a union for social workers" (*Social Work Today* 1978a).

Thus came into being the British Union of Social Workers (BUSW). By the end of October its membership had crept up to 633, an accomplishment BASW leadership viewed as "encouraging." But some within the Association felt the formation of a union by BASW had been a mistake (*Social Work Today* 1978e). The events surrounding the launching of the NALGO strikes and the formation of a counter-union posed major dilemmas for the social work professionals. BASW leaders sought to reconcile their ethical standards with strike activity. A proposed draft of a code of practice asserted that a strike was acceptable only after "proper consultation," and it implied that a major concern was the protection of clients' interests (Pryce 1978a).

The question for BASW was not simply one of whether strikes were ethical or unethical. Rather, said General Secretary Chris Andrews, one had to weigh the total situation. The increased demands on social workers justified higher salaries, he said, but first it was necessary to exhaust all alternatives, consider more limited action and make sure one could justify a strike on the basis of expected gains for consumers. In the event of a strike, it was necessary to set up machinery to protect life, make arrangements to protect the most vulnerable clients, and prepare clients in advance for the job action (Andrews 1978).

At points, BASW seemed unsure of the proper course to pursue. Its action in launching BUSW had brought down criticism upon the leadership. Having antagonized NALGO by this move, BASW later sought to enlist the union in supporting an appeal to Secretary of State for Social Services David Ennals to set up an independent inquiry regarding the strike issues (Wilton 1979b).

One dilemma was posed for professional social workers by the shortage of field training opportunities for social work students. As is true in the United States, British social work education includes direct experience in social agencies. The local authority social service departments were used extensively for this purpose, reflecting in part the more "public" nature of social service delivery in Britain, as compared to the United States. Now, as the strikes spread, social work schools found themselves unable to place many of their students. Deep into the school year, the school at the University of Liverpool was still trying to find training locations for thirty of its students (Wilton 1979a). Thus, the strike was obstructing professional development in a tangible way, further exacerbating the internal tensions in the social work community.

Escalation. Despite the misgivings of the professional leadership, the strike spread rapidly as additional locals joined the movement. A one day sympathy strike in September called by a group described as "Trotskyist" by the *Times* brought two thousand social workers onto the streets of London in a show of unity. Counterpart demonstrations were held in other cities. The action temporarily brought operations to a halt in a number of places (Thomas 1978; Wilton 1978a; Wilton 1978d).

By mid-October, eleven hundred social workers in five locals were off the job. By early November, twelve weeks into the strike, two thousand workers in nine areas had joined in. At its peak, the action idled twenty-eight hundred workers in fourteen localities (*Social Work Today* 1978d; Wilton 1978; Wilton 1979e).

Yet the strikes remained local actions against selected local authorities to the end. NALGO gave its official blessing and contributed funds for strike benefits, but there was no move by the national leadership to call for a general walkout of its social worker members across the country. In addition, the support at

the local level by non–social work NALGO members was uneven. This only served to deepen the suspicion among some
striking social workers that they were being used by NALGO.
At one point a group of strikers sat in at NALGO headquarters
demanding increased response from its officers (Wilton 1978b).
It is clear that the strikers had a real sense of abandonment. By
this time, however, the strikes had taken on sufficient momentum to be difficult to stop, especially with a hardline stance on
the part of management and a feeling that the strikers could not
capitulate without something to show for their trouble.

Impact of the Strikes.   It was mainly social workers themselves who appeared to be concerned about the effects on consumers. Some clients spoke in support of the striking social
workers, identifying with them as fellow captives of the system.
But for most, personal concerns loomed largest. Many stopped
asking for help except in cases of emergency. Those who did ask
were referred to other service agencies, particularly the health
service. Some clients sought out their workers on the picket
line. Said one picket,

> You cannot turn away from them when they come up
> to you on the picket lines. We cannot do much for
> them except offer advice. But I have noticed that one
> of my clients turns up every so often with her children,
> just to make sure I am still around (Healy 1978c).

For one group of consumers, the strikes provided a means
of escape from unwanted interference in their lives. These were
families mandated by the court to receive services because of
child neglect and abuse and other forms of "behavior problems." It was this sort of impact that disturbed the news media
most at the outset of the strikes. The press even expressed concern for the lives of children exposed to parental abuse without
the watchful eye of the social worker (Healy 1978a; Parker
1978a).

A very different and potentially more devastating reaction
began to set in as the strikes continued. This was a "ho hum"
attitude—that, far from endangering their clients by their ab-

sence, social workers were hardly missed. The clients seemed to survive somehow. This public apathy would come back to haunt the strikers repeatedly, well after the strikes were over. "Unnoticed Absence," editorialized the *Daily Telegraph,* which felt that the action had demonstrated how well the country could get along with far fewer social workers on the public payroll (1979b). The major lesson to some local authorities was that they were saving money during the strikes. Said the *Daily Telegraph* at the height of the strikes,

> The result has proved far from catastrophic. Even some of their most dedicated admirers have been moved to question whether quite so many of them . . . are really necessary. As for those who are under their care, the impression is that they have shown no new symptoms of privation (1979a).

The problem of public apathy about the social work strikes was made even more glaring by the manifest concern about other strikes occurring at the time. For truck drivers and school janitors and hospital porters to be off the job created a crisis in millions of people's lives; not so the absence of social workers from the social service offices.

Despite the rather cavalier attitude in the news media and the less tangible nature of social services, however, it is clear that many vulnerable persons suffered as a result of the strikes. One study of the impact on the London Borough of Tower Hamlets, carried out under the auspices of the Department of Health and Social Security, described breakdowns in foster child placement and protective services, physical and mental problems left unattended, and severe staff morale problems (Howard and Briers 1980). One infant's death was attributed to the failure of her mother to gain admittance to a shelter, a direct result of the walkout. Yet the researchers could cite only anecdotal material; and, in selecting Tower Hamlets, they had chosen to focus on the social service department which had been strikebound for longer than any other—in an area with a high rate of social problems. On the other side, residential care workers had expanded their roles to compensate for the loss of the social service workers, and some clients took the initiative to find other resources (Howard and Briers 1980; see also Clayton 1978).

At one point, strikers in one district tried to dramatize their case by leaving a fourteen-year-old girl in need of care at the town hall. Local officials claimed they had no difficulty in handling the situation and that the girl was not upset by the experience (Morrow 1979).

In either event—whether viewed as a sign of social worker indifference to human need or as demonstrating their irrelevance—the strikes were posing a major image problem for the social work profession. Even more devastating for social workers was their own disillusionment over the affair. Terming it "a shambles," *Social Work Today* editorialized,

> Social Workers allowed themselves to be marched to the barricades behind a leadership with more heart than head. The profession has been seen to be disunited and inept in its own cause. The main union involved, NALGO, half-heartedly . . . supported the strikers financially, whilst inadequately representing the social work case publicly and politically. The non-social work members of NALGO finally became bored with the whole business, leaving the social workers as disillusioned with their union colleagues as they were with the employers (1979a).

Meanwhile, BUSW, the social workers' union spun off by BASW, continued to expand its membership during the strikes. By February 1979, when the strikes were already winding down, BUSW numbered fifteen hundred—miniscule compared with the twenty-five thousand social workers in NALGO, but a respectable number considering that BUSW had been in existence only since the previous September. More crucial was the question of the proper function and direction of BUSW. Founded for basically negative reasons—as an alternative to NALGO, or perhaps more accurately as a protest statement—the fledgling organization sought to define its mission at its first Annual General Meeting in late February. Some elements in BASW were saying BUSW should never have been formed. There was also talk of joining forces with the small National Union of Social Workers (*Social Work Today* 1979d).

The Strikes Subside.   By January, various parties, including NALGO, were looking for a way out of what had become an abortive movement. Already NALGO national leadership had been rebuffed by the branches for proposing a strike settlement. Now the leaders were pressing for an end to the impasse. For their part, local authorities were facing the possibility of a new rash of strikes by workers in residential institutions, a more serious threat to operations than the idling of field social service workers (Wilton 1979c; *Social Work Today* 1979b).

Early in February, NALGO made a partial capitulation at a meeting of the NJC. But although it agreed to a formula for ending the walkout, it refused to order its local branches back to work. For their part, the locals showed no inclination to return to the job (Wilton 1979d). The end would be anticlimactic. One by one, local units made their peace with management, generally seeking to find a face-saving way to give in.

By the end of March, four hundred workers in three locals were still out. It was not until June 11—almost ten months to the day after the first walkout—that the last holdouts voted to return to work. They were one hundred forty social workers in Tower Hamlets, one of the first locals to go out. Seventy of their coworkers had resigned in the interim, and Tower Hamlets authorities indicated they would not be replaced (Wilton 1979e).

In the wake of the long struggle, there was no dearth of post-mortems. The simplest analyses came from those most removed from the scene. For the *Daily Telegraph,* the strikes demonstrated that there were too many social workers around, and that their ranks should be cut sharply. Beyond this, the shift from specialist to generalist social worker should be abandoned forthwith. Generalists "cannot possibly be 'skilled' in treating everything from mental illness to housing allocation" (1979b).

Studies by social work professionals were more reflective of the complexity of the issues. A study of two locals carried out during the strikes revealed an increase in social workers' identity with unionization but not with NALGO. Despite the fact that NALGO had paid 55 percent of the strikers' regular wages, "for most social workers the major opponent in the strike, with the same antipathy as management, was that same trade union" (Brogden and Wright 1979, p. 14). It was found that social workers did not see themselves as being like other workers. A major factor in this was their service ideology. In addition, the isolation of one branch from another and the diversity of occupational interests and levels within locals vitiated the sense of worker solidarity. This study also found that BUSW, the union founded by BASW, suffered from the double handicap of the "pious" opposition of BASW to the strikes and a lack of potential power in the short run (p. 15).

Another survey found that there were too many alternative resources for consumers to be referred to. The lack of a clear image of social workers as distinct from other helpers further weakened the monopoly control that the strikers needed in order to impact on services (Keidan 1979).

All of the above factors came together to make the task of the NALGO strike leaders a difficult one. One researcher posited that any group of strikers needs (1) a cause or grievance which is viewed as legitimate both internally and externally; (2) a potential impact on management, consumers and other workers in allied fields; and (3) a monopoly in a particular sector so that the impact of their action can be measured quickly and effectively. The NALGO strikers lacked all three, by and large. As to the impact on management, some local councils appeared happy that the strike was reducing their operating costs, a fact which had particular appeal to a relevant constituency, the taxpayers (Keidan 1979).

An Attempt to Revive a Coalition. It was natural enough for social workers to blame the NALGO strike for the growing problem of cutbacks in social service programs. But there were larger forces at work as the Conservative government of Margaret Thatcher set a new direction for the nation in the spring of 1979, amid widespread support. The threat drove the social workers together as the issue of the cuts dwarfed their internal differences. "The cuts" soon became the new battle cry, and BASW sought to form a coalition to fight the inroads on services (*Social Work Today* 1979g). In a spirit reminiscent of the earlier fight over the Local Authority Social Services Act, the social workers launched a vigorous campaign to minimize the service cutbacks.

In September, under BASW's leadership, thirty organizations joined to form a "social priorities alliance." The groups were all working in the field of personal social services. Out of necessity they assumed a defensive posture. They could not necessarily maintain the existing complements of workers in the local authority social service operations, they said; but the cuts should be based on coherent policies, and not be haphazard (Fletcher 1979). At the same time, BASW appeared to be less of an insider than it had been under the more friendly Labour government. At the very least, the atmosphere appeared to be more chilly between officialdom and BASW.

THE LICENSURE CAMPAIGN

The history of efforts to obtain licensure of social workers in the United States has epitomized the dilemma between altruism and self-interest. Espoused as a way of protecting the public, particularly consumers of services, the legal regulation of the field has also been seen as a way of establishing a professional monopoly over a sector of work, thus protecting the field against outside competition. As between these two concerns—public interest and self-interest—the latter appears to have been the more salient, judging from the timing of the major drives for licensure.

There have been two periods of major licensure activity by social work professional groups: the first just prior to and during the Great Depression, when social workers' new-found professional identity was threatened by the entry of large numbers of uncredentialed persons into welfare work; and the second in the 1970s, when health insurance legislation threatened to exclude unlicensed persons from receiving "third party" vendor payments for services rendered. Particularly in the latter period, the internal cohesion of social work was severely tested by the issue of licensure.

The Problem of Professional Unity. From its beginning, American social work has had, at best, a tenuous basis of professional cohesion. As a bureaucratically based field, social work has always been reflective of the specialized agencies within which it was practiced (Richan 1973). Early social work education had strong overtones of apprenticeship, with a greater emphasis on field training in service settings than was true of other professional fields (Lubove 1965, pp. 137–56). It is not surprising, therefore, that professional identity tended to be with specialized agencies more than with a single professional community.

As social workers organized themselves into professional associations, these were identified mainly with special fields— medical social work, psychiatric social work, school social work, and the like. The special associations did not amalgate into a single organization, the National Association of Social Workers (NASW), until 1955, a half-century after social work began claiming professional status. Since then NASW has consistently sought greater integration of its disparate constituency. By extending membership rights to persons with less than a Master's degree in 1969, it expanded its potential control of the social service work force, a majority of which did not have training at the Master's level.

Even as NASW sought professional unity, there were strong forces in social work that were pulling in the opposite direction. The urban crisis of the 1960s generated deepening divisions within social welfare. As unrest spread among racial minorities in the cities, the government sought to dampen the explosive potential by pouring large amounts of money into a bewildering range of antipoverty programs. Not only did many social workers take jobs in these programs, but the field as a whole seemed to get caught up in the fervor of social reform.

The pages of the professional journals were filled with calls to militant activism. No longer content with the traditional roles of enabler and broker and therapist, writers urged their colleagues to be "partisan in social conflict" (Grosser 1965), and "mercenaries" in the service of the clients (Miller 1968). It was no time for social workers to be squeamish about tactics, either. Manipulation and disruptive tactics were considered legitimate parts of the social worker's weaponry (Brager 1968; Specht 1969).

The professional institutions themselves were a major target of criticism and attack. In 1968, the Annual Forum of the National Conference on Social Welfare—a broad amalgam of social work professionals and social welfare organizations—was disrupted by blacks and other dissident elements, who claimed it was supporting institutional racism. The confrontation culminated in the formation of the National Association of Black Social Workers in clear repudiation of the National Association of Social Workers (NCSW 1968, pp. 156–63). The following year the Conference was physically taken over by members of the National Welfare Rights Organization (Borders 1969). Meanwhile, the schools of social work were criticized for failing to train their students for practice relevant to the needs of the poor and minorities in America's inner cities and for not allowing students a genuine voice in school governance (Peirce 1970).

The professional institutions sought to respond to the challenge in various ways. Some social work schools expanded their minority enrollment dramatically (Glasgow 1971), and social work educators urged the schools to advocate for students whose activism got them into difficulty with their field work agencies (Wineman and James 1969). The curricula in social work schools were suddenly including more courses on racism, advocacy, and social change. The National Conference on Social Welfare sought to revamp itself to become more responsive to political issues (NCSW 1969, pp. 178–95).

The National Association of Social Workers (NASW) moved in several ways to deal with the pressure. It committed 75 percent of its annual budget to the fight against racism and poverty, although the action was largely a symbolic redefinition of existing functions. In 1968, an Urban Crisis Task Force was set up by NASW to promote activism and consumer advocacy.

Steps were taken to strengthen NASW machinery for protecting workers' rights to advocate for their clients.

Even as these modest steps were taking place, a backlash within the profession began to emerge. Clinicians and others identified with traditional practice had been relatively quiet during the height of the militancy of the 1960s. Now, as a national trend toward conservatism surfaced, traditionalists in the profession became more outspoken. There was concern about "reverse racism"—discrimination against white social workers in behalf of their black colleagues. Most of all, the failure of the schools to teach practice skills was decried.

The countermovement in social work found a rallying cry in "deprofessionalization," a term introduced by social work professor Harry Specht, who only a few years before had espoused disruptive tactics for social change. By embracing activism, anti-individualism, communalism, and environmental determinism, said Specht, social work was jeopardizing its hard-won professional standing. As for the concern with "institutional racism," Specht considered this "an excellent example of dogma without content" (1972, p. 5).

Having so recently come under the withering attack of activists, the schools of social work now found themselves the major target of the counterthrust. The deteriorating relations between the schools and many social agencies led the Council on Social Work Education in 1972 to form a Task Force on Practice and Education. This body sought to repair "an unfortunate splintering . . . within the profession" (Dolgoff 1974, p. 1).

Just as the earlier protest against racism had found organizational form in the establishment of the National Association of Black Social Workers, clinical social workers began to set up their own organizations in a number of major metropolitan areas. In 1971, they formed the American Federation of Societies for Clinical Social Work (Richan 1973). These schismatic movements threatened NASW's role as the unifying organization for social workers. Its executive director, Chauncey Alexander, declared,

Probably the most persistent obstacle to social work unity that we note from the national vantage point is the dichotomy of clinical practice versus social action. NASW has made much headway in the last year in combatting this destructive polarization, but old experiences and attitudes die hard (1971).

Looming in the background of these internal struggles were much more threatening developments: the growing restrictions on governmental funding for social programs and the increasingly unfriendly climate in which the profession operated. These conditions made social workers aware of the fragility of their gains of the 1960s and intensified their concerns about professional turf. Not only were social service programs falling by the wayside, but a major movement to "declassify" public social service positions (that is, strip them of professional credentialing requirements) was occurring at the state level. The two forces—the resurgence of clinical forces within the profession and the threat to social work careers from without—now combined to set off a major drive for professional licensure.

The Licensure Issue. Several factors have made the licensure movement in American social work rather distinctive. To start with, licensing is a matter for the several states, so any campaign is really fifty-odd campaigns. For a professional community that is still struggling to attain national unity, this presents special problems. Second, the entire movement toward professional licensure of American social workers has been more halting than in many other fields. The historic mistrust of elitism among social workers is only one factor in this. Probably more important has been the close involvement of the profession with social service bureaucracies throughout its existence. The agencies have provided their own system of regulation of their employees, lessening the public concern about control by the professional community.

A complicating factor in the licensing campaign has been the great premium which social workers historically have placed on university-based education as the hallmark of professionalism. Even the description of licensing categories has been based, not on tasks to be done, but on levels of formal education. Neither medicine nor law approached licensure in the same way. It was after most states had adopted licensing laws for physicians that Abraham Flexner conducted his famous study in which he found standards of medical training to be abominably low (1910). Until a few decades ago, one could become a lawyer in some states by "reading law" in the offices of a practicing attorney and passing the bar examination, never having set foot inside a university. Meanwhile, states have been induced to license a variety of human service occupations—ranging from practical nurses to undertakers—with much lower educational requirements than those in the social work profession.

By 1960, only California and Puerto Rico had acted on the regulation of social workers. Puerto Rico adopted title registration in 1934, and then licensing in 1940. California's registration bill was passed in 1945 (Johnson 1974). Registration simply prohibits the use of the term social worker by a person who does not meet certain standards. Theoretically, licensing both protects the title and limits certain practices to the credentialed; but policing of the wide and poorly defined range of activities of social workers presents mammoth problems.

In the mid-sixties interest in licensing had begun to pick up among NASW members. An interim policy statement in 1964 called for title protection as a first step toward licensure (Agostinelli 1973). By 1970, however, only five more states had acted on registration; and one more, California, had adopted licensing (Johnson 1974). Whatever the concern for protection of consumers, at its height in many quarters of the profession in the mid-1960s, it did not mobilize the social work community to campaign for licensure at that point.

In 1972, social workers in Utah and Louisiana pushed through licensing laws, and the Michigan and Iowa legislatures were considering similar bills. The following year saw a sudden upsurge of activity with bills either submitted or in preparation in thirteen states. In 1974, nine more states had joined the movement; another four in 1975, and two more in 1976 (Johnson 1974).

This was not the late sixties, the time of militant alliance with consumers and advocacy in their behalf, but a period when social action in the profession had become relatively quiescent. The goad to action was clearly the threat to social workers posed by insurance carriers who limited third party vendor payments to services rendered by licensed practitioners. On the horizon loomed the prospect of a comprehensive national health insurance which would drastically alter the financing of clinical services. Although the rapidly growing body of private practitioners stood to lose most without licensure, hospitals and clinics which received per-patient funding for social work services would also be affected (Phillips 1977, p. 623). In actuality, reimbursement provisions allowed payment for services provided by an unlicensed person if under supervision of a licensed practitioner; the shape that national health insurance might take was unknown. Yet social workers balked at the idea of making their right to reimbursement dependent on a senior professional. Thus, a combination of pragmatic economic concerns and an underlying anxiety about social work's professional status helped to fuel the licensing drive.

Now NASW found itself fighting on two fronts at once: against the clinical social work societies that sought restrictive licensure that would exclude large numbers of NASW members, and against many black social workers and union members, who saw licensure of any kind as a potential threat. NASW President Lorenzo Traylor—himself a black—said of one set of critics that they "seem convinced that the only function of licensure is to establish a right to private practice." And then, as if to say, a curse on both your houses, he attacked those who described licensing as "elitist" and "inherently discriminatory," saying that this line of argument "tends to contradict itself" (1975).

As NASW chapters in different states sought to enact licensing laws that conformed with the Association's national standards, they ran into opposition in both quarters. Sometimes it was the clinical social workers who were the chief antagonist. When the clinical forces in Connecticut and Texas promoted bills covering only advanced clinicians, NASW intervened to try to abort the licensing effort. This angered clinical social workers, who saw NASW as acting in the role of the spoiler (Kasser 1974; Reposa 1974).

In New York State, the combined opposition of black social workers and other groups was instrumental in a gubernatorial veto in 1974 of an NASW-backed bill that had cleared both houses of the State General Assembly by heavy margins (*NASW News* 1974). During the seventies, however, the licensing movement continued to rack up victories in several states. By the end of the decade, twenty-three states had licensing or registration laws.

Throughout the period, NASW stood resolutely by two principles that accentuated the split with the two critical constituencies. One was the insistence on multiple-level bills, that is, those that recognized more than a single social work category based on educational background. The other principle called for "requirements for specific educational attainment" at all levels (Stern 1979). Thus, NASW's historic commitment to the principle that professional practice required professional education, together with its inclusion of social workers with different levels of education, limited the extent to which it was willing to accommodate to other interests in the professional community.

By 1979, the period of rapid expansion of social work licensure was over. Some NASW chapters had invested large amounts of time and money in licensing drives, only to see them defeated repeatedly, and the NASW leadership recognized a "changing political climate which has brought a public questioning of the value of legal regulation" (Stern 1979).

Meanwhile, NASW sought other ways of protecting its members' interests. One was to promote a bill that would allow health insurance reimbursement of clinical social work services as third party vendors with or without licensure (*NASW News* 1977a). To counteract the lure of the clinical social work societies, it developed its own registry of clinical social workers (*NASW News* 1975; 1977b). This only served to intensify the hostility of the Federation of Societies for Clinical Social Work, which was trying to develop its own registry (*NASW News* 1978). Toward the end of the seventies, NASW made several efforts toward rapprochement with the clinical groups. In 1979, incoming NASW President Nancy Humphreys called clinical social work "the backbone of the profession," but acknowledged that it had its problems, "as backbones sometimes do" (*NASW News* 1979).

A more obstinate problem presented itself regarding relations with black social work groups. Many blacks remained in NASW or held dual membership there and in the National Association of Black Social Workers (NABSW); but NABSW had, by this time, developed its own momentum and appeared to be a permanent feature of the social work landscape. On the question of legal regulation, there was no sign of compromise from NABSW. Even if licensing or registration were to include a category without any formal educational requirement, regulation itself was anathema.

The licensing issue had from the beginning provided a rallying point for black social workers, as they sought to develop their own association. NABSW included in its ranks many uncredentialed social service workers brought into the field during the expansive days of the 1960s. It was feared that these and other nonprofessional workers would be excluded from licensed status either by formal educational requirements or by state licensing examinations, which were viewed generally as being racially biased. Thus, while the licensing controversy did not cause the original schism between many black social workers and the established professional institutions, it gave it added momentum and helped to perpetuate it.

The NASW staff member with primary responsibility for the licensure drive feels the foregoing account overstresses the role of the NABSW (Johnson 1980). It is true that the alignment of forces has varied from state to state, and black opposition has been most visible in large, urban states. Yet licensing must be seen in the context of larger political forces; for social work in the past decade and a half, race has been a central issue.

Depending on local circumstances in a particular state, the licensing drive has attracted different critics. For instance, where a single-level bill called for a Master of Social Work degree as the minimum requirement, undergraduate social work educators, persons with the Bachelor of Social Work degree, and social work unions might be found in opposition. Union opposition, centered in governmental social service agencies, could sometimes be blunted by a clause that exempted public agency positions from the licensing requirement. For an unknown number of social workers, licensure still smacked of the kind of self-oriented professionalism associated in many minds with the medical profession.

Given these sources of internal opposition and the need to find common ground on which to unify social workers, it was likely that the licensing drive would spend itself, if other ways could be found to protect the vendor payment rights of social workers. The growing resistance in state legislatures to the licensing of new professions would serve to accelerate this trend.

One State's Struggle over Licensing. Since licensing of professions is a state matter, the dynamics of the process and its relationship to professional unity can best be seen by examination of the campaign in one state. The problems in Pennsylvania—where after an intensive five-year campaign licensure still eluded the social workers in 1980—typify many of those found in others states.

The third largest state, Pennsylvania runs the gamut in social, economic, and political complexion. It includes the fourth and twelfth largest metropolitan areas in the United States, industrial complexes, mountainous coalmining regions, and farmlands. It has direct access to Atlantic shipping on the east, abuts on one of the Great Lakes on the northwest, and stretches to the Mason Dixon Line, the historic boundary of the Old South. Its people represent every racial, ethnic, and religious strain; and politically, its state government and congressional delegation have shifted back and forth between the two major parties. Philadelphia's role in the nation's founding is well known; and because of its geography, the state figured prominently in both the American Revolution and the Civil War. Thus, in many ways Pennsylvania captures in microcosm the country and its history.

In 1974, the state's thirty-three hundred NASW members voted to form a single state chapter out of eleven local units rather than waiting for the deadline imposed by a national reorganization of the Association. Opposition to the Pennsylvania consolidation was centered in the two largest cities, Philadelphia and Pittsburgh, which would be forced to give up elements of their local operations. Particularly in Philadelphia, the controversy over reorganization came on top of the more basic schisms with blacks and with clinical social workers. The licensure issue now crystallized these tensions.

From the start, the new Pennsylvania State Chapter of NASW made licensing its number-one action priority. This cause, it was hoped, would help to unite dissident elements in NASW still unhappy over reorganization. To an extent, the strategy worked, as Philadelphia and Pittsburgh social workers took the lead in the licensure effort, even though for some the reconciliation was begrudging. It rapidly became evident that the drive would aggravate other rifts in the professional community.

In 1974, the new Pennsylvania Society of Clinical Social Workers began agitating for licensure. At the time the Society numbered less than a hundred, mainly in Philadelphia and Pittsburgh. The proposal was for a single-level bill that would restrict clinical social work practice to people with a Master of Social Work degree and a designated amount of supervised experience. The fledgling organization was miniscule in comparison with the thirty-three-hundred–member NASW chapter, but its assertive leadership and talk of raising a large war chest for the licensing effort caused consternation in NASW. Some elements in NASW also favored a single-level bill; but the chapter was expected to abide by the policies of National NASW, which stood for multiple-level legislation, covering persons at least down to the baccalaureate level.

In order to head off an abortive confrontation, NASW brought together four Pennsylvania organizations of social service workers: the clinical social work group, the Alliance of Black Social Workers (ABSW), and two social service unions representing public welfare personnel. From the start, it was clear that unity would be difficult to achieve. The unions approached the matter in a tentative and pragmatic spirit, apparently willing to wait and see what came forth from the effort. The clinicians wanted a bill tailored to their specifications, and urged NASW to join them rather than risk a split that would surely kill all licensing efforts in the legislature.

The most adamant opposition came from black social workers. Some Pittsburgh ABSW members were willing at least to discuss the issue, and consider various formulas that might protect their constituency's interests, but the larger Philadelphia-based group of blacks were solidly opposed to licensing.

Various drafts of legislation had been in the works since 1974. An initial version, which followed the NASW national "model" bill, had included a laundry list of professional activities to be covered by the legislation (Pennsylvania State Chapter, NASW 1974). It called for three classes of worker: "registered social work associate," with an associate in arts degree; "licensed social worker," with a baccalaureate degree; and "certified social worker," who would need to have a Master of Social Work degree and two years of supervised experience in his or her field of specialization.

In 1975, the NASW chapter decided to abandon this multi-level approach for a single-level, master's degree–only bill as a way of avoiding a split with the clinical social workers. This, in turn, created dissension within NASW, although the chapter leadership was prepared to go ahead on that basis.

The tenuous relationship with the clinical social work society was shattered in the spring of that year, when it was discovered that the latter group had gone ahead and submitted its own clinical licensing bill (Pennsylvania, General Assembly, House 1975). NASW claimed that this violated an earlier understanding among the five-group "coalition" that none would submit a bill without consulting with the others. It was to be the first of many instances in the ensuing months when the fragile link with the clinical social workers would break down amidst charges of bad faith.

NASW decided to go ahead with its own licensing bill. No

longer intent on wooing the Pennsylvania Society of Clinical Social Workers, it reverted to the multi-level concept, in accord with national NASW policy. In November 1975, such a bill was introduced in the State Senate (Pennsylvania General Assembly, Senate 1975). It called for two levels: a "social worker," requiring a Bachelor of Social Work degree or another baccalaureate degree and three years of experience; and a "certified social worker," requiring a Master of Social Work degree. In going for such a definition, NASW was, in effect, writing off the support of both the clinical social workers and the Alliance of Black Social Workers.

The intraprofessional maneuvering became moot, however, when both licensure bills died in committee. By now, however, the NASW licensing drive had gained sufficient momentum that the initial setback was only a minor interruption of ongoing activity. The next push for licensure would have active support from an unexpected quarter: the black administrative aide to the black speaker of the Pennsylvania House of Representatives, Dr. Rufus Lynch.

Dr. Lynch had ties in both Philadelphia and Pittsburgh. He had received his Master of Social Work degree at the University of Pittsburgh and his doctorate at the University of Pennsylvania. After an unsuccessful bid for a State Senate seat in Philadelphia, he eventually became the administrative assistant to House Majority Leader, then Speaker, K. Leroy Irvis of Pittsburgh. Lynch had always been something of a maverick among black social workers; and he had maintained close ties with NASW.

In 1977, Lynch assumed a broker role in the licensure struggle. He convened a series of meetings which included representatives of all sides of the issue: NASW, ABSW, the Society of Clinical Social Workers, and the unions. Even to get the different factions talking with one another at this point was a major achievement. The rudiments of a three-pronged strategy emerged out of these meetings.

Instead of one bill, which Lynch felt was confusing to legislators, the strategy was to submit three companion bills. The plan had something for everybody: the designation of "certified social worker" would conform to the standards for which the clinical social workers had been pressing; it would be aimed primarily at regulating private practitioners. Licensed social workers would be required to have a baccalaureate degree, in line with NASW's first level. In a major bid for support from blacks, a category of "registered social workers" would require only a designated period of work in the field and an agreement to abide by a social work code of ethics. This would prevent anyone's being totally excluded from social work practice by any licensing legislation that set minimal educational requirements; yet it would regulate those persons intervening in the lives of others in the name of social work. By framing these categories in separate bills, the scheme allowed NASW to abstain from the registration bill, which was out of compliance with National NASW's insistence on educational credentials for any level of practice covered by licensing legislation.

In the end, a single bill (HB 2300) went into the hopper, cosponsored by Lynch's boss, Irvis, on April 5, 1978. It was reported out by the House Committee on Professional Licensure on May 31, but it faced opposition of most black legislators and the social service unions, as well as a general reluctance to license more professions. Finally, Irvis himself was said to have backed off from active promotion of the bill because of the resistance.

By early 1980, there had been two more attempts by NASW to launch social work licensure legislation. The latest bill, still alive as of this writing, includes two levels—one requiring a Bachelor of Social Work degree, and the other calling for a Master of Social Work degree. Explicitly excluded from coverage would be workers under civil service, a move that might avert the opposition of the social service unions, whose membership is made up of government workers (Pennsylvania State Chapter, NASW 1980).

Thus, by the end of the seventies, the drive for licensure, nationally and in Pennsylvania, appeared to have slowed but not stopped. Meanwhile, a new threat emerged in the form of state "sunset" laws. In the movement to reduce government's regulatory role and save tax money, several states enacted legislation making it easier to dismantle obsolete and superfluous boards and agencies. A prime target of such efforts was the proliferation of licensing boards for various occupational groups. By the end of 1979, all such attempts to eliminate social work licensing bodies had been beaten back (*NASW News* 1980).

DILEMMAS OF SELF-INTEREST: BRITISH AND AMERICAN STYLE

In the case of the NALGO strikes in Britain and the licensure campaigns in the United States, social workers presented their claims in the language of both public interest and self-interest. They were indeed concerned about their own futures, they said, but ultimately the ones who would suffer most from failure to meet their demands were the consumers of service and, therefore, the public at large. For substantial numbers of social workers in both instances, however, the message was not convincing.

Many British professionals were offended by the disruption of vital social services in a fight over the obscure issue of local bargaining rights. American black social workers were alienated from the main body of the professional community by what appeared to them to be a drive motivated by elitist and monopolistic sentiments. Nor were they alone in this; many students and younger members of the social work community were similarly turned off by the licensing campaigns.

The question here is neither the actual motives of the proponents of these two sets of actions nor the merits of their claims. Let us assume, in fact, that for some of the main movers in the NALGO strikes, the months of picketing and existence on union handouts were endured primarily for the good of the consumers. Let us assume that the concern of American social work leaders over protecting the consumers from unlicensed charlatans was what drove them forward in their licensure efforts. Let us further assume that success in these two movements would in fact have benefited consumers. The point is that major elements in the two professional communities did not believe in the rightness of what was being done. Thereby, the respective professional communities fell to internal squabbling.

The internal divisions undercut the social workers' effectiveness in the political arena. In the United States, legislatures were reluctant to license a professional community that could not agree on what it wanted. In Britain, the results may have been even more disastrous; in the eyes of at least some social workers, the strikes made the sharp cutbacks in social services more palatable to the public than they might otherwise have been. This is not to say that united social work communities could have altered the outcomes in either case, but it is safe to say that they did not help their respective causes by turning upon one another.

Part Three
Analysis

9
Political Resources and Political Influence

THE PUBLIC HAS LONG SINCE BEEN DISABUSED OF THE CIVICS BOOK view of policy making in which the public good prevails out of the sheer logic of the democratic process. What has replaced this benign view of politics, however, is a cynicism that is equally misleading and troublesome. Now we are told that a mysterious and all-powerful "they" pull the strings while the rest of us dance.

MONEY AND VOTES
It goes without saying that money and large blocs of voters are key elements in policy making. If they were the only elements, then a book such as this could be very short, if somewhat depressing, since social workers are notably lacking in direct control over both money and voting blocs. These easy generalizations, however, are defied at many points in our case histories. For example, Presthus's finding (1974), to the effect that interest groups with the largest treasuries and voting blocs do not necessarily have the best success rating in influencing policy decisions, should act as a useful counter to the conventional thinking.

The most obvious use of money in the political arena is to influence elections and obligate the holder of elective office to assumed benefactors. The scale of such spending is out of the reach of social workers, even if they were given to engaging in such pressure tactics, although occasionally unions in which social workers are members may wield this kind of power.

Interest groups can also use their financial resources to set up an office in the proper location and pay for research, lobbying, and clerical staff. This sort of resource—the paid political operative—appears to be more readily available to American social service professionals than to their colleagues in Britain. The British Association of Social Workers could make only part of the time of one professional staff member available to work on social policy matters. The National Association of Social Workers has a number of professionals on staff to work full time on such issues and can call upon others for spot assignments.

Access to a constituency which is large, committed, and politically sophisticated is certainly a great advantage to the policy advocate. One of rehabilitation lobbyist E. B. Whitten's basic assets was the fact that in every state in the union was a cadre of professionals and clients to whom rehabilitation issues were vital. Beyond this, the client population could evoke sympathy from a much larger segment of the voting public.

Judith Hart and Baronness Serota were invited to join the Wilson government in part because they were heavily involved in politics—Hart in the Labour party and Serota in London local government. They had to be listened to because of the constituencies they represented, aside from the fact that both were well informed and intelligent regarding the substance of policy. The Child Poverty Action Group, on the other hand, could safely be ignored at certain points because it could threaten no serious consequences to policy makers who did not respond.

Professor Morris, Lane, and Barratt were important members of the Seebohm Committee, not because they persuaded their colleagues of the wisdom of their views, but because they represented politically potent groups. Even though they departed from the majority on many issues within the Seebohm Committee, they had to be listened to. As it turned out, these constituencies—the doctors and the local authority organizations—could not prevail because they could not turn that potential power into actual influence on policy. They were significant enough, however, that Lord Seebohm and Robin Huws Jones spent a great deal of time wooing Professor Morris; they also viewed the local authority constituency as the main audience for the Seebohm Report.

Certain members of the Social Services Coalition that fought the battle of the HEW regulations were influential because of the powerful constituencies they represented. Mary Logan, the AFL-CIO representative, was listened to largely because of this connection. Allen Jensen represented the politically powerful National Governors' Conference, and this contributed to his leadership position in the Coalition.

Jensen is also a good illustration of a problem facing the representative of a political constituency: the need to avoid getting too far away from the interests of one's supporters. Jensen could not act independently lest he lose his support and, with it, much of his usefulness to the Social Services Coalition (SSC). Aware of this fact, Allison took special pains to keep the group from forcing Jensen to make a choice; inevitably, it would have been to leave the SSC.

The extent to which a constituency holds a representative accountable varies greatly. Generally, the less organized the group, the freer the agent is to depart from its wishes. Unorganized, low-income residents of an area may have exceedingly little impact on the actions of a designated representative because they are in a poor position to hold him or her accountable.

This also happens among professionals. Glenn Allison was guided by the general outlook of the membership of the National Association of Social Workers as he participated in the Social Services Coalition; and he made it a point to keep the executive and the board informed. Yet, he had considerable autonomy in his daily functioning. One indicator of this is the fact that the direction in which the SSC moved was in agreement with his preferences—according to Taggart's (1977) analysis—but contrary to what Allison perceived to be the preferences of his organization.

Allen Jensen's special province on the staff of the National Governors' Conference (NGC) was human resources policy. This involved him in a close working relationship with the NGC's Human Resources Committee. Jensen experienced markedly different degrees of autonomy under different committee chairmen. Overall, however, he was under far greater direct pressure from the constituency of governors than was Allison with the social workers' constituency.

As both Jensen, in relation to social service funding in the United States, and Professor Morris, as a member of the Seebohm Committee, discovered, it is very easy for a representative to become suspect in the eyes of a constituency. Morris was in no sense an agent of the medical profession—in fact, he was not particularly identified with the profession's mainstream. But his willingness to go along with the final recommendations of the Seebohm Committee caused resentment among doctors, particularly the medical officers of health. Ironically, the medical domination of mental health services at the local level, of central importance to the medical officers of health, was the one issue in which Morris was most isolated from his fellow committee members. Thus, despite his efforts in behalf of medical interests, he was nonetheless viewed as something of a traitor to his constituency.

In what Mott (1976) has described as mass politics versus coalition politics, the Nixon administration sought to go over the heads of vested interest groups and appeal to "the silent majority." Its lack of success raises a real question as to whether the silent majority was more than an abstraction when it came to political bargaining. The groups that acted in concert against the administration had identifiable constituencies with a vital stake in the outcome of the struggle. The fact that they were able to generate over two hundred thousand adverse comments on the initial draft of the HEW regulations in 1973 suggests that it was they, not the administration, who were able to succeed at mass politics, because those who made up the "mass" were also members of more narrowly focused constituencies.

FORMAL AUTHORITY

The vested power to make decisions, formally sanctioned authority, does not have to be purchased by means of trade-offs, as does informal political influence. We have seen differences in the ways in which formal authority affected decision making in the two national settings. Not only is such authority much more centralized in the British government than in the administration in the United States, but the channels for action are much more clearly spelled out. Thus, more may hinge on one's formal position in Britain than in the United States. This does not necessarily mean that a British government minister is freer of political pressure than his or her American opposite number. In fact, the image of authority which must be maintained—lest one appear to be losing control, as Prime Minister Wilson warned Richard Crossman—can thus impose a major burden on the person so vested.

Paradoxically, then, the greater centralization of formal control in Britain robs government officials of a kind of flexibility available to their American counterparts. Crossman could never have openly promoted a doomed policy such as the Allied Services Act and come away unscathed, as Elliot Richardson did. What sometimes appears to be procrastination on the part of Whitehall is actually a careful weighing of what the government can afford to espouse in Parliament without losing face.

Formal authority does provide important leverage over policy. Judith Hart recognized this fact and used it to promote reorganization of local social services in Scotland. It was at the point that the Labour party assumed control in 1964 that she became the Under Secretary of State for Scotland, and thus was able to set in motion the process by which the Kilbrandon proposals were drastically altered. Similarly, Baronness Serota's influence on social service policy was suddenly multiplied when she became the Minister of State for Health under Richard Crossman. As a member of the Seebohm Committee she had seen her ideas frequently defeated in the deliberations, dominated as they were by another committee faction. But later, as a high-ranking official in the government, she was able to promote the policies she was most interested in.

At certain points, British social workers found themselves in a position to affect policy in vital ways by virtue of their official status. Catherine Carmichael and Megan Browne could have rallied their supporters against the Kilbrandon Report, but it is doubtful they could have had a key role in formulating the eventual policy if they had not been named to the Kilbrandon Study Group. Conversely, social workers in the position of professional advisers in Edinburgh and London were required to defer to the authority of the civil service administrators on matters of policy, even though the professionals had greater expertise. Again, the formality of the British system and the readiness to observe the rules give extra weight to the authority with which one is vested.

Although a person may have little control over the extent to which powers are conferred on him or her, it is possible for some people actively to improve their position. The ability to be where decisions are being made when they are being made is partially subject to external and often unpredictable factors. When Christopher Cross was reassigned to the minority staff of the House Education and Labor Committee, after having served within HEW, it was not as a result of a carefully conceived campaign by him to move to where he would be in a better position to promote the Allied Services Act, in which he had a major investment; yet the move did have that effect. As a congressional staff member, he was able to take the steps necessary to assure that hearings would be held on the measure. In addition, Cross's files contain carefully prepared questions which were fed to the committee members for use in the hearings. Education Subcommittee Chairman John Brademas would do favors for his minority members and their staff which he might have been much less willing to do for people in the Nixon administration.

Persons connected with the National Institute for Social Work (NISW) in Britain assured the writer that they did not set out intentionally to dominate either the group that called for an official committee of inquiry regarding social services or the resulting Seebohm panel. As one civil servant involved in the selection of Seebohm Committee members stated, they were simply the logical choice in view of their knowledge and experience. This fact, however, gave the NISW a strategic role in the determination of the Seebohm proposals.

One way to affect the relationship between one's position and the locus of decision making is to move the locus of decision making. The battle over social service funding in the United States was largely a struggle to determine where the battlefield would be: within the administration, in the writing of regulations, or in Congress, through development of new legislation. Often congressmen who receive assignments to minor committees try to enhance their position by making those committees the scene of important action.

It is probably easier to cultivate one's access to the people formally vested with making policy—especially at the national level—than it is to gain the mantle of authority oneself. The Standing Conference of Organizations of Social Workers' (SCOSW), Scottish Branch, was advised by a former civil servant to deal directly with the civil service administrators rather than with professional advisers only. This made it possible to bring pressure to bear directly on the people who had greater power to make decisions. But here, too, fortuitous circumstances play a major part. Social worker Kay Carmichael got her views into the debate of the Scottish Grand Committee in Parliament, when the Kilbrandon Report was being discussed, because she was the wife of a prominent member of that committee.

In many instances, groups must earn their way into a position of access to formal authority. In the British system, the process of consultation, by which outside interests have an opportunity to influence policy in the making, draws important distinctions among groups. The British Association of Social Workers (BASW) is a body whose views need to be taken into consideration, along with other established constituencies. The Child Poverty Action Group (CPAG) on the other hand has traditionally assumed the role of the outside critic. Its arguments may be based on better data than those of BASW—this is the view of at least one "neutral" observer—but the points made by the latter organization will be given more weight simply because of its status.

Aware of the importance of the opportunity to influence decision makers, American professionals, both inside and outside the government, take care to preserve their channels of access. This has sometimes led them to shy away from controversial positions on issues. HEW staff members in the Nixon administration who were restive under the policies emanating from the Department in early 1973 were constrained to avoid too vocal a stand in opposition for fear of cutting themselves off from such access. Likewise, one factor influencing the National Association of Social Workers to tread lightly in some areas has been the belief, not only that they might be pursuing lost causes, but that in so doing they might isolate themselves and thus weaken their potential influence over future policies.

Access is thus something that, while it can be affected by deliberate action, is also affected by the actions of others. Social workers can sharply reduce access to formal decision makers by making the wrong moves. But the converse does not necessarily follow. The group that seeks to ingratiate itself with the policy maker will not necessarily be rewarded with a responsive audience. This was apparently one factor that led NASW and other members of the Social Services Coalition to take a strong approach against the regulations: They had little to lose.

There is another sense in which one can increase or decrease access to the decision-making process. This is through geographical location. Over the past few decades, there has been a major migration of interest groups' headquarters to Washington, D.C. For example, the State of Illinois was able to maximize its use of the 75-25 federal funding formula for social services partly because it had an office in the nation's capital. The National Rehabilitation Association as an organization, and E. B. Whitten as a lobbyist, both greatly increased their access to the decision process when they became part of the Washington scene. In like manner, the National Governors' Conference, the National Association of Social Workers, the American Public Welfare Association, and the National Conference on Social

Welfare have all either moved their headquarters or major parts of their operations to Washington.

In these days of instant communication and rapid transportation, the geographical factor may seem less important. But one soon learns in talking with political activists in Washington that daily access to others, to documentary materials and to congressional hearings, floor votes, and the like can be crucial to one's impact on policy.

In view of all this, one must wonder at the effect of the British Association of Social Workers' decision to move from London to Manchester. It was apparently dictated by economic necessity. The chief legislative representative of BASW asserts that he is "closer" to London—in terms of time—than many persons living in the suburbs. Out of necessity, however, he spends only part of his week there, and thus cannot be in daily and direct contact with the process through which national policy is being fashioned. As will become evident later in this chapter, personal relationships built up over time are a major factor in one's ability to affect policy. These are face-to-face contacts, made through both formal meetings and informal gatherings in which much of the policy-making process goes on. The world of national policy is high-pressured in both Britain and the United States. Time, then, becomes a precious commodity that decision makers guard jealously and dole out parsimoniously. In such circumstances, geographical proximity can be a critical factor.

CONTROL OVER INFORMATION

Information can be thought of in two senses: as a means of determining strategy, and as a rhetorical weapon. In the first case, the actor needs to know where and when key decisions are to be made, who the important decision makers are, and who or what influences those decision makers. In the second case, the actor must determine the biases of target audiences, the arguments that will be most compelling for those audiences, and then obtain the information to underpin the arguments.

The information one needs in order to maximize one's potential influence on policy runs the gamut of policy content and political process, broad principles and minute detail. While some of this can be obtained through formal training, a great deal of such information never finds its way into textbooks or lecture notes. It comes only through living and breathing the political experience. One effective, if potentially expensive, teacher is mistakes.

Dr. Gill Michael admits candidly that some of her learning came by means of her own mistakes. As described in an earlier chapter, she refused to accept the official "laundered" minutes of a meeting her organization had had with civil servants, whereupon she received a brisk lecture and a warning that she should learn the way things were done. After that, she accepted the official minutes but also kept her own set.

It was important for Dr. Michael and her group, the Scottish Branch of the Standing Conference of Organizations of Social Workers, to know with whom to negotiate inside the government. On the advice of a former civil servant, they insisted on dealing with civil service administrators, not just with professional advisers. The senior civil servants were reluctant to meet with the social work group, but eventually agreed to do so, greatly enhancing the influence of the social workers.

Experience may be a hard teacher, but this appears to be how most persons learn the ins and outs of the process. Social workers in Scotland and England started at a rather naive level when they sought to promote social service reform. By the time they were through, they were acting in a far more sophisticated manner, outmaneuvering more experienced groups in the process. It was vital, for instance, that they understand the importance of direct lobbying with backbench MPs from the three major parties. A superficial reading of the situation might have led them to focus all their attention on the government and its partisans in Parliament. That would have been a mistake.

Even seasoned veterans in the political arena can fall victim to their own mistaken assumptions, a fact that underscores the importance of adequate information. This is the lesson to be learned in the failure of medical professionals to appreciate the importance of the Seebohm Committee at the point that they had the opportunity to influence the selection of its members. In the case of social services reform in both Scotland and England, the medical officers of health, potentially a powerful political group, failed to act in a timely fashion, despite the fact that their vital interests were at stake. The doctors and the local authority associations—well experienced in the political world—both missed opportunities to avert policy changes that they were later to view as inimical to their interests.

The task of understanding the policy-making process in the United States is even more formidable, both because of the division of responsibility among the different branches of government, and because there are fewer formal rules governing the process. Even such an old hand as Elliot Richardson was blinded to the political realities by his own assumptions as he sought to promote the Allied Services Act. Richardson had previously been directly involved in handling congressional relations for HEW. And yet, as Secretary, he was unprepared for the reaction to his "modest proposal" for social service reform. Paradoxically, staff members working under him were aware of the dismal prospects for the bill. Unlike his predecessor, Robert Finch, Richardson at least understood welfare policy. Finch, it was said, knew little about either Washington or welfare, and thus, suffered from a double disadvantage.

One of the natural advantages of long-term veterans in Washington is their accumulated wisdom regarding the policy-making process. This was clearly a major asset for E. B. Whitten, former head of the National Rehabilitation Association. He knew rehabilitation, the intricacies of parliamentary and administrative procedures, and, particularly important, he knew whom to approach and how to make the approach.

In the second effort to enact an Allied Services Act, the question of congressional committee jurisdiction became crucial. Instead of leaving this to chance, Christopher Cross went to considerable lengths to have the bill referred where it could expect to get a reasonable reception. Later, in an effort to generate support, Cross applied pressure, through Representative Quie, to get public hearings on the bill. The hearings were held, despite the resistance of the committee leadership.

As one moves from the national to the state level in the

United States, the problems in trying to acquire strategic knowledge are multiplied. As the National Association of Social Workers sought to mount a major licensure campaign in the 1970s, it was faced with having to deal with some fifty different jurisdictions with as many different political environments. The difficulties are aggravated by the fact that state government is least well known in the United States, with the result that social workers within a state have frequently been relatively ignorant about the political forces with which they were dealing.

We are left to ask, then, Are there any generalizations regarding strategic intelligence other than the one that says there are no generalizations? To a large extent that appears to be true. Notwithstanding the great volume of political science analyses of the political process, the operatives in the field rely almost exclusively on direct experience—their own and that of trusted advisers.

The Rhetorical Uses of Information. In one sense, any attempt to influence policy decisions is rhetorical, even if the ultimate argument is, "it will benefit your campaign fund." The discussion here, however, is addressed more to the kind of argument grounded in universal principles of the public interest. It is tempting for cynics to write off such attempts to persuade as so much window dressing, a diversion from the "real" influencers. Window dressing it may be in some cases, but if so, then we must ask why vast amounts of money and energy are expended on research to bolster such universalistic arguments. Why, for instance, does a powerful oil company hire legal and communications experts at very high salaries to prepare its case in asking for a tax break? Is it not aware that Senator Long will look after its interests? The answer is that both the oil company and Senator Long are compelled to justify what they do in the wider political arena.

The need for justification is greater in relation to social service policy than oil policy, because the former so clearly involves issues of basic human needs. Unfortunately social service professionals have frequently relied on such broad moral principles as the only justification for their views on policy.

Convinced of the rightness of their position, they believe others should share the conviction. Leaders of the National Association of Social Workers have been conscious that the profession has tended to trade on virtue, meanwhile neglecting the need for evidence to back up its claims. For this reason, there has been concern about strengthening the research capacity of the organization.

Nor are American social workers the only ones susceptible to this tendency. One professional adviser in the British civil service observed that social workers had a tendency to talk about issues of concern to them but of little interest to the administrators they were trying to influence. Similarly Catherine Carmichael believes, in retrospect, that she and Megan Browne were sometimes talking professional issues in the Kilbrandon Study Group on the mistaken assumption that the civil servants were also thinking in the same terms.

American social workers promoting licensure were careful to emphasize the protection of the consumer and, ultimately, the general public in their arguments. Conversely, the NALGO strikers were never able to translate their insistence on local wage negotiations into a crusade for the welfare of consumers.

How does one justify fighting a limitation on social service spending to a skeptical Congress, when funds are knowingly diverted to nonsocial service uses in many states? By arguing that it would be unfair to states that had been late in cashing in on the bonanza; they should have a chance to catch up with the rest. How does the British Medical Association argue against intrusion on their control over local authority mental health services, seemingly for a more rational service delivery system? By espousing the principle of confidentiality; asserting that to put services under social work domination would endanger the protection afforded patient privacy by the existing arrangement of doctor-to-doctor communication.

Of a different order is rhetoric used to rally a special constituency in support of a viewpoint. During the campaign for passage of the Local Authority Social Services bill, there was concern that different groups of social workers might be split off in pursuit of their special interests. Thus, literature directed to the professionals urged that they "advocate total Seebohm" (Hall 1976, p. 150).

The Components of Argument.   Argument involves several components: *audience, issues, evidence,* and *credibility.* Illustrations of how each of these enters into the argument can be found in the case studies.

Audience.   During the Nixon years, it was particularly difficult to read audiences. This was no more true than when appeals were pitched to a mass audience. Both in the case of Nixon's New Federalism and Elliot Richardson's promotion of services integration, the appeals received mixed reactions, depending on the constituency concerned. The heady experience of the sixties was in decline but far from dead in the minds of social workers and their allies in Congress. As it turned out, these forces were strategically more important than the general public, which did not get sufficiently excited about governmental efficiency and the prerogatives of state governments.

Although coming from a very different viewpoint, the Fabian Society and the Child Poverty Action Group in England used an approach not too different from that of the Nixon administration. Instead of seeking to persuade government officials directly, a strategy which would have required them to modify their approach drastically, they chose to pose fundamental issues to the British public. It appears from these cases that, as a general rule, such mass appeals are relatively ineffective in influencing specific policies. Instead, it is necessary to identify key decision makers and those individuals and groups who influence them, and tailor arguments to their concerns.

The rhetorical strategy used in the writing of the Seebohm Report is an illustration of this approach. The committee leadership consciously directed its arguments to the local authority interests, believing that in the end this was the critical audience. Unfortunately it is not possible to assess whether this was a wise judgment, although it is true that the local authority representatives on the committee went along with the majority in the end, and the opposition to the Seebohm proposals at the local level was eventually defeated.

Issues. The selection of issues on which to argue has a major influence on the outcome of the argument. It grows directly out of the analysis of the audience, for this determines which are the most important issues to deal with. If Richard Titmuss had been addressing his remarks of April 1965, to a different audience he presumably would have focused on different issues. As it was, he skillfully selected those issues that had special meaning for his listeners. Others have been cited in the case studies for their special skills in focusing arguments and selecting pertinent issues. In the Seebohm Committee, Roy Parker, an "outsider," became particularly important because of his ability to develop compelling arguments. In like manner, a special quality attributed to both Glenn Allison and Elizabeth Boggs in the Social Services Coalition was skill in focusing on relevant issues.

Skill in undermining arguments is also of value. Representative John Brademas, chairman of the Select Subcommittee on Education of the House Education and Labor Committee, was opposed to the Allied Services Act, but did not wish to attack it directly. Instead, he raised questions in committee hearings in such a way as to put witnesses on the defensive without explicitly stating his own position. It was incumbent on the proponents of Allied Services to demonstrate the inadequacy of present arrangements and the superiority of their own scheme. Brademas was aware of how difficult it would be to muster strong evidence on either score. If a few cases are cited to support an argument, the questioner can say they are not enough. If many cases are cited, the quality of the research—or even the ability of empirical research to answer such questions—can be challenged. Under the circumstances, the witness—in this case, HEW Under Secretary Frank Carlucci—had little choice but to seek additional data if he wished to present convincing arguments. Both Carlucci and Brademas were aware that, regardless of the content of the hearings, Brademas would oppose Allied Services. Brademas needed justification for doing so, and it was Carlucci's task to make that difficult.

Evidence. The quality of one's evidence is far more important than the quantity. As to what kind or amount of evidence is sufficient, that varies widely with the audience and the circumstances. An audience already disposed to believe an advocate will have a low "credibility threshhold." On the other hand, sometimes no matter how much or how excellent empirical evidence may be, an obdurate listener will not be swayed, Carlucci discovered in trying to convince Chairman Brademas of the merits of the Allied Services bill.

In recent years, the credibility threshold has risen noticeably in both the United States and Britain, as more sophisticated information techniques have become available. The Seebohm Committee's report reflected norms of an earlier era, when rigorous scientific analysis was not the rule in policy documents. Much of the criticism of the Seebohm Report focused on the weakness of the research on which conclusions were based (Hall 1976; Sinfield 1970; Smith 1971; Townsend 1970). In the years since, the general level of expectation for such reports has become higher.

Yet, looked upon as a piece of political rhetoric, the Seebohm Report must be judged on the basis of both the audience to which it was directed and the cogency of its case in the eyes of that audience. The report was aimed at local authority interests, government officials, and members of Parliament. All of these read the material in terms of their political interests. The committee could afford to be much less concerned about the reactions of the academicians. It should be noted that its membership included a first-rate scholar, Roy Parker. It appears that the biggest weakness of the Seebohm Report, from a rhetorical standpoint, was that it failed to excite much interest among policy makers.

Most of the serious opposition to the report's conclusions came from interest groups concerned about the impact on them. The more searching criticisms of a scholarly sort focused mainly on the narrow scope of the findings, rather than their quality. The Seebohm Committee had accepted the prevailing assumptions about the validity of current social service interventions and had neglected to raise fundamental questions about human needs. They had failed to survey the concerns and attitudes of consumers of social services, relying instead on the conventional wisdom of the professionals, on the grounds that they did not have enough time to seek out the views of those impacted by services.

Would a more solid base in empirical data have strengthened the Seebohm Report's chances of positive action in the political arena? This seems to the author to be questionable. It is doubtful that the Cabinet ministers would have been any more impressed, since they were reading it primarily from the standpoint of the political impact on the Wilson government. The medical, local authority, and other interest groups also would not have been dissuaded from attacking it. The harshest criticisms of the document's scientific quality came from individuals on the left, who would have been satisfied only if the evidence had bolstered their own challenge to fundamental assumptions about the social services. As for the constituency on which the Seebohm Report depended for active political support, the social workers, a searching critique of prevailing assumptions could well have divided them down the middle.

One must add, however, that political success is not the same as policy effectiveness. Many social workers have been disillusioned with the reforms that resulted from the Local Authority Social Services Act. There is no question that a better analysis of the problem could have pointed to better solutions. It is a very old and familiar question in policy making: are conclusions that are comprehensive and well-grounded, but end up on the shelf, preferable to mediocre ones that are weakly support but end up on the Queen's desk awaiting her signature? In theory, there are alternatives other than these two, but in the British political arena in 1970, there may, in reality, have been none.

The elusiveness of empirical data in rhetorical communication can be seen from the history of the services integration issue in the United States. People on opposite sides of the question have used data from the same study by Perlman (1975) to support their respective positions (see Austin 1978; Morris and Hirsch-Lesochier 1977; U.S., Congress, House, Committee on Education and Labor 1974). One may then be tempted to say that empirical data are meaningless, a tool of mere sophistry. But this is to misunderstand the nature of argument. In scientific research, the integrity of the process is protected by universal canons of scientific inquiry and the ability of the investigator to set aside value preferences in behalf of objectivity. In contrast to this, political arguments involve both empirical and value questions, as does any process involving choices. In this way, the preferences become part of the argument. The integrity of this process is protected insofar as all parties have equivalent access to relevant information and equivalent freedom to participate in the deliberative process. The solution, then, is neither to rule out rhetoric as illegitimate nor try to divest it of biases, but to maximize the participation of all interests.

Credibility. The final component of argument to be discussed is credibility. Impeccable logic and evidence, it appears, are not enough. Spokespersons for the Child Poverty Action Group, despite the high quality of their work, had low credibility among some policy makers. The Nixon administration had low credibility with congressional liberals; thus, no matter how well it argued for services integration, the assumption would remain that this was a subterfuge for services retrenchment.

Source credibility is not distributed fairly among the populace. Old associations may give one advocate presumed credibility, while a newcomer with equally good data may be treated skeptically. In the population as a whole, social workers seem to have a low credibility rating. In the actual policy-making process, many have been able to overcome this problem. Glenn Allison of the National Association of Social Workers and Robin Huws Jones in Britain were able to come across to key audiences as trustworthy sources of information because of an accumulation of past experiences. In the next section we look at a central factor in source credibility, personal relationships.

PERSONAL RELATIONSHIPS
A superficial and misleading view of personal relationships in the political arena focuses on charm, attractiveness, and personal friendship. British civil servant Jimmy Johnston had charm, but he was mistrusted by the social workers, and thus, was less able to be persuasive with them than he might otherwise have been.

Richard Nixon's long-standing personal friendship with Robert Finch did not protect Finch from dismissal as Secretary of Health, Education, and Welfare. Nor should this be looked upon as one more sign of Nixon's baseness; retaining Finch in that position would have been damaging to the programs he oversaw. Need we mention the more recent departure of Jimmy Carter's close friend, Bert Lance, from government when the scandals surrounding him made him a liability? Conversely, people override personal distaste to ally themselves with others.

The significance of personal relationships lies somewhere other than in charm or friendship. At some point, virtually every informant with whom the author talked brought personal ties into the discussion. As the author pursued this term, the crucial factor appeared to be trust; and a central component of trust was credibility. As one thinks about the nature of policy it is not hard to fathom the reasons for this. Those charged with responsibility for making policy are constantly deluged by an enormous volume of information. In spite of valiant efforts at simplification, the amount of data committed to paper and magnetic tape continues to grow to astronomical proportions. Even the specialist working within a narrowly circumscribed area has trouble absorbing the relevant content in his or her own field. For the policy maker in general government, the task may seem to be impossible.

THE CUING PROCESS

Under these circumstances, it is necessary for those engaged in making policy to rely on cues about how to respond to issues. The most natural source of such cues is the individual or group on whom one feels able to rely with confidence. This is true not only of policy makers but also voters as they seek guidance in making their choices in an election (Lazarsfeld, Berelson, and Gaudet 1948). The medium for this sort of political shorthand may be only a facial expression or vocal inflection.

In the preceding section, two uses of information were discussed: as a basis for mapping strategy and as a tool of persuasion. In relation to the first of these, personal relationships are a major means of access to information. A dramatic example

of this is the fact that E. B. Whitten of the National Rehabilitation Association had better information about the Allied Services Act and its prospects in Congress than did its chief spon-
sor, HEW Secretary Elliot Richardson. In relation to his ties
with people inside HEW, Whitten told the writer, "we never
had any secrets from each other." This is probably not completely true. In any such relationship, the parties understand that
some bits of intelligence must be withheld, lest other personal
relationships inside one's own organization be jeopardized.
What Whitten was actually saying was that he and his contacts
inside HEW could trust one another.

The same kind of relationship, based on trust without
necessarily total disclosure, was described by Scottish social
worker Gill Michael. In her dealings with the professional
adviser in the civil service, Marjorie McInnes, Dr. Michael
knew there were state secrets she could not be privy to. McInnes
was forthright about this fact, thus protecting the integrity of
the relationship.

Such personal relationships are cemented in place by the
exchange of favors. These are not gifts in a material sense but
most commonly exchanges of information. Information is the
lifeblood of the policy-making process. By giving or withhold-
ing vital information, a participant in that process can make or
break a colleague; and, of course, there is more to be gained by
making than breaking. Despite the contentious nature of policy,
relations among the persons involved are generally extremely
amicable. That is a major reason that the abrasive behavior of
some HEW officials during the Nixon years so shocked and
antagonized those on the outside.

The exchange of favors is not a matter of strict accounting,
according to veteran HEW professional Michio Suzuki. Rather,
a person develops a general reputation for being helpful or un-
helpful; and it can be overdone. In Suzuki's words, "you don't
go around stroking people all the time—that's false, and people
recognize it."

From the vantage point of seeking to promote one's views,
the exchange of favors is useful in getting the ear of the strategic

person, according to the National Association of Social Workers' chief lobbyist, Al Gonzalez. The influencing process can be separated into two parts: gaining access, and giving advice and information. Gonzalez claims that the exchange of favors can affect the first of these but not the second.

Breaches of faith—or behavior that appears to be that, however well-intentioned—can cause rifts that are hard to repair. The case of the Pennsylvania social workers seeking licensure is illustrative. Members of the National Association of Social Workers came out of a meeting in the summer of 1974 with what they thought was a firm agreement among all participants that none would submit its own licensing bill without consulting with the others. When NASW discovered that the Pennsylvania Society of Clinical Social Workers had gone ahead and introduced its own bill, the reaction was predictable. Infuriated, NASW retaliated with its own bill, aware that this might well doom both bills.

Outright betrayal in the eyes of one's allies is not the only way to lose credibility. One of the quickest ways to destroy your credibility, says HEW's Michio Suzuki, is to show that you do not know what you are talking about. This is understandable, since the policy maker needs to be assured that he or she will not be embarrassed by presenting faulty information. Furthermore, once tagged as an untrustworthy source of advice or information, it is extremely hard for an individual to change that perception. On the other hand, an individual who is personally disliked may still be a trusted source. One informant alluded to a high HEW official, personally very unpopular because of his brusque manner, who nevertheless could be trusted "because he did his homework."

Personal relationships become especially important when there is a potential for suspicion and misunderstanding. The close working relationship between Gill Michael, representing the Scottish Branch of the Standing Conference of Organizations of Social Workers, and Marjorie McInnes, the professional civil servant in the Scottish Office, was a vital factor in making collaboration possible. Michael was aware that some of her colleagues were uneasy about McInnes. She managed to maintain the trust of her constituency by being open with them regarding her discussions with McInnes.

In the Social Services Coalition, Glenn Allison faced a similar problem with respect to Allen Jensen. Coalition members were concerned that Jensen might be playing a dual role, in effect selling out their cause in his dealings with the governors. Allison's trust in Jensen and, in turn, his credibility with the rest of the coalition members as the one with the least vested special interest allowed the relationship to continue. When Jensen began negotiating directly with HEW staff members, however, trust was not enough. At that point, it was insisted that Allison attend also. On the other side, Jensen's insistence on collaborating with the Social Services Coalition caused some strain in his relationship with the National Governors' Conference. His credibility with certain governors was an important factor in preventing this from disrupting a delicate process.

THE WEB OF RELATIONSHIPS

A distinctive feature of the American governmental process which is not found in Britain is the frequent movement of specialists both in and out of government, and between branches of the government. Christopher Cross's progress—from HEW to the staff of the House Committee on Education and Labor to a private consulting firm, all within less than a decade—is not unusual. Allen Jensen moved the other way: from the National Governors' Association to the staff of the House Committee on Ways and Means.

As a result of this constant movement and interaction, shared outlooks on policy tend to cut across jurisdictional lines. The individual is aware that he or she may run into a colleague in a new context a few years hence. Thus, there are potential costs involved in wandering too far from the commonly shared view of what is sound, constructive, realistic, and so forth. Although informants tended to deny that they were influenced by any such consideration, there were clear commonalities in the underlying assumptions of many persons interviewed. It was this set of shared expectations that made it possible for people of diverse political outlooks, professional backgrounds, and locations in the policy-making arena to come out with the same view of the unsoundness of the Allied Services Act. Herein, of course, lies a danger. Issues may not be joined sharply, and policy options beyond the pale of what is commonly viewed as "safe" may remain unstated, not because one fears being unpopular, but rather to maintain credibility in the eyes of the informal network.

In Britain, there appears to be less of this kind of movement in and out of the government. Party affiliation is a more important consideration than in the United States; and the tenure of people at the ministerial rank is contingent on which party is in power. Since ministers are also members of one of the Houses of Parliament, they simply return to the back benches if their party loses the election. Civil service, on the other hand, is a permanent career. This is particularly so for administrators, who are ordinarily trained specifically for the role. Within government, they are presumed to be able to move from one special area to another. While the civil service professionals are more specialized, they also tend to stay put. Some kinds of lateral mobility do occur. Andrew Rowe, one of the civil service administrators who, as part of the Kilbrandon Study Group, developed the white paper that was the basis for the Social Work (Scotland) Act, later joined the staff of the Conservative party at its London headquarters.

The general lack of horizontal mobility does not mean necessarily that issues are drawn any more sharply in Britain, or that the thinking about policy options is therefore more daring. Within the government, the civil service administrators are seen as a restraining force on innovation; and because of their position, they are able to filter the communications between the civil service professionals and the ministerial level, effectively killing proposals they disagree with. Dependent on the administrators to have an impact on policy, the professionals try to be selective in what they put forward. As a result, their view of what is sound and realistic may be just as conforming as that of their American counterparts. However, professionals outside of government, being more clearly set apart from the careerists inside, may be freer to depart from conventional wisdom, since, in a sense, they have less to lose.

The official structure for bringing in consultants provides professional groups with access to the government at the policy-making level. Yet, if they are too radical or antagonistic in their approach, they may find themselves dropped from the list of insider groups with a recognized advisory role. This, in fact, appears to have happened to the Child Poverty Action Group (CPAG). As one civil service professional put it, the government has to listen to what the British Association of Social Workers thinks about a policy in its area. It does not have to listen to CPAG.

Informal circles of acquaintances appear to be important in providing access to government officials in Britain. Several examples emerge from the case of the Seebohm Committee. In the beginning, the group that first sought establishment of a committee of inquiry identified intermediaries who could broach the idea to the appropriate ministers. Richard Crossman, the Secretary of State for Social Services during that era, developed close personal ties with some of the Seebohm principals. Through his friend Richard Titmuss he met Professor Morris. Lady Serota entered the "inner circle" after she became Minister of Health; and the informal access made her especially effective in lobbying for the report. Lord Seebohm himself, however, appears not to have become a Crossman intimate during the period leading up to enactment of the Local Authority Social Services Act, judging from the sparse references to Seebohm in the Crossman diaries.

Although the lines of such relationships appear to be looser and perhaps less stratified in the United States, the use of intermediaries is just as important as in British policy making. For members of the Social Services Coalition, Allen Jensen's access to influential governors and Elizabeth Bogg's relationship with HEW official Suzanne Woolsey were crucial links in the cuing process.

In the fragmented policy system of the United States, the ties between middle-level functionaries in congressional staffs and the administration are particularly important. This is especially so when different parties are in control of Congress and the White House, as happened during the period in which the Allied Services Act, the ceiling on social services spending, and Title XX were under consideration. Congressional committee chairpersons and senior administration officials frequently got involved in political posturing in their relations with one another—both because of party affiliation and in relation to the issue of executive or congressional dominance.

The importance of easy and continuing communication at the staff level is underscored by what happens when this is shut off, as during the controversy over the social service regulations of HEW. HEW staff members were explicitly forbidden, at one point, to have any traffic with members of the Social Services Coalition. In the words of one HEW informant, "while they were making policy [with Congress], we were writing position papers to each other." Faced with the possibility of excluding itself from any voice in the emerging policy, the HEW leadership eventually dropped the ban on communication with "the enemy." It was then that the various interests were able to hammer out compromise legislation.

COALITION POLITICS

Social service professionals lack vast sums of money and large voting blocs. Their access to positions of formal authority is largely fortuitous and dependent on the decisions of others. They, thus, must rely on the quality of their information and their ability to develop strategic personal ties. In effect, they must borrow strength from others; the characteristic way for them to do this is through coalitions with allied interests. (The quest for licensure in Pennsylvania was jeopardized by the fragility of the coalitions that NASW members moved in and out of. Conversely, it was through the combined strength of organizations in the Social Services Coalition that NASW was able to contend with an adamant and powerful Nixon administration.)

The efforts of social workers in Scotland and England to promote social service reorganization were true coalition activities, for their interests were diverse, and they lacked the organizational unity of NASW. Yet, because of their common concern about some of the issues involved, they did band together effectively, overcoming internal differences in the process. One explanation for their ability to prevail against the opposition of the doctors in the case of Seebohm was the doctors' lack of unity. The British Medical Association appears to have been too removed from the problems of the Society of Medical Officers of Health, whose very future was at stake. Meanwhile the Royal Colleges, the third major component of organized medicine in Britain, seem to have been entirely uninvolved.

In Scotland, the sheriffs, probation officers, medical officers of health, and educators had far more potential political power than the social workers. If at any point they had decided to band together, they could easily have averted the Social Work (Scotland) Act. However, the educators and medical officers did not come to the aid of the court people; the probation officers had no direct interest in whether social education or social work was the dominant orientation in the field agencies. In the case of the Seebohm Report, too, the doctors and the local authority groups spent more time and energy fighting each other than they did fighting implementation of Seebohm.

Several leaders engaged in successful coalition politics. Glenn Allison and Allen Jensen had a major role in maintaining the internal unity of the Social Services Coalition and the ongoing relationship between the SSC and the National Governors' Conference. At strategic points both contributed to the achievement of policy aims—Jensen by injecting the more national perspective of the SSC in the deliberations of the governors, and Allison by offering the NASW social services bill when the Chicago Fifteen were casting about for content of their legislative proposal.

In the case of the Local Authority Social Services Act, Robin Huws Jones and Lord Seebohm maintained their influence over a considerable period of time. Not only did Lord Seebohm chair the Committee, he also was active in the campaign for the bill that followed its dissolution. Huws Jones, who was among those who first called for an inquiry, helped the factions in the Seebohm Committee resolve their differences and work toward common goals, and after their work was complete, helped obtain foundation money for the campaign for the Local Authority Social Services bill.

Obviously political coalitions of the kind described here have a limited life expectancy. Nor should the passing of such instrumentalities necessarily be mourned. A particular policy issue can draw together strange bedfellows. It was characteristic of the social workers who sought to affect policy that they collaborated at various points with groups with whom they would ordinarily have had little in common.

This basically pragmatic approach to working relationships is the only viable one for those wishing to have an impact on policy decisions, given the nature of political life in the United States and Britain. Occasionally, an organization that is strongly ideological in nature can have a significant impact on policy. Its most effective role usually will be, not as part of a coalition of diverse interests, but as an external critic and analyst. To get too involved in collaboration with alien groups jeopardizes the ideological integrity of the group and, thus, the loyalty of its own membership. The Child Poverty Action Group and the Fabian Society are examples of such external organizations.

Coalition politics is by no means a cure-all. For one thing, the less a constituency has in the way of resources of its own, the less powerful a role it will play within the coalition. Inevitably, the views expressed in behalf of the whole will reflect less of that particular constituency's interests. NASW staff members have long felt a lack of sufficient research capacity in the Association. To some extent this has been compensated for by scholars on leave of absence and student internes working for the organization.

Social workers may err in either of two directions as they venture into coalition politics. On the one hand, they may work in isolation in order to avoid contamination, and thereby limit their political power. On the other hand, they may allow their basic values to become eroded, as they enter into the compromises which necessarily attend any coalition effort. Only as they understand the underlying rationale behind any sets of "principles" can they see which ones are, or are not, negotiable.

From time to time, manipulation and other covert tactics become a controversial issue for social workers. Is not manipulation—and with it implied coercion—contrary to the basic principle of self-determination? Are not all covert tactics dishonest? In a pure sense this is so. Yet, principles derived from direct practice with clients cannot be transferred *in toto* to the context of political action. One avoids manipulation of clients because of their vulnerability and the corresponding responsibility of the professional for their welfare. In the political arena, however, the parties are, in a sense, forewarned; and the contending interests share a common set of assumptions regarding "fair play." This does not relieve the social professional of the responsibility for attending to the moral and ethical implications of his or her behavior. On a purely practical level, disregard for personal integrity can undermine one's credibility, which, once lost, may be impossible to regain.

INVESTMENT

There is, finally, a factor in political influence that is completely within the control of the constituency itself, and which can be a powerful determinant of its fortunes in the policy-making process. It is: an investment in the issue at hand. To the degree that a constituency makes an intense and sustained commitment of its resources to a cause, it will be able to actualize its potential influence. The readiness of social workers to make such an investment in particular issues is the subject of the final chapter.

10
Social Work's Mixed Agenda in the Political Arena

WE HAVE SEEN INSTANCES IN OUR CASE HISTORIES WHERE THE investment of social workers in an issue was a major determinant of their impact on the outcome. Working in their favor has sometimes been the relative apathy of other, more powerful interests. For example, at the time of the unveiling of the Kilbrandon Report, Scottish social workers were politically weak, naive, and unorganized. With the exception of the child care workers, they were politically inactive. The majority of them looked on political action as slightly tainted and of questionable professional relevance.

The Goliaths of social service politics—the sheriffs, the educators, and the medical officers of health—managed to squander their advantage and so give the initiative to the social workers. The social workers were able to influence policy against the wishes of much more powerful interests because they seized and kept the initiative. The medical profession and the local authority associations were both preoccupied with reform legislation in their respective bailiwicks. This gave the highly committed social workers the necessary advantage to see the Local Authority Social Services Act through to completion.

Conversely, the Allied Services Act was killed, as much by the apathy of its potential friends as the opposition of its enemies. In the case of the 2.5-billion-dollar ceiling of social service spending in the United States, the reluctance of the National Association of Social Workers to make a major investment in its defeat meant that the rank and file were never aroused to the point of widespread political effort. Yet, a few months later, the social work community found a rallying point in the opposition to the restrictive regulations promulgated by the Department of Health, Education, and Welfare. Although other more powerful forces brokered the final version of the Title XX amendments to the Social Security Act, the social workers had a significant role in helping to abort the HEW regulations and develop the substance of Title XX.

In the cases of the NALGO strikes and the drive for social work licensure in the United States, the investments were intense, but often at cross-purposes. The results were disastrous in the case of the strikes, and only partially successful in the case of the licensure campaign. Although we cannot attribute the outcomes solely to the internal bickering of the social workers in these cases, the dissension within clearly detracted from the efforts.

ASKING THE RIGHT QUESTIONS

Are social workers willing to invest their time and energy in political action? This question is too global to yield useful answers. Epstein (1968) tried to refine the issue by asking which tactics of political intervention are most acceptable to social workers. It may come as no surprise to learn that he found consensual strategies generally preferable to more militant ones. Lees (1972) found a similar tendency among British social workers. Thursz (1973) further clarified the question by asking, Are certain kinds of social workers more prepared to enter the political arena than others? His solution was to accept different levels of readiness among different specialists and to gear the training of clinical practitioners to less direct involvement in the political process.

Several factors have been cited as weakening social workers' willingness to get directly involved in political action. Ribi-coff's (1962) assertion that many social workers view politics as "an undignified business" may have been more accurate when he wrote it than it is today. The readiness of many American social workers, including clinical social workers, to lobby for licensure in recent years suggests, indeed, that times have changed. Brager's (1968) view that many social workers are concerned that manipulative political tactics violate ethical prin-ciples appears to be closer to the mark.

There is still one element that none of these analysts address-es: the social workers' choice of substantive policy questions to get involved in politically. It is the author's view that this is a critical element. There is, first of all, some evidence that social workers stay out of fights they believe they have no chance of winning. For example, the limited involvement of NASW in the struggle over the 2.5-billion-dollar ceiling on social service expenditures was only partly dictated by the moral ambiguity of the issue. Also at work, according to one informant who was close to the situation, was NASW's belief that any such efforts were doomed to failure. Similarly, NASW avoided entering the lists against Richard Nixon's candidacy for re-election in 1972; Nixon was probably as hated a figure among social work-ers as any in recent history, but NASW did not want to be caught backing a sure loser.

There is, finally, the way in which policy questions speak to social work's multiple concerns and interests. Chetkow and Nadler (1978) hint at this factor when they note that Israeli social workers have pressured politicians on issues involving benefit to the community and to their own professional en-hancement. In essence, social workers appear to become most active when they perceive that both the public interest and their own interest are at stake.

THE NATURE OF THE "MIXED AGENDA"

Every organized profession is by definition committed to pub-lic, as well as parochial, ends. It is, after all, by dint of the service mission of a professional field that society affords it monopoly over a given sector of work and the right to professional autonomy, that is, freedom from external control. The duality of these concerns among social workers makes them distinctive among professional fields. Historically the service mission overshadowed the proprietary interests of the field. Begun as voluntary charity, social work came late to the status of an organized body that attends to its corporate interests. Even today there are those within the profession who feel uncomfortable about matters of self-interest that are taken for granted in other fields.

On the basis of our six case studies, it is possible to discern a pattern in the way this mixed agenda is played out in social work. Social workers are most likely to make a united, intense, and sustained investment in those issues in which they perceive that both public interest and self-interest are at stake. If they perceive that an issue contributes to the public good, but not to their own vital interests, they tend to be apathetic. If, on the other hand, an issue is seen as serving mainly the self-interest of social workers but only secondarily the public interest, internal unity is weakened, thus undercutting political effectiveness.

Nor do these perceptions on the part of professionals have to be accurate. The crucial question is what is believed to be true by most social workers. The tendency toward apathy on issues which are not seen as serving the vital interests of the profession is the more familiar pattern, noted by most analysts of interest group politics. What has been overlooked in the past has been the importance of the other side of the mixed agenda, concern for the public interest.

Here we must recall two important characteristics of social work. The first is its adherence to the model of the "professional altruist." No matter how cynical or self-oriented the individual social worker, he or she is constantly admonished to care for others. The selection process in schools of social work, the ethical prescripts of the profession, and the social work literature bombard the individual member with that message. Social workers may feel defensive about it in a society that sneers at "do-gooders" and "bleeding hearts"; but among colleagues, the social worker subscribes to these values.

A second important characteristic is the fragmentary and

loose-knit character of social work as compared with most other professions. Having had its roots in several fields that were determined more by their respective organizational settings than any central model, social work has constantly had a tendency toward schism. Professional unity is, therefore, a hard-won and tenuously held goal. Because of the strong ideological flavor of the field, internal conflicts over value issues are particularly troublesome.

With a strong emphasis on public service and a tendency toward schism—social work is particularly vulnerable regarding those issues that seem to place professional self-interest above public interest. We can see this clearly in relation to the NALGO strikes and the licensure campaign, where many in the social work community perceived them as motivated basically by the proprietary concerns of their colleagues. Some NASW members characterized the clinical social workers' quest for special licensing legislation as exclusionary, elitist, and geared to the concern of private practitioners about their income—strikingly similar to the way in which NASW's own licensing efforts were characterized by members of the National Association of Black Social Workers and by left-wing social work groups.

The mixed agenda of social workers thus helps to determine how they will respond to a particular policy issue. When social workers perceive both parts of the agenda as being served by the policy, they are most likely to come together in united action. Their readiness to do so is a major factor in their ability to participate in coalition politics. When the implications either for the public interest or for the self-interest of the social workers are ambiguous or negative, it becomes difficult to predict how the professional community will react. It is an oversimplification to say that low public interest and high self-interest will always lead to schisms, just as we cannot always predict apathy in cases in which the public interest is served, but not the vital interests of the social workers themselves.

The Allied Services Act failed to light a fire under social workers, in terms of either the public good or the professional community's welfare. There were elements in the profession that did identify services integration as the wave of the future, as did their British counterparts. There was also the lurking fear that Allied Services was part of a grand plan of the Nixon administration to cut back on services, even though the British experience offered evidence to the contrary.

The harsh and repressive nature of the regulations promulgated by HEW in early 1973 embodied a direct threat to everything for which social workers stood—both in terms of the deprived populations, which would suffer severely, and the social workers' own interests. The regulations thus effectively mobilized the disparate parts of the professional community and allied groups in opposition; in addition, within the Social Services Coalition, tensions were suppressed.

The NALGO strikes seemed to social work professionals to be so clear a case of self-interest that the agreement that clients would ultimately benefit was lost from view. The result was a debilitating conflict within the social workers' ranks, one that left a bitter residue after the strikes were over. Similarly, the licensure campaign in the United States, while gaining the official support of NASW, alienated significant groups in the social work community. Here, too, the wounds did not heal quickly.

Does the converse hold? If an issue is seen as being of vital interest both to social workers and their clients or the wider public, does this guarantee that social work will mobilize its forces in the political arena? Not always, as demonstrated in the case of the 2.5 billion dollar cap on social service funding in the United States.

Scottish social workers reacted strongly when they perceived that the Kilbrandon Report would make them subservient to educators in the local authorities. They saw this in more than terms of professional dominance. At stake also was the guiding philosophy underlying the delivery of services—a traditional educational orientation that was rigidly authoritarian versus a social work philosophy of humane concern for the consumer. The policy that emerged, however, spoke to more than personal social services; it called for a positive, preventive approach to the meeting of basic human needs.

The psychiatric social workers who participated in the Kilbrandon Study Group were motivated by a broad, humanitarian concern. Psychiatric social workers were viewed in some quarters as an elite; and there was resentment of the fact that both social workers involved came from this field. Given the fragmentary nature of the field in Scotland at that time and the uncertain impact of the emerging policy on different elements in social work, it would have been easy for the different factions to turn against one another, as happened in some of the licensing efforts in the United States. By casting the struggle in broader terms of human welfare, however, the Scottish social workers were able to unite in a common effort.

It will be recalled that in the case of the Seebohm Committee, the origins of the inquiry lay in an issue of how broadly social services were to be defined. Was Britain to move in the direction of a family service focused primarily on the rehabilitation of malfunctioning families, or toward a comprehensive and integrated service to meet the range of human needs? The first conception, of a narrow family service, might have served the proprietary interests of child care workers. Being the most politically active faction among social workers, they might well have mounted their own campaign for such a model. This would surely have alienated other social workers, who did not share this view. As it was, the notion of an integrated service delivery system, responsive to varied service needs, provided a common theme around which the diverse social work elements could rally. In that professional unity lay their political strength.

In the fight over the 1973 HEW social service regulations, different social service groups formed a successful coalition. The Social Services Coalition was held together through the leadership of Glenn Allison. Allison's organization, the National Association of Social Workers, had a vital interest in the welfare of its members. The battle over the regulations concerned more than the self-interest of the professionals, however. At stake also were client populations that would suffer if the regulations were put into effect. Because this was a fight in behalf of social workers and their clients, it was possible to enlist a broad alliance of interests.

IMPLICATIONS FOR ACTION

Possibly most important is a recognition of the potential of social workers for influencing the policy-making process. In both Britain and the United States, social workers have demonstrated their ability to take on ostensibly more powerful forces, and come out, if not with shining victories, at least having mitigated the worst effects of the opposition. Those of more radical disposition may look on tactics of compromise and stand-off as defeatist, but there are times when the alternative is total surrender.

Social workers need to assess their potential strengths, as well as the weaknesses, which have been so often discussed in the literature. Lacking money and voting blocs, they must rely on their access to superior information. And they must identify potential allies. It should be noted that every success or partial success recorded in the case studies involved an alliance; and the coalition process required that pure positions be modified.

A most vital resource is something entirely under the control of the social workers: their own investment in a particular question. Only as long as social workers are willing to commit their resources to a particular cause can they maintain the fight long enough to have a significant impact. Here, one of social work's virtues—its concern for the full range of human problems—is potentially its undoing, for if one tries to deal with all problems the likelihood is that no problem will be dealt with successfully.

Finally, we have considered how investment in a policy issue is influenced by social work's mixed agenda, the combination of public interest and self-interest. The implications seem clear: in selecting issues for political action, social workers should try to identify those that have clearly understood significance for both public interest and their own self-interest. Accordingly, it is important for the leadership to be able to interpret to the membership the relevance of an issue to both sets of concerns.

IMPLICATIONS FOR RESEARCH

A loosely framed survey of six cases in political action can provide only a beginning in the development of propositions for further study. But based on the present study, some questions for future research emerge:

1. Information appears to be one of social workers' most potent assets. In matters of social service policy, they are the presumed experts. Yet, they frequently labor under an image of being well-intentioned but naive do-gooders. What are the conditions under which they are able to cast off this image and establish credibility in the eyes of policy makers?

2. Given the emphasis on interpersonal relationships in social work practice and education, social workers should be particularly skilled at developing personal ties with key individuals in the policy-making process. Are the skills involved in establishing effective working relationships in the clinical setting and in the political arena the same, or different? Are the processes involved in developing one type of working relationship supportive of the other?

3. It has been proposed that, lacking tangible political resources such as money and votes, social workers often need to rely on coalition politics. To what extent does the fragmentation within social work and allied fields hinder the formation of effective coalitions?

4. Does the mixed agenda affect different social specialties in different ways? In time of retrenchment and political conservatism, does the self-interest side of the agenda tend to predominate, as social workers feel more threatened about their future?

As social workers move into the uncertain eighties, they are aware that the political drift to the right in the United States and Britain imperils past gains in social services. Yet they can take heart in the fact that they are far from powerless, in a political sense. They have demonstrated an ability to influence policy decisions, against heavy odds. It is the author's hope that the present volume will help them capitalize on their potential more effectively in the future.

Bibliography

Index

Bibliography

INTERVIEWEES

United States
Glenn Allison
Mark Battle
Charles Berman
Robert Cohen
Christopher Cross
Jack Duncan
Al Gonzalez
Allen Jensen
Martin LaVor
Robert Morris
Paul Mott
Edward Newman
Hon. Elliot Richardson
Benjamin Schuster
Leonard Stern
Michio Suzuki
Stephen Taggart
Richard Verville
Edward Weaver
E. B. Whitten

Great Britain
Megan Browne
Alison Campbell
Catherine Carmichael
Nancy Drucker
Neil Fraser
E. Matilda Goldberg
Phoebe Hall
Vera Hiddleston
David Holroyd
Robin Huws Jones
David Jones
Marjorie McInnes
Gillian McMillan
F. M. Martin
Gill Michael
Baroness Serota
Alice Sheridan
Gilbert Smith
William Utting

PUBLISHED SOURCES

Agostinelli, A. J. 1973. *The legal regulation of social work practice* (pre-publication copy). Photocopy. Washington: National Association of Social Workers.

Alexander, C. A. 1971. Enigma of unity. *NASW News* 16, no. 2 (Feb.): 2.

Allport, G. W. 1955. The limits of social service. In *National policies for education, health, and social services,* ed. J. E. Russell, pp. 194–214. New York: Doubleday.

American Public Welfare Association (APWA). 1977. *Integrated social services: A comparison between an integrated and a categorical social service system.* Washington: APWA.

Andrews, C. 1978. Advice to strikers. *Social Work Today* 10, no. 9 (Oct. 24): 28.

Association of Child Care Officers (ACCO), Scottish Region, n.d. *Report of the Committee of Children and Young Persons (Scotland).* Memorandum on the report prepared by the Association of Child Care Officers (Scottish Region). Edinburgh: photocopy.

Association of Child Care Officers, et al. n.d. Detailed comments on the Social Work (Scotland) Act prepared by a professional working party representing the Association of Child Care Officers, the Association of Family Caseworkers, the Association of Psychiatric Social Workers, the Association of Social Workers, the Institute of Medical Social Workers, the Moral Welfare Workers Association and the Society of Mental Welfare Officers. Photocopy.

Austin, D. M. 1978. Consolidation and integration. *Public Welfare* 36, no. 3 (Summer): 20–28.

Axinn, J., and Levin, H. 1975. *Social welfare: A history of the American response to need.* New York: Harper and Row.

Bamford, T. 1979. Comment: Thou shalt not kill, but. . . . *Social Work Today* 11, no. 5 (Oct. 2): 1.

Beer, S. H. 1956. Pressure groups and parties in Britain. *American Political Science Review* 50, no. 1 (March): 1–23.

Beer, S. H., and Ulam, A. B., eds. 1962. *Patterns of government: The major political systems of Europe.* 2d ed. New York: Random House.

Bell, W. 1965. *Aid to dependent children.* New York: Columbia University Press.

Beloff, M. 1975. Introduction. In *American political institutions in the 1970s,* ed. M. Beloff and V. Vale. Totawa, N.J.: Rowman and Littlefield.

Benemy, F. W. G. 1965. *Whitehall-Town Hall: A brief account of central and local government.* 5th ed. New York: Taplinger.

Benjamin, R. W. 1977. Local government in post-industrial Britain. In *Comparing urban service delivery systems: Structure and performance,* ed. V. Ostrom and F. P. Bush. Urban Affairs Annual Reviews, vol. 12. Beverly Hills, Calif.: Sage.

Bernard, S. E. 1975. Why service delivery programs fail. *Social Work* 20, no. 3 (May): 206–12.

Bibby, J., and Davidson, R. 1967. *On Capitol Hill: Studies in the legislative process.* New York: Holt, Rinehart, and Winston.

Borders, W. 1969. Welfare militants disrupt meeting to press reforms. *New York Times* (May 26): 1.

Brager, G. 1968. Advocacy and political behavior. *Social Work* 13, no. 2: 5–15.

Brogden, M., and Wright, M. 1979. What about the workers? *Social Work Today* 10, no. 37 (May 22): 12–14.

Bryce, J. 1915. *The American commonwealth.* 3d ed. vols. 1 and 2. New York: Macmillan.

Buell, B., et al. 1952. *Community planning for human services.* New York: Columbia University Press.

Campbell, A. 1978. The origins and implementation of section 12 of the Social Work (Scotland) Act 1968. Ph.D. diss., University of Edinburgh.

Carmichael, C. M. 1969. Developments in Scottish social work: Changes in the law and implications for the future. *Applied Social Studies* 1, no. 1 (Jan.): 35–42.

Cartwright, D., and Zander, A., eds. 1968. *Group dynamics: Research and theory.* 3d ed. New York: Harper and Row.

Chetkow, B. H., and Nadler, S. 1978. Community social workers and political leaders in municipal settings in Israel. *Journal of Social Service Research* 1, no. 4: 257–72.

Clayton, P. 1978. Who needs the social workers anyway? *Social Work Today* 10, no. 37 (May 22): 12–14.

Community Service Society of New York. 1974. *125th anniversary symposium of the Community Service Society of New York.* New York.

Coughlin, B. J. 1973. The rights of children. In *The rights of children,* ed. A. E. Wilkerson. Philadelphia: Temple University Press.

Crossman, R. H. S. 1972. *The myths of cabinet government.* Cambridge, Mass.: Harvard University Press.

———. 1977. *The diaries of the cabinet minister.* vol. 3, *Secretary of State for Social Services, 1968–1970.* New York: Holt, Rinehart, and Winston.

Daily Telegraph. 1979a. Servants or masters? Jan. 11, p. 12.

————. 1979b. Unnoticed absence. June 7, p. 18.

————. 1979c. Social workers face loss of credibility. June 8, p. 8.

Davie, J. 1967. Letter to William Ross. July 26.

Deaton, R. 1972. The fiscal crisis of the state and the revolt of the public employee. *Our Generation* 8 (Oct).

Delaney, P. 1970. Richardson firmly in charge at Health, Education, and Welfare after six months. *New York Times,* Nov. 20, p. 77.

Departmental Task Force on Social Work Education and Manpower, HEW. 1965. *Closing the gap in social work manpower.* Washington, D.C.: G.P.O.

Derthick, M. 1975. *Uncontrollable spending for social services grants.* Washington: Brookings Institution.

Dolgoff, R. 1974. *Report to the task force on social work practice and education.* New York: Council on Social Work Education.

Donnison, D. 1954. *The neglected child and the social services.* Manchester: Manchester University Press.

Drucker, N. 1980. Letter to the author. July 17.

Dye, T. R., and Zeigler, L. H. 1975. *The irony of democracy: An uncommon introduction to American politics.* 3d ed. North Scituate, Mass.: Duxbury Press.

Eckstein, H. 1960. *Pressure group politics: The case of the British Medical Association.* London: George Allen and Unwin.

Edelman, M. 1964. *The symbolic uses of politics.* Urbana, Ill.: University of Illinois Press.

Epstein, I. 1968. Social workers and social action: Attitudes toward social action strategies. *Social Work* 13, no. 2: 101–108.

Epstein, L. D. 1980. What happened to the British party model? *American Political Science Review* 74, no. 1 (March): 9–22.

Ergang, R. 1948. *Europe in our time: 1914 to the present.* New York: D. C. Heath.

Evans, R., Jr., and Novak, R. D. 1971. *Nixon in the White House: The frustration of power.* New York: Random House.

Federal Register. 1973a. "Proposed rules, Part 2." 38, no. 32. Washington, D.C.: G.P.O. (Feb. 16).

————. 1973b. "Proposed rules, Part 2." 38, no. 33. Washington, D.C.: G.P.O. (May 1).

Fergusson, R. M. 1884. *Rambles in the far north.* 2d ed. London: Alex Gardner.

Fletcher, D. 1979. Social Groups Unite. *Daily Telegraph,* Sept. 7.

Flexner, A. 1910. *Medical education in the United States and Canada*. New York: Carnegie Foundation.

Fraser, N. 1979. Labor market structure and social policy: Great Britain and the United States. Unpub. paper. Photocopy.

Galloway, G. B. 1955. *Congress and Parliament: Their organization and operation in the U.S. and U.K.* Planning Pamphlet no. 93. Washington: National Planning Association.

Galper, J. H. 1975. *The politics of social services*. Englewood Cliffs, N.J.: Prentice-Hall.

Gans, S. P., and Horton, G. T. 1975. *Integration of the human services: the state and municipal levels*. New York: Praeger.

Gilbert, N., and Specht, H. 1977. *Coordinating social services: An analysis of community, organizational, and staff characteristics*. New York: Praeger.

Glasgow, D. 1971. The black thrust for vitality: The impact on social work education. *Journal of Education for Social Work* 7, no. 2 (Spring): 9–18.

Goldberg, E. M. 1978. *Social work since Seebohm: All things to all men?* London: National Institute for Social Work.

Goodwin, R. N. 1974. *The American condition*. Garden City, N.Y.: Doubleday.

Grant, W. 1977. Corporatism and pressure groups. In *New trends in British politics,* ed. D. Kavanagh and R. Rose, London: Sage.

Great Britain. 1959. *Report of the Working Party on Social Workers in the Local Authority Health and Welfare Services* (Younghusband report). London: Her Majesty's Stationery Office.

———. 1960. *Report of the Committee on Children and Young Persons* (Ingleby Report). London: Her Majesty's Stationery Office.

———. 1963a. *Children and Young Persons Act 1963*. London: Her Majesty's Stationery Office.

———. 1963b. *Prevention of neglect of children—Report of the Committee of the Scottish Advisory Council on Child Care* (McBoyle Report). London: Her Majesty's Stationery Office.

———. 1964a. *Children and young persons in Scotland* (Kilbrandon Report). London: Her Majesty's Stationery Office.

———. 1964b. *Crime: A challenge to us all; Report of a Labour Party study group* (Longford Report). London: Her Majesty's Stationery Office.

———. 1964c. *Parliamentary debates* (Commons). Scottish Grand Committee, *Official Report* (Kilbrandon Report), 23d July, pp. 55–100.

———. 1966. *Social work and the community; Proposals for reorganising* local authority services in Scotland. London: Her Majesty's Stationery Office.

---------. 1968a. *The report of the Committee on Local Authority and Allied Personal Social Services* (Seebohm Report). London: Her Majesty's Stationery Office.

---------. 1968b. *Social Work (Scotland) Act 1968*. London: Her Majesty's Stationery Office.

---------. 1970. *Local Authority Social Services Act 1970*. London: Her Majesty's Stationery Office.

Great Britain, Central Office of Information. 1978. *Criminal justice in Britain*. 2d ed. Central Office of Information Reference Pamphlet 129. London: Her Majesty's Stationery Office.

Greve, F. 1979. Viet veterans find a new foe: Their fathers. *Philadelphia Inquirer,* Feb. 20, p. 1.

Grigsby, J. 1979. Social workers' strike is off. *Daily Telegraph,* Jan. 27, p. 2.

Grosser, C. F. 1965. Community development programs serving the urban poor. *Social Work* 10, no. 2 (July): 15–21.

Gurteen, S. H. 1882. *A handbook of charity organization*. Buffalo, N.Y.: S. H. Gurteen.

Hall, P., Land, H., Parker, R., and Webb, A. 1975. *Change, choice, and conflict in social policy*. London: Heinemann.

Hall, P. 1976. *Reforming the welfare: The politics of change in the personal social services*. London: Heinemann.

Handler, J. F. 1973. *The coercive social worker: British lessons for American social services*. Chicago: Rand McNally.

Havemann, J. 1974. Welfare report/impasse over social services regulations appears broken. *National Journal Reports* 6, no. 49 (Dec. 7): 1840–44.

Healy, P. 1978a. Social workers' strike will affect children and aged. *Times of London,* Aug. 12, p. 2.

---------. 1978b. Social workers decide to form union and open membership. *Times of London,* Sept. 16, p. 4.

---------. 1978c. Social workers' strike expected to spread. *Times of London,* Oct. 9, p. 4.

Herbers, J. 1978. Special interests gaining power as voter disillusionment grows. *New York Times,* Nov. 1, p. 1.

Hofstadter, R. 1944. *Social Darwinism in American thought*. Philadelphia, Pa.: University of Pennsylvania Press.

Hoshino, G. 1969. Britain's debate on universal or selective social services: Lessons for America. *Social Service Review* 43 (Sept.): 245–58.

Howard, A., and Briers, J. 1980. *Investigation into the effects on clients of industrial action by social workers in the London borough of Tower Hamlets.* Stanmore, England: Department of Health and Social Security.

Iglehart, J. 1973. New federalism report: Governors lose enthusiasm for Nixon's revenue sharing programs. *National Journal* 5, no. 26 (June 30): 935–43.

Iglehart, J. K. 1972. Welfare report/Nixon, Congress decline to check soaring social service costs. *National Journal Reports* 4, no. 33 (Aug. 12): 1300–1303.

Iglehart, J. K., Lilley, W., and Clark, T. B. 1973. New federalism report/HEW department advances sweeping proposal to overhaul its programs. *National Journal Reports* 5, no. 1 (Jan. 6): 1–3, 5–7, 10.

Indianapolis Chapter, American Association of Social Workers (AASW). 1952. What happened in Indiana. *Social Work Journal* 33, no. 1 (Jan.): 35–37.

Institute of Medical Social Workers (IMSW). 1966. *Evidence to be offered to the Committee on Local Authority and Allied Personal Social Services.* London: photocopy.

Institute of Medical Social Workers (IMSW), Scottish Region. 1967. *Newsletter.* Edinburgh: (August) photocopy.

Johnson, M. 1974. Memorandum to NASW licensing coordinators: Summary of NASW chapter activity on state regulation of social work. Washington, Jan.

———. 1980. Letter to the author. June 4.

Kahn, A. J. 1976. Service delivery at the neighborhood level: Experience, theory, and fads. *Social Service Review* 50, no. 1 (March): 23–56.

Kahn, A. J., and Kamerman, S. B. 1978. The course of personal social services. *Public Welfare* 36, no. 3 (Summer): 29–42.

Kasser, J. T. 1974. Letter to Chauncey A. Alexander. April 10.

Kavanagh, D. 1977. Party politics in question. In *New trends in British politics,* ed. D. Kavanagh and R. Rose. London: Sage.

Kavanagh, D., and Rose R., ed. 1977. *New trends in British politics.* London: Sage.

Keidan, O. 1979. Alternatives to social workers. *Social Work Today* 10, no. 37 (May 22): 16–17.

Kennedy, J. F. 1962. *Message from President John F. Kennedy: February 1, 1962* (House Doc. no. 325). Cited in J. Axinn and H. Levin, *Social welfare: A history of the American response to need,* pp. 255–62. New York: Harper and Row, 1975.

Klein, R. 1976. The rise and decline of policy analysis: The strange case of health policy-making in Britain. *Policy Analysis* 2, no. 3 (Summer): 459–76.

Larsen, L. M. 1924. *History of England and the British Commonwealth.* New York: Henry Holt.

Lazarsfeld, P. F., Berelson, B., and Gaudet, H. 1944. *The people's choice.* New York: Duell, Sloan, and Pearce.

Lees, R. 1972. *Politics and social work.* London: Routledge and Kegan Paul.

Lubove, R. 1965. *The professional altruist: The emergence of social work as a career, 1880–1930.* Cambridge, Mass.: Harvard University Press.

Lydon, C. 1970. The choice at H.E.W.: Elliot Lee Richardson. *New York Times,* June 8.

Lyons, R. D. 1970. New HEW head calls selection "Out of the Blue": Richardson reports Rogers told him only 24 hours before announcement. *New York Times,* June 8, p. 1.

Marcus, E. P. 1977. Options for a revised allied services bill. Memorandum to Glenn Allison, March 28.

Marmor, T. R., and Thomas, D. 1972. Doctors, politics, and pay disputes: Pressure group politics revisited. *British Journal of Political Sciences* 2, no. 4 (Oct.).

McKenzie, R. T. 1974. Parties, pressure groups, and the British political process. In *Pressure groups in Britain: A reader,* ed. R. Kimber and J. J. Richardson. Totowa, N.J.: Rowman and Littlefield.

Miller, H. 1968. Value dilemmas in social casework. *Social Work* 13, no. 10 (Jan.): 27–33.

Miller, H. N. 1977. Future research on parliament. In *New trends in British politics,* ed. D. Kavanagh and R. Rose. London: Sage.

Morris, R., ed. 1974. *Toward a caring society.* New York: Columbia University School of Social Work.

Morris, R., and Hirsch-Lescohier, I. 1977. Services integration: To what problems is it the presumed solution? Paper prepared for Conference on Issues in Service Delivery in Human Service Organizations, Ann Arbor, Michigan, June. Photocopy.

Morrow, A. 1979. Girl, 14, left at Town Hall. *Daily Telegraph,* Jan. 22.

Mosher, F. C. 1968. *Democracy and the public service.* New York: Oxford University Press.

Mott, P. E. 1976. *Meeting human needs: The social and political history of Title XX.* Columbus, Oh.: National Conference on Social Welfare.

Mowat, C. L. 1955. *Britain between the wars, 1918–1940.* Chicago: University of Chicago Press.

Moynihan, D. P. 1972. *The politics of a guaranteed income.* New York: Vintage Press.

Muir, R. 1930. *How Britain is governed.* New York: Richard R. Smith.

NASW News. 1974. N.Y. governor vetoes licensure bill. 19, no. 8 (Sept.): 3.

————. 1975. Model being developed for register. 20, no. 7 (July): 12.

————. 1977a. Vendorship bill introduced. 22, no. 3 (Mar.): 1.

————. 1977b. Certification okayed as register standard if ACSW equivalent. 22, no. 7 (July): 14.

————. 1978. NASW/clinical federation relations hit snag. 23, no. 7 (July): 3.

————. 1979. Clinical specialty examined by profession; some common ground for definition sought. 24, no. 7 (July): 1, 4–7.

————. 1980. Chapters battle anti-regulation trend. 25, no. 2 (Feb.): 12.

National Association of Probation Officers (NAPO), Scottish Branch. 1965. *Observations on the Kilbrandon Report.* Edinburgh: photocopy.

National Association of Social Workers (NASW). 1973. *Principles for guidance in revision of social services regulations and/or possible legislation.* Washington, D.C.: photocopy.

National Conference on Social Welfare (NCSW). 1968. *The Social Welfare Forum, 1968.* New York: Columbia University Press.

————. 1969. *The Social Welfare Forum, 1969.* New York: Columbia University Press.

National Journal. 1972. Federal report/Revenue sharing bill authorizes sweeping innovation in federal aid system. 4, no. 41 (Oct. 7): 1553–66.

————. 1973. Elliot Richardson's tenure as HEW secretary: Many defeats and frustrations, taken in a spirit of loyalty. 5, no. 1 (Jan. 6): 8–9.

Newman, E. 1968. A case study of social planning opportunities and limitations. Ph.D. diss. Brandeis University.

Newman, E., and Demone, H. W., Jr. 1969. Policy paper: A new look at public planning for human services. *Journal of Health and Human Behavior* 10, no. 2: 142–49.

Newman, E., and Turem, J. 1974. The crisis of accountability. *Social Work* 19, no. 1 (Jan.): 5–16.

Nicholas, H. G. 1975. The insulation of the presidency. In *American political institutions in the 1970s,* ed. M. Beloff and V. Vale. Toto-wa, N.J.: Rowman and Littlefield.

O'Donnell, P. 1978. *Social services: Three years after Title XX.* Washington: National Governors' Association.

Orten, J. D. 1972. Political action: End or means? *Social Work* 17, no. 6 (Nov.): 4, 105–106.

Parker, R. 1978a. Fears that lives may be at risk as social workers go on strike. *Times of London,* Aug. 15, p. 2.

———. 1978b. NALGO warning of extending social work strikes. *Times of London,* Aug. 16, p. 2.

Pearson, G. 1978. To strike or not to strike. *Social Work Today* 10, no. 10 (Oct. 31): 9–10.

Peirce, F. J. 1970. Student involvement: Participatory democracy or adult socialization? *Journal of Education for Social Work* 6, no. 2 (Fall): 21–26.

Pennsylvania, General Assembly, House. 1975. An act regulating the practice of clinical social work. (House Bill 1024): Apr. 15.

———. 1978. An act relating to the regulation of social workers. (House Bill 2300): Apr. 5.

Pennsylvania, General Assembly, Senate. 1975. An act relating to the licensing of social workers. (Senate Bill 1195): Nov. 24.

Pennsylvania State Chapter, NASW. 1974. "An act relating to the regulation of social workers (second draft for discussion only)." Harrisburg, Pa.: photocopy.

———. 1980. "New licensure bill introduced." *Pennsylvania Chapter Newsletter.* 5, no. 6 (Mar.): 1.

Perlman, R. 1975. *Consumers and social services.* New York: Wiley.

Perlman, R., and Jones, D. 1967. *Neighborhood service centers.* Washington: HEW.

Phillips, B. 1977. Health services: Social workers. In *Encyclopedia of Social Work,* vol. 1, ed. J. B. Turner, pp. 615–25. Washington: National Association of Social Workers.

Piven, F. F., and Cloward, R. A. 1971. *Regulating the poor: The functions of public welfare.* New York: Pantheon Books.

Polsby, N. W. 1971. *Congress and the presidency.* 2d ed. Englewood Cliffs, N.J.: Prentice-Hall.

Presthus, R. 1974. *Elites in the policy process.* London: Cambridge University Press.

Professional Caseworkers' Working Party. 1962. *Statement by Professional Caseworkers' Working Party.* Edinburgh: photocopy.

Pryce, M. 1978a. BASW debates its strike code of practice. *Social Work Today* 10, no. 11 (Nov. 7): 3.

Pryce, M. 1978b. A traumatic year for social work. *Social Work Today* 10, no. 17 (Dec. 19): 12–14.

Publius. 1972. The *Publius* symposium on the future of American federalism. 2, no. 1 (Spring): 95–146.

Pym, B. 1974. *Pressure groups and the permissive society.* Newton Abbott, England: David and Charles.

Rand Corporation. 1975. *Census of local services integrations: A working note.* Santa Monica, Calif.

Reiselbach, L. N. 1977. *Congressional reform in the seventies.* Morristown, N.J.: General Learning Press.

Reposa, R. E. 1974. The social worker as professional advocate: An incomplete gestalt. *Clinical Social Work Journal* 2, no. 2 (Summer): 135–41.

Richardson, E. L. 1972. *Responsibility and responsiveness: The HEW potential for the seventies.* Washington: HEW.

———. 1973. *Responsibility and responsiveness (II): A report on the HEW potential for the seventies.* Washington: HEW.

———. 1976. *The creative balance.* New York: Holt, Rinehart, and Winston.

Rimlinger, G. V. 1971. *Welfare policy and industrialization in Europe, America, and Russia.* New York: Wiley.

Ribicoff, A. 1962. Politics and social workers. *Social Work* 7, no. 2: 3–6.

Richan, W. C. 1973. The social work profession and organized social welfare. In *Shaping the new social work,* ed. A. J. Kahn, pp. 147–68. New York: Columbia University Press.

———. 1978. Personnel issues in child welfare. In *Child welfare strategy in the coming years,* pp. 227–81. Washington, D.C.: HEW.

Rose, R. 1971. The political ideas of English party activists. In *A comparative study of party organization,* ed. W. E. Wright, pp. 290–311. Columbus, Oh.: Charles E. Merrill.

Safire, W. 1975. *Before the fall: An inside view of the pre-Watergate White House.* Garden City, N.Y.: Doubleday.

Scarrow, H. A. 1971. Policy pressures by British local government. *Comparative Politics* 4, no. 1 (Oct.).

Schlesinger, A. M. 1951. *The rise of modern America, 1865–1951.* 4th ed. New York: Macmillan.

Schlesinger, A. M., Jr. 1959. *The coming of the New Deal.* Boston: Houghton Mifflin.

Schneiderman, L. 1978. Collaboration between the health and social services in England. *Social Work* 23, no. 3 (May): 192–97.

Schwartz, J. E. 1980. Exploring a new role in policy-making: The British House of Commons in the 1970s. *American Political Science Review* 74, no. 1 (March): 23–37.

Seebohm, F. 1974. Reorganization of British personal services. Paper delivered at 125th Anniversary Symposium of the Community Service Society of New York, Oct. New York: Community Service Society of New York.

Seyd, P. 1976. The child poverty action group. *Political Quarterly* 47, no. 2 (April–June): 189–202.

Sharpe, L. J. 1975. The social scientist and policy-maker: Some cautionary thoughts and transatlantic reflections. *Policy and Politics* 4, no. 2 (Dec.): 7–34.

———. 1977. Whitehall—structure and people. In *New trends in British politics,* ed. D. Kavanagh and R. Rose, pp. 53–81. London: Sage.

Siegel, S. 1975. *Social service manpower needs: An overview to 1980.* New York: Council on Social Work Education.

Sinfield, A. 1970. Which way for social work? In *The fifth social service: A critical analysis of the Seebohm proposals,* ed. P. Townsend, pp. 23–58. London: Fabian Society.

Smith, G. 1971. Some research implications of the Seebohm report. *British Journal of Sociology* 22: 295–310.

Social Security Bulletin. 1979. *Social Security Bulletin* 42, no. 4 (April).

Social Work Today. 1978a. BASW ousted from joint consultative committee. 10, no. 6 (Oct. 3): 3.

———. 1978b. The social workers' union? 10, no. 7 (Oct. 10): 1.

———. 1978c. Strike question posed in four more areas. 10, no. 7 (Oct. 10): 2.

———. 1978d. Liverpool and Lewisham now out on strike. 10, no. 8 (Oct. 17): 2.

———. 1978e. BASW "encouraged" by early membership total. 10, no. 10 (Oct. 31): 4.

———. 1978f. Striking social workers occupy NALGO headquarters. 10, no. 10 (Oct. 31): 3.

———. 1979a. Comment. 10, no. 19 (Jan. 9): 1.

———. 1979b. Residential strike a possibility. 10, no. 20 (Jan. 16): 3.

———. 1979c. The strikes: picking up the pieces. 10, no. 24 (Feb. 13): 1.

———. 1979d. How BUSW is facing up to the realities of trade unionism. 10, no. 25 (Feb. 20): 3.

————. 1979e. A review of the issues to be debated this week. 11, no. 5 (Oct. 2): 7–8.

————. 1979f. Sink or swim time for year old union. 11, no. 5 (Oct. 2): 9–10.

————. 1979g. SWT fighting fund is swelled by conference. 11, no. 7 (Oct. 16): 6.

————. 1979h. Jenkin on cuts. 11, no. 9 (Oct. 30): 10–13.

Sorauf, F. J. 1968. *Party politics in America*. Boston: Little, Brown.

Specht, H. 1969. Disruptive tactics. *Social Work* 14, no. 2 (April): 5–16.

————. 1972. The deprofessionalization of social work. *Social Work* 17, no. 2 (March): 3–15.

Stern, L. 1979. On the Record. *NASW News* 24, no. 6 (June): 32.

Stewart, J. D. 1974. British pressure groups: A conclusion. In *Pressure groups in Britain: A reader,* ed. R. Kimber and J. J. Richardson. Totowa, N.J.: Rowman and Littlefield.

Taggart, S. P. 1977. *The coalition that built Title XX: An analysis of the infra-structure of the social services coalition.* Master's Thesis, School of Social Administration, Temple University.

Thomas, C. 1977. NALGO urges strikes against cuts in services. *Times of London,* June 17, p. 3.

————. 1978. Social workers called out on a day's strike. *Times of London,* Sept. 27, p. 2.

Thursz, D. 1973. Professional education for expected political action by social workers. *Journal of Education for Social Work* 9, no. 3 (Fall): 87–93.

Time. 1978. The swarming lobbyists: Washington's new billion-dollar game of who can influence whom. *Time* 112, no. 6 (Aug. 7): 14–22.

Times of London. 1968a. Social services under one roof would improve lives of most vulnerable. July 24, p. 4.

————. 1968b. The welfare machine. July 24, p. 9.

————. 1977. Unions alarmed by change of regime. May 7, p. 3.

————. 1978. Local bargaining on local conditions. Sept. 27, p. 15.

Titmuss, R. M. 1950. *Problems of social policy*. London: Her Majesty's Stationery Office.

————. 1968. *Committment to social welfare*. New York: Pantheon Books.

Townsend, P., ed. 1970. *The fifth social service: A critical analysis of the Seebohm report*. London: Fabian Society.

Traylor, L. 1975. NASW president Traylor responds to licensing critics. *NASW News* 20, no. 3 (March): 1, 32.

Tropman, J. E. 1971. Community welfare councils. In *Encyclopedia of Social Work,* ed. R. Morris, vol. 1, pp. 150–56. New York: National Association of Social Workers.

United Nations, Department of International Economic and Social Affairs. 1978. *Statistical Yearbook 1977.* 29th ed. New York: United Nations.

United Nations, General Assembly. 1960. *Official records of the general assembly: Fourteenth session,* Sup. no. 16. New York: United Nations.

United Services Agency Evaluation Project. 1977. *The service delivery system of the United Services Agency.* Philadelphia, Pa.: School of Social Administration, Temple University.

U.S., Congress. 1956. *Amendments to the Social Security Act, Title III, Part II.* Public Law 880, 84th Cong. Washington, D.C.: G.P.O.

U.S., Congress, House. 1975. *The Allied Services Act of 1975.* 94th Cong., 1st sess.

U.S., Congress, House, Committee on Education and Labor. 1974. *Allied Services Act of 1974:* Hearings on H.R. 12285, 93d Cong., 2d sess., May 29, 30; July 10, 11.

U.S., Congress, House, Subcommittee on Fiscal Policy of the Joint Economic Committee. 1972. *Open-ended federal matching of state social service expenditures authorized under public assistance titles of the Social Security Act:* Hearing, 92d Cong., 2d sess., Sept. 12, 13.

Vale, V. 1975. The collaborative chaos of federal administration. In *American political institutions in the 1970s,* ed. M. Beloff and V. Vale, pp. 35–51. Totowa, N.J.: Rowman and Littlefield.

Virtue, M. B. 1952. *Public services to children in Michigan: A study of basic structure.* Ann Arbor: University of Michigan Press.

Wall Street Journal. 1973. Washington Wire. May 18, p. 1.

Warman, C. 1978. Tories gain power in most London boroughs. *Times of London,* May 5, p. 1.

Washington Report. 1979. British approach to personal social services explained. 14, no. 2 (Feb.): 1.

Watson, F. D. 1922. *The charity organization movement in the United States: A study in American philanthropy.* New York: Macmillan.

Weber, S. 1974. Social work in Scotland: Lessons for America. *Social Work* 19, no. 3 (May): 298–304.

White, T. H. 1969. *The making of the president, 1968.* New York: Atheneum.

Wilcox, C. 1969. *Toward social welfare.* Homewood, Ill.: R. D. Irwin.

Wilensky, H. L., and Lebeaux, C. N. 1958. *Industrial society and social welfare.* New York: Sage.

Williams, R. M., Jr. 1963. *American society: A sociological interpretation.* New York: Knopf.

Wilson, D. J. 1975. *Power and party bureaucracy in Britain: Regional organization in the Conservative and Labour parties.* Lexington, Mass.: Lexington Books.

Wilson, J. H. 1971. *A personal record: The Labour government, 1964–1970.* Boston: Atlantic/Little, Brown.

Wilton, G. 1978a. All standing firm in eighth week of strike. *Social Work Today* 10, no. 6 (Oct. 31): 2–3.

————. 1979b. Anger and disappointment after NJC meeting. *Social Work Today* 10, no. 19 (Oct. 31): 2.

————. 1978c. 2000 out as four more areas join strike. *Social Work Today* 10, no. 11 (Nov. 7): 2.

————. 1978d. How the strikes developed: A diary by Gill Wilton. *Social Work Today* 10, no. 17 (Dec. 19): 15–17.

————. 1979a. Four more authorities out in new year. *Social Work Today* 10, no. 18 (Jan. 16): 2.

————. 1979b. Strike in 22nd week continues to spread. *Social Work Today* 10, no. 19 (Jan. 9): 2.

————. 1979c. NALGO leaders urge a strike settlement. *Social Work Today* 10, no. 20 (Jan. 16): 2.

————. 1979d. Both sides agree on formula to end the strikes. *Social Work Today* 10, no. 24 (Feb. 13): 2.

————. 1979e. Return to work in Tower Hamlets. *Social Work Today* 10, no. 39 (June 12): 3.

Wineman, D., and James, A. 1969. The advocacy challenge to schools of social work. *Social Work* 14, no. 2 (April): 23–32.

Wiseman, H. V. 1966. *Politics in everyday life.* Oxford: Basil Blackwell.

Wish, H. 1955. *Contemporary America: The national scene since 1900.* Rev. ed. New York: Harper.

Young, K. 1977. Environmental management in local politics. In *New trends in British politics,* ed. D. Kavanagh and R. Rose. London: Sage.

Younghusband, E. 1964. *Social work and social change.* London: Allen and Unwin.

Index

Association of Municipal Corporations, 36
ASW (Association of Social Workers), 83
Audience. *See* Argument, components of

Backbenchers. *See* House of Commons; Parliament
Barratt, Sir Charles. *See* Seebohm Committee
BASW (British Association of Social Workers): advice of, to government, 215; and BUSW, 183–84, 190; coalition organized by, to fight service cutbacks, 191; criticism of NALGO by, 184; expulsion from Joint Consultative Committee, 184; formation of, 60; headquarters of, moved from London, 217; staff resources of, 210; and strikes by social workers, 184–85
Beveridge, Sir William H., 53–54
BMA (British Medical Association), 47–49, 113–14, 221; and government committees, 48; and Seebohm Report, 113–14, 221
Boggs, Elizabeth, 169, 223. *See also* Social Services Coalition
Brademas, John: and Allied Services Act, 140, 142, 147, 148–49; role of, in hearings on Allied Services Act, 142–44, 223
Browne, Megan, 70, 74–76, 89, 214. *See also* Kilbrandon Study Group
Bureaucracy. *See* Civil servants
BUSW (British Union of Social Workers), 184, 188–89. *See also* BASW

Cabinet: in Canada, 41; career in, and legislative defeats, 121, 213; and civil servants, 134–36; committees of, 21; conflicts within, 96, 98, 109; and fiscal policy, 17; in Great Britain, 17, 21, 22, 96, 98, 109; and interest groups, 41; and president, 23; turn-over in, 41; in U.S., 22–23, 41, 134–36
Callaghan, James, 96, 109
Canada, interest groups in. *See* Presthus, R.
Carlucci, Frank C., 138, 143, 170, 223
Carmichael, Catherine M., 73, 75–77, 89, 214. *See also* Kilbrandon Study Group
Carmichael, Neil, 73, 75
Carp, Bertram W., 168, 171, 176. *See also* Social Services Coalition
Carter, James Earl (Jimmy), 3, 142, 148, 161, 227
Centralization, 6, 15, 28, 213
Chancellor of the Exchequer, 21
Charity organization societies, 123
Children Act of 1948, 54, 93, 94
Children and Young Persons Act of 1963, 67
Children and Young Persons in Scotland. See Kilbrandon Committee, report of
Children and youth: services for, 52, 61–62, 65, 94, 153; in Great Britain, 52, 65, 94; in U.S., 153
Citizen panels. *See* Kilbrandon Committee, report of
Civil servants: administrators and professional advisers among, in Great Britain, 26–27, 76–77, 214; American and British, compared, 231; and cabinet members, 134–35; and cabinet ministers, 25; careers of American and British, compared, 24–25; careers of, in Great Britain, 26, 50; careers of, in U.S., 27, 142, 230; and Congress, 174–75;

Gonzalez, Al, 229
Governors, 161, 162–63, 173. *See also* NGC
Great Britain: civil servants in, 24–28; class consciousness in, 6, 52; committees and commissions in, 33; compared with U.S., 6–7; conditions in, after World War II, 65; executive function in, 21–24; interest groups in, 44–49; labor movement in, 51; legislative function in, 15–18, 19; local government in, 35–36; political parties, 28–30; political philosophy in, 6, 36–37; social service reorganization in, 65–120; social service work force in, 58–59, 180–90; strikes by social workers in, 180–90; welfare state in, 52–55
Green paper, 77. *See also* White paper

Hall, Phoebe, 9, 11, 98
Hart, Judith, 70, 72, 74–76, 210, 213; formal authority of, 213; and Kilbrandon Study Group, 74–76; political constituency of, 72, 210; and Social Work (Scotland) Act, 72; speech by, to social workers on Kilbrandon Report, 70; and working parties on Kilbrandon Report, 74, 77
Health and Human Services, U.S. Department of. *See* HEW
Health and Social Security, Department of, 45
HEW (U.S. Department of Health, Education and Welfare): attempts by Nixon administration to control, 128; officials of, and interest groups, 167; restrictions on social service funding by, 165–67, 169–72; underestimation of opposition by, 170

Hiddleston, Vera, 84
Home Office, 95–97. *See also* Callaghan, James
House of Commons, 16, 19, 21, 73, 85, 89, 117. *See also* Parliament
House of Representatives (U.S.), committees of, 136, 147, 158. *See also* Congress
House of Lords, 19, 89. *See also* Parliament
Huston, Thomas C. (Tom). *See* New Federalism, conception of
Huws Jones, Robin, 99, 100, 102, 226

IMSW (Institute of Medical Social Workers), 70–71, 82–83, 103
Information: and policy influence, 7, 42, 217–26; use of, by Allied Services Act opponents, 149; use of, by Kilbrandon Study Group, 77. *See also* Argument, components of; Evidence; Strategic intelligence
Ingleby Report, 66–67, 68, 94
Insider strategy, 45, 108–12, 215–16. *See also* Formal authority, access to; Personal relationships
Interest groups, 38–50; adaptability of, 39; in Canada, 39; and civil servants, in U.S., 145; and Congress, 39; conservative bias of, in U.S., 39; effectiveness of, in U.S., 38–39, 41–43; essential to government, 39; and government officials, in Great Britain, 46–49; in Great Britain, 44–50; as initiators of policy, 32; leaders of, 43; leaders of, and constituencies, 229; lobbying by, against funding ceiling, in U.S., 158–59; migration of headquarters of major, to Washington, 138–39, 216–17; mobilization of rank and file in, in U.S., 166–

67, 170; myth of non-existence of, in Great Britain, 44; and political parties, in Great Britain, 46; reaction of, to HEW restrictions on social service funding, 166; sectional and promotional, in Britain, defined, 44–45; use of paid lobbyists by, in U.S., 38, 138–39. *See also* "Iron triangle"

Investment: factors in social workers' policy issues, 238–41; importance of, 237–38; and policy influence, 8, 236, 237–43. *See also* Mixed agenda

"Iron triangle," 25, 43–44, 140, 223. *See also* Interest groups

Issues. *See* Argument, components of

James, Lady. *See* Seebohm Committee

Jensen, Allen E.: and constituency of governors, 169, 177, 211, 230; role of, in development of social service funding policy, 173, 174, 175–76, 177; role of, in Social Services Coalition, 167–68, 169

Johnston, James O. (Jimmy), 74, 226. *See also* Kilbrandon Study Group

Joint Working Group of Local Authority Associations, 74, 77

Jones, David, 97–98, 118

Kennedy, John F., 20, 154, 156

Kilbrandon, Lord, 67–68

Kilbrandon Committee, 66–70, 73–82; focus of, on juvenile justice, 68–69; opposition divided by, 72; report of, 68–70; Scottish Education Department letter on, 73–74; Scottish Grand Committee report to Parliament on, 73; social education

emphasis in, 82; social workers' reaction to, 70–72; white paper on, 74–82

Kilbrandon Study Group, 74–79; composition of, 74–76; role of, re content of white paper, 79

Labor movement. *See* Organized labor

Labour Party, 28–30, 46, 52, 66, 72

Lane, W. N., 100, 210–11. *See also* Seebohm Committee

Legislative function, 15–20

Leonard, Peter. *See* Seebohm Committee

Liberal Party, 29

Liberalism, history of, in U.S. and Great Britain, 6

Licensure of social workers, 8, 10, 191–205; black social workers and, 197, 199, 201, 202, 203, 204; clinical social workers and, 197–99, 201–2, 203; comparison of, with other occupations, 196; educational credentials, NASW stand on, 195–96, 198, 199–200; growth of, 196; multiple-level bills, NASW stand on, 198; Pennsylvania campaign for, 200–204; resistance of state legislatures to, 200; retarded by bureaucratic nature of profession, 195; slowing of momentum of campaigns for, 198; and social activism, 197; social workers divided over, 197–98, 241; state jurisdiction over, 195; vendor payments and, 197; veto of, by New York governor, 198

Lobbyists, 39–50, 211-12. *See also* Interest groups

Local authorities: associations of, 114–15; intended audience of Seebohm Report, 222; lack of

Local authorities: lack of power (*cont.*):

power, 35; leeway afforded to, by Local Authority Social Services Act, 115; reaction of, to white paper on Kilbrandon Report, 80–81; representation of, on Seebohm Committee, 100. *See also* Centralization

Local authority social service departments. *See* Local Authority Social Services Act; Seebohm Committee, report of; Social Work (Scotland) Act; Social workers, strikes by, in Great Britain

Local Authority Social Services Act, 9, 92–120; attitude of American social workers toward, 122; effects of, on services, 118–19, 180–81; enactment of, 112, 118; relation of, to National Health Service and local authority reforms. *See also* Seebohm Committee; Services integration

Local Government Act, 35

Long, Russell B.: and ceiling on social service funding, 160–61; chairman of Senate Finance Committee, 130; and Hew restrictions on social service funding, 171; and services for families on AFDC, 153; and social service funding bill, 174

Longford Committee, 94–95

Lords, House of. *See* House of Lords

Lynch, Rufus, 203–4

McBoyle Committee, 66–68

McInnes, Marjorie, 87–88

Mahon, George H., 158–59

Mass politics, compared with interest group politics, 212

Maud Report, 111–12

Medical profession (Great Britain), 113, 218–19. *See also* BMA; SMOH

Mental health, issue of jurisdiction over, 106

Michael, Gill, 82–83, 87–88, 218, 228

Mills, Wilbur D., 129, 136, 161

Mixed agenda, 237–43; of British social workers, 120; defined, 239–40; failure of, to explain inaction of social workers on funding ceiling, 242; and HEW restrictions on social service funding, 243; of Scottish social workers, 91; and social service reorganization in Great Britain, 242–43; of social workers, 205; of U.S. social workers, 5. *See also* Investment

Model cities program, 125

Mondale, Walter F., 171, 173–74

Money, and policy influence, 7, 209–10

Morrill, William A., 175

Morris, J. N., 99; and constituency of doctors, 102–3, 210–11; personal relationships of, as source of influence, 110; role of, in Seebohm Committee, 100–101, 102–3, 106

MP (Member of Parliament). *See* House of Commons; Parliament

NALGO (National and Local Government Officers' Association), 180–91; attitudes of social workers toward, 189–90; conflict within, 183; difficulty of, in interpreting strikes, 183; expulsion of BASW by, 184; pressure on, by militants, 182; reluctance of leadership of, to strike, 182; weak support of social work strikes by wider membership of, 185–86

130; and formal authority, 213; as HEW Secretary, 129–37; in Massachusetts state government, 132–34; and social service spending, 157–58; testimony of, for Allied Services Act, 143; underestimation of opposition by, 134, 137, 219

Rogers, Walter E., 144–45

Rowe, Andrew, 74–75, 231. *See also* Kilbrandon Study Group

Royal Colleges, 48. *See also* Medical profession (Great Britain)

Royal commissions. *See* Committees and commissions

Safire, William, 127, 130. *See also* New Federalism, conception of

SCOSW (Standing Conference of Organizations of Social Workers), 82–83, 87–89, 103

Scotland: legal system of, 66; social service reorganization in, 65–91; traditional view of education in, 66, 69–70

Scottish Advisory Council on Child Care, Committee of. *See* McBoyle Committee

Scottish Office, 79

Secretary of State for Scotland, 67, 74

SED (Scottish Education Department), 73–74

Seebohm, Lord (Frederic), 99, 100. *See also* Seebohm Committee

Seebohm Committee, 9, 33, 98–103, 105-8; and coalition politics, 234–35; composition of, 98–100; criticism of, 115–16; definition of "family" by, 105; emphasis on training in, 107–8; internal dynamics of, 100–103; quality of evidence in, 224; question of jurisdiction over,

by departments, 95; report of, 9, 105–8, 224

Senate (U.S.), 22, 158, 170. *See also* Congress

Serota, Lady (Beatrice), 99–102, 110, 213; formal authority of, and policy influence, 213; Minister of State for Health, 102, 110. *See also* Seebohm Committee

Services integration, 93–94, 95–96, 122–26, 143. *See also* Allied Services Act; Local Authority Social Services Act; Social Work (Scotland) Act

Sheriffs (Scotland), 66, 80

SIAG (Seebohm Implementation Action Group), 116–17

Simson, Michael R. F. *See* Seebohm Committee

SMOH (Society of Medical Officers of Health), 78–80, 113–14. *See also* BMA

Social class, consciousness of, 52

Social Darwinism, 36–37

Social education departments, 69–70. *See also* Kilbrandon Committee, report of; Kilbrandon Study Group

Social promotion, concept of, 78, 107

Social Security Act, 40, 55–57; categorical assistance under, 152; 1956 amendments to, 153–54; 1962 amendments to, 57–58, 154; 1967 amendments to, 155; Title XX of, 10, 43, 176–78

Social services: advocates of, in U.S., 42; ceiling on, in U.S., 156–62; defined, 5–6; demand for, 60–62; demand for, in U.S., 149–50; in England and Wales, 8, 92–120; expenditures for, 6, 58–59; expenditures for, in Great Britain, 52, 54, 181–82, 190–91; expenditures for, in

Social services: expenditure for, in U.S.: (cont.):
U.S., 58; federal government role in, in U.S., 151–54; fragmentation of, in U.S., 124–25; funding of, in U.S., 54–58; as an industry, 58–62; management of, in U.S., 8, 122, 128, 130–48; modeled on British prototypes, 6; politics of, 4, 10; post-World War II developments in, in Great Britain, 4, 54; post-World War II developments in, in U.S., 4, 57–58; primitive state of, in Scotland, 66, 68; public v. voluntary auspices of, in U.S., 125; purchase of, in U.S., 155; reorganization of, in Great Britain, 8, 65–120; reorganization of, in Scotland, 8, 65–91; reorientation of, in 1980s, 4; as strategy against poverty, in U.S., 126; use of, by nonrecipients of public assistance, in U.S., 155, 161–62; work force in, 9–10, 58–62; work force in, in Great Britain, 93–94, 180–91

Social Services Coalition, 167–69, 211, 232, 234

Social unrest, as impetus to reform, 58

Social Work and the Community. See Kilbrandon Committee, report of; Kilbrandon Committee, white paper on

Social Work (Scotland) Act, 8, 65–91; enactment of, 89–90; impact of, on services, 90–91; finding and training provisions of, 89–90

Social Work Services Group (Scotland), 88–89

Social Work Today, 181, 188. See BASW

Social workers: and Allied Services Act, in U.S., 9, 138, 142, 143–44, 149; altruism of, 239–43; ambivalence of, re political action, in U.S., 5; black, and licensure issue, in U.S., 197, 199, 201, 202, 203, 204; and ceiling on social service funding, in U.S., 163–64; changing political role of, in U.S., 4–5; clinical, in U.S., 194–95, 197, 198–99, 201–2, 203; coalition organized by, to fight cutbacks in services, in Great Britain, 190–91; and coalition politics, 167–69, 211, 232, 234–36; concern of, re access to decision makers, in U.S., 5, 145, 167, 216; concern of, re social service funding, in Scotland, 84–85; conflict among, over strikes, in Great Britain, 9–10; dealings of, with civil servants, in Great Britain, 117; dealings of, with civil servants, in Scotland, 87–89; defined, 6; generalist role of, 189; generalist role of, in Great Britain, 104, 106–7; growth of, in Great Britain 59–60; and HEW restrictions on funding, 5, 166–68, 178–79; history of professionalization of, in U.S., 123; lack of political experience of, in Scotland, 85–86; licensure campaigns of, in U.S., 191–205, 229; mixed agenda of, in U.S., 5, 237–43; pessimism of, in 1980s, 4; political action by, American and British compared, 179; political action by, in Great Britain, 82–89, 116–20; political action by, in Scotland, 82–89; political effectiveness of, 7, 10; political effectiveness of, in Great Britain, 119–20; political effectiveness of, in Scotland,

91; political effectiveness of, in U.S., 9; political resources of, 209–36; public image of, in Great Britain, 9–10, 186–87; reactions of, to conservative trend, in Great Britain, 3, 181, 190–91; reactions of, to conservative trend, in U.S., 3, 151; reactions of, to Kilbrandon Report, in Scotland, 71; repercussions of political action by, 5; repercussions of political action by, in U.S., 5; and Seebohm Committee, 99–100, 103; and Seebohm implementation campaign, 116–17; self-interest of, 180–206, 242–43; and social service reorganization, in Great Britain, 65–120; strategic intelligence as a resource for, in Scotland, 218; strikes by, in Great Britain, 180–91

Socialism, British, 52

Special interests. *See* Interest groups

States (U.S.): continuing importance of, 34–35; and HEW funding restrictions, 165; New Federalism and role of, 127–28; noncompliance of, with federal regulations, 152–53; revenue sharing and role of, 160; "rights" of, and conservatism, 34–35; role of, in policy innovation, 55–56; use of federal social service funds by, 156–57, 163–64

Strategic intelligence, 7, 217–20

Strikes by social workers. *See* NALGO

Suitable home laws, 153

Sunset laws, 204–5

Supreme Count (U.S.), 21, 34, 56

Taggart, S. P., 168–69

Thatcher, Margaret, 3, 190–91

Titmuss, Richard M., 46; member of Kilbrandon Study Group, 75, 99; personal relationships of, 110; and Seebohm Committee, 99; speech by, on social service reorganization, 97–98, 100, 223

Traylor, Lorenzo H., 197

Twiname, John D., 165

Ullman, Al, 175

Ultra vires, principle of, 35. *See* Local authorities

Uncontrollables. *See* Social services, funding of, in U.S.; Social services, ceiling on, in U.S.

United States: civil servants in, 25, 27, 30–32; courts, role of in social policy, 21; executive function in, 20, 22–24; individualism, philosophy of, in, 36–37; interest groups in, 40–44; labor movement in, 51; legislative function in, 17, 18–19, 20–21; political parties in, 30–32; political philosophy, 6, 15, 36–37, 57; social service expenditures in, 58–59, 154–63; social service funding, politics of, in, 151–79; social service reform in, 121–79; social service work force in, 59–60; states, role of, in, 33–35; welfare state in, 55–58, 151–56

Veneman, John G., 165

Voters, constituencies of, and policy influence, 7, 210–12

Weaver, Edward T., 156

Weinberger, Caspar W., 137–38, 147, 164–65

Welfare state, 51–62; defined, 51; differences between American and British, 6; in Great Britain, 52–55; in U.S., 55–58